POWER

How Influence, Authority,
and Control Shaped Civilizations

by

JOEL THOMAS

Also by Joel Thomas

THEMATIC SERIES

Forthcoming in 2026

Power

How Influence, Authority, and Control Shaped Civilizations

Information

How Knowledge, Secrecy, and Lies Built the Modern World

Risk

How Civilizations Gamble, Hedge, and Get the Math Wrong

Wealth

How Fortunes Are Built, Inherited, and Taken Away

Influence

How Persuasion, Propaganda, and Belief Move the World

Fear

How Fear Built Empires and Governed Humanity

Trust

How Belief in Strangers Built Markets, Nations, and Everything Between

Authority

How the Right to Command Is Won, Imposed, and Lost

Control

How Surveillance, Systems, and Algorithms Shape Modern Life

Resistance

How Defiance, Dissent, and Revolution Reshape the World

Legitimacy

How Power Earns Belief, Demands Obedience, and Loses Both

NOMICAL HISTORY

Monthly Series

October	*The Brave Advance, the Mighty Stumble, and History Laughs Last*
November	*Between Chaos and Consequence*
December	*When Calendars Close but History Refuses to Rest*
January	*When the Machinery of History Grinds to Life*
February	*Lincoln, Darwin, Yalta, and the Modern World*
March	*Ideas, Inventions, and the Days That Wouldn't Behave*
April	*Wars, Wonder, and the Month That Never Sits Still*
May	*Where Flowers Meet Gunfire*
June	*The Longest Days and the Shortest Fuses*
July	*Where Freedom Meets Fire*
August	*Where Crowns Fall and History Draws Blood*
September	*Where Empires End and Everything Else Begins*

Published by Nomical Books
nomicalbooks.com

POWER

HOW INFLUENCE, AUTHORITY, AND CONTROL SHAPED CIVILIZATIONS

JOEL THOMAS

NOMICAL BOOKS, LLC

ISBN: 978-1-972041-00-0
Published by Nomical Books
Printed in the United States of America

For information, permissions, or bulk orders, contact: contact@nomicalbooks.com

First edition 2026

For Kim —
who supported, listened, and encouraged
through every doubt and every draft.

Without you, I would never have gotten here.

CONTENTS

INTRODUCTION

THIS IS A BOOK about power. Not the inspirational kind that decorates office walls and graduation speeches, the power to believe in yourself, the power of positive thinking, the power of showing up. That kind of power is a greeting card with ambitions. This book is about the other kind. The kind that determines who eats and who does not. Who speaks and who is silent. Who makes the rules and who discovers, usually too late, what the rules are. The kind that builds empires, funds armies, shapes economies, and arranges the world so thoroughly that the arrangement feels like nature rather than design. That kind of power. The kind that matters.

The subject is not new. Machiavelli wrote about how to get power. Hobbes wrote about why we need it. Locke wrote about how to restrain it. Marx wrote about who has it and why. Foucault wrote about where it hides. The conversation is centuries old and not close to finished, because power is one of those subjects that becomes more complicated the longer you look at it. The fish studying water has a methodological problem, and the problem does not get smaller with a bigger microscope.

This book does not attempt to resolve that problem. It attempts something more modest and, I hope, more useful: to examine power as a structural phenomenon rather than a personal one. Most accounts of power focus on the people who wield it—the kings, the presidents, the generals, the executives, the founders. The focus is understandable. People make good stories. Structures make good insomnia cures. But the focus on personalities obscures the more important truth, which is that the structures persist long after the personalities are gone. The pharaoh is dust. The bureaucracy he built to manage grain distribution is the ancestor of every tax authority on the planet. Napoleon is a tomb in Paris. The civil code he imposed is still governing property disputes in Louisiana. The person is temporary. The structure is the thing that lasts, and the thing that lasts is the thing worth understanding.

This book is part of the Nomical History series. It is organized thematically rather than chronologically, because the patterns it describes are not confined to any single era. The dynamics through which a Mesopotamian priest-king maintained authority in 3000 BCE are structurally analogous to—different in scale, technology, and historical context, similar in the underlying dynamics of resource control, legitimation, and institutional self-preservation—to the dynamics through which a modern corporation maintains market dominance. The corporation will return throughout this book as a running example, not because it is uniquely powerful but because it is the institution in which the dynamics this book describes are most legible to anyone willing to look past the language of business. The technology differs. The scale differs. The underlying mechanics—control over scarce resources, information asymmetry, institutional self-preservation, the conversion of one form of power into another—do not differ in any way that matters for structural analysis.

The book begins with fundamentals: what power is, how it operated before states existed, and the forms it took as human organization scaled. It then examines power domain by domain—sacred, military, political, economic, imperial, and so on—because each domain has its own structural mechanics. The book's second half examines the dynamics that cut across all domains: fear, consent, decline, hidden power, cyclical patterns, and the structural constants that persist across every form of power the book has described.

This book is not a manual for acquiring power, a moral evaluation of it, or a comprehensive survey of every civilization that exercised it. It is a structural analysis—neither optimistic nor pessimistic but diagnostic—that treats understanding power's mechanics as more useful than judging its morality or cataloging its every manifestation.

The chapters are designed to be read in order but do not depend on sequential reading. Each chapter introduces its subject, develops its structural argument, and connects to the broader themes of the book with enough context that a reader who begins partway through will understand what is being argued. That said, the book builds cumulatively, and the reader who begins at the beginning will have a richer experience of the later chapters—not because the later chapters are incomprehensible without the earlier ones but because the connections between chapters are part of the argument. Power does not operate in isolated domains. Neither does this book.

One final note. This book was written with the conviction that understanding power is not a luxury but a necessity—not for scholars, who have plenty of books on the subject already, but for anyone who lives within a power structure, which is everyone. The mechanic who understands the engine is better positioned than the driver who does not. The patient who understands the disease is better positioned than the one who only knows it hurts. The citizen who understands the structural dynamics of power is better positioned than the citizen who experiences power only as weather—something that happens to them, unpredictably, from above. This book aims to replace the weather experience with the structural one. It cannot make anyone powerful. It can make the machinery visible, and visibility is the prerequisite for every other form of engagement. You cannot fix what you cannot see. You cannot challenge what you do not understand. And you cannot participate meaningfully in the governance of your own life if you do not understand the systems that govern it for you. This book is an attempt to help with that understanding. Whether it succeeds is, appropriately, the reader's call.

Core Concepts

Tʜᴇ ᴄʜᴀᴘᴛᴇʀs ᴛʜᴀᴛ ꜰᴏʟʟᴏᴡ return to a small set of terms with enough regularity that they function as the working vocabulary of the book. They are defined where they first appear, but readers may find it useful to have them collected in one place. The list is not exhaustive. It is the minimum set required to follow the structural argument.

Power.
The capacity to determine outcomes, including what does not occur.

Power concerns control over results, not necessarily direct control over people or territory. Those are often mechanisms through which power operates rather than power itself.

Authority.
The recognized right to issue commands and expect compliance.

Authority reduces the need for force because people enforce its rules upon themselves. The difference between governing a continent and merely occupying a city is often the difference between authority and coercion.

Coercion.
Compliance produced through threat, punishment, or force.

Coercion is expensive to sustain and difficult to scale. Systems rely on it most heavily when legitimacy and authority have weakened or failed.

Legitimacy.
The belief that a system has the right to operate as it does.

Legitimacy does not require admiration or agreement. It requires only enough acceptance that most people continue acting within the system without constant enforcement.

Legitimacy lowers the cost of rule by making authority effective and coercion infrequent.

Visible Power.
Forms of power openly recognized, exercised, and contested as power.

Laws, military force, executive decisions, and corporate directives belong to visible power because they are openly acknowledged, debated, and contested.

Visible power can be challenged because it presents itself openly.

Invisible Power.
The shaping of perception, assumptions, and available choices.

Invisible power shapes which questions are asked, which possibilities are perceived as natural, and which arrangements become difficult to imagine otherwise.

It is more difficult to challenge because it is not often recognized as power at all.

Institutional Power.
Power embedded within positions, offices, and systems rather than individuals.

Individuals leave, but institutions persist. The office survives the office-holder.

This transfer of power from person to position is one of the foundational developments of complex societies.

Resource Conversion.
The ability to transform one form of power into another.

Military force can become territorial control. Territorial control can become economic extraction. Economic extraction can become political loyalty. Political loyalty can become renewed military capacity.

Power compounds because these conversions reinforce one another over time.

Self-Preservation.
The tendency of institutions to direct resources toward their own continuation.

Once an institution acquires the ability to act independently, preserving itself becomes part of its operational logic.

Self-preservation is not necessarily corruption. It is a structural consequence of institutional existence.

Normalization:
The process by which a particular arrangement comes to be perceived as natural rather than constructed.

Arrangements that are perceived as natural do not need to be defended, because they do not appear to be choices.

Normalization stabilizes systems by removing the perception of alternatives.

These concepts provide the structural vocabulary for the chapters that follow. The terms recur because the dynamics they describe recur. Power changes appearance across societies, institutions, and historical periods. Its underlying mechanisms change far less than its surface forms.

1
POWER DEFINED

"Power tends to corrupt;
absolute power corrupts absolutely."

Lord Acton
Letter to Bishop Creighton (1887)

POWER IS THE MOST discussed and least examined word in political life. Everyone uses it. Politicians claim it, protestors challenge it, historians trace it, philosophers build careers debating it. Yet for all the attention, the word remains functionally vague, treated as self-evident, something people recognize when they see it but rarely bother to take apart. The vagueness is not an oversight. It is a feature. Power benefits from imprecision the way a pickpocket benefits from a crowd. The less clearly it is understood, the harder it is to resist, redirect, or dismantle. Clarity is not in power's interest, which is reason enough to pursue it.

What Power Actually Is

At its most fundamental level, power is control over outcomes. Not control over people, though that is often a consequence. Not control over territory, though that is often a mechanism. Power is the capacity to determine what happens—and, equally important, what does not happen. A king who decides tax policy exercises power. So does the advisor who determines which policy options the king ever sees. So does the bureaucrat who decides how vigorously the policy is enforced. So does the merchant who decides whether to comply or to develop a creative interpretation of the relevant statute. Power is distributed across these actors in different concentrations, but it is present in each case because each one shapes what actually occurs. The king gets the portrait. The advisor gets the outcome.

The definition is deliberately broad, and it needs to be. One of the persistent errors in how power is discussed is the tendency to locate it in a single point—usually the most visible one. We speak of the power of presidents, generals, and CEOs as though authority flows downward from a single source, a waterfall model of governance that is flattering to the people at the top and inaccurate about everything else. Power in practice is relational. It exists between people, not within them. A president who issues an order that no one follows has a title. A prisoner who convinces a guard to look the other way has power. The title confers the expectation. The relationship determines whether the expectation is met.

This relational quality makes power inherently dynamic. It shifts without any formal change in structure. A parliament may hold identical legal authority from one decade to the next while its actual capacity to shape outcomes quietly evaporates. A corporation may hold no official governing role while its decisions reshape the lives of millions of people who never voted for its board of directors and could not name them under oath. Understanding power requires looking past the organizational chart and examining where outcomes are actually being determined. This is harder than it sounds. Organizational charts are printed, laminated, and hung in lobbies. Actual power flows are none of these things.

A few distinctions are worth drawing before we proceed, because the words that cluster around power are used interchangeably by people who should know better. Influence is the capacity to shape decisions without direct control over them. A newspaper editorial board influences policy; it does not set policy. The distinction matters because influence operates through persuasion, which requires at least the appearance of voluntary agreement, while power can operate through compulsion. Dominance is the ability to override resistance. A military occupation is dominance. But dominance without legitimacy is expensive and unstable, as we will see with monotonous regularity throughout this book. Power in its most effective form requires neither constant persuasion nor constant compulsion. It operates through systems that make compliance the default—the path of least resistance in a landscape that someone else designed.

AUTHORITY VERSUS COERCION

The distinction between authority and coercion is the first great fault line in understanding power. Both produce compliance. Both result in people doing things they would not otherwise do. But the mechanism is entirely different, and the mechanism determines how long the compliance lasts and how much it costs to maintain.

Coercion operates through the threat or application of harm. Do this or something bad will happen to you. The logic is straightforward, the implementation is direct, and the results are immediate. A conquering army coerces a population into submission. A feudal lord coerces peasants into labor. A government coerces tax payment through the threat of imprisonment. In each case, compliance is achieved not because the subject agrees with the demand but because the cost of resistance exceeds the cost of submission. The math is simple. The human experience of it is not, but coercion has never been particularly interested in the human experience.

Authority operates through recognized legitimacy. People comply not because they fear punishment but because they accept the right of the authority to make the demand. A judge sentences a defendant, and the defendant accepts the sentence—not because the judge has a weapon, but because the defendant recognizes the court's authority to pass judgment. A parent instructs a child, and the child obeys—not from fear of violence, but from an internalized recognition of the parent's role. The outward compliance is identical in both cases. The cost of maintaining it is radically different, and the difference is where the interesting analysis begins.

Coercion requires constant surveillance and the credible threat of enforcement. Every act of disobedience must be detected and punished, or the system loses its deterrent effect. This is enormously expensive. The Soviet Union maintained one of the most extensive internal security apparatuses in human history, employing millions of informants and security officers, and it still could not prevent the slow erosion of compliance that eventually contributed to its collapse. Coercion works in the short term. Over years and decades, it generates resistance, resentment, and the constant search for opportunities to defect. It is governance by exhaustion—and the governed are not the only ones who get tired.

Authority is largely self-enforcing. When people accept the legitimacy of a system, they police themselves. They pay taxes without auditors checking every return. They follow laws without a police officer on every corner. They defer to institutional decisions they personally disagree with because they accept the framework in which those decisions were made. This self-enforcement represents an enormous efficiency advantage—one so large that it is, in structural terms, the difference between a system that can govern a continent and one that can barely hold a city. Legitimate governments operate with far smaller security forces relative to their populations than illegitimate ones. The ratio is diagnostic. When the security budget grows faster than the economy, something has gone wrong with the legitimacy, not the security.

The line between authority and coercion is rarely clean. Most functioning systems employ both. A democratic government relies primarily on authority—citizens accept the legitimacy of elected officials—but it maintains police forces and prisons for those who do not comply voluntarily. A colonial administration relies primarily on coercion—the conquered population has not consented to being governed by strangers who arrived on boats—but it typically seeks to develop at least some appearance of authority through co-opted local elites, legal frameworks, and institutional trappings that lend an air of permanence to what is essentially an occupation with stationery. The ratio of authority to coercion in any given system is one of the best indicators of its long-term prospects. Systems heavy on coercion are fragile. Systems heavy on authority are resilient. The history of power is substantially the history of this conversion—the ongoing, never fully completed effort to transform force into legitimacy and compliance into something that resembles consent.

Legitimacy as Efficiency Multiplier

If authority is self-enforcing compliance, then legitimacy is the mechanism that produces authority. Legitimacy is the widespread belief that a given arrangement of power is proper, justified, or at least tolerable. It does not require enthusiasm. It does not require agreement with every decision. It requires only the general acceptance that the system has the right to operate as it does—a bar so low that it is remarkable how many regimes fail to clear it. This acceptance, once established, transforms the economics of power entirely.

Consider the difference in cost between a legitimate and an illegitimate regime attempting the same task—collecting taxes equal to twenty percent of economic output. A government with strong legitimacy achieves this through a relatively modest tax administration. Citizens file returns, businesses withhold wages, banks report interest income. The vast majority comply voluntarily, enforcement resources concentrate on the small minority who do not, and the cost of collection is a fraction of the revenue generated. The system runs on trust, habit, and the quiet understanding that everyone else is also complying, which makes non-compliance feel antisocial rather than heroic.

Now consider the same task under a military occupation that the population regards as illegitimate. Every transaction must be monitored. Evasion is not a crime that citizens report; it is a form of resistance that neighbors celebrate and assist. Enforcement requires soldiers, not auditors. The cost of collection rises dramatically, the revenue collected falls, and the process of collection itself generates the resentment that erodes compliance further. Same task, same population, radically different costs—the only variable is whether the population regards the entity collecting the money as having the right to collect it. Legitimacy does not create power from nothing. A legitimate government with no army, no bureaucracy, and no treasury still cannot govern. But legitimacy amplifies the effectiveness of every instrument of power that does exist. An army fights harder for a cause its soldiers believe in. A bureaucracy functions better when its officials believe in its mission. A treasury fills faster when citizens believe the system is fair. Every component of the power apparatus works better with legitimacy beneath it. Without it, every component works worse, costs more, and eventually breaks.

The sources of legitimacy have varied enormously across history—divine mandate, military conquest, democratic election, revolutionary struggle, economic performance, tradition, personal charisma. What they share is that legitimacy is always granted from below, even when it appears to flow from above. A king claims divine right, but the claim only works because the population believes it—or at least does not disbelieve it forcefully enough to act on the disbelief. An emperor claims the mandate of heaven, but the mandate holds only as long as enough people accept the premise. Legitimacy is a collective fiction—not because it is false, but because it exists only as long as enough people act as though it is true. This makes it both powerful and fragile. Powerful because when it holds, it makes governance almost effortless. Fragile because when it cracks, no quantity of force can fully substitute for what has been lost.

The fragility explains a pattern that recurs throughout this book: the disproportionate response of power to symbolic challenges. Regimes that tolerate significant material threats sometimes react with extraordinary violence to symbolic ones. A government may accept smuggling, tax evasion, and petty corruption as manageable costs of doing business while treating a protest movement, a satirical newspaper, or a dissident intellectual as existential threats requiring the full attention of the security apparatus. This is not irrational. It is structurally logical. The smuggler costs the state revenue. The dissident threatens the state's legitimacy. Revenue can be replaced. Legitimacy, once lost, is extraordinarily difficult to rebuild—a fact that explains why the satirist has historically been treated as more dangerous than the thief, and why the satirist has historically been right to take the compliment seriously.

Power, then, is control over outcomes—relational, multi-dimensional, and often invisible. It operates most efficiently when supported by legitimacy rather than sustained by force. It functions on multiple levels simultaneously, from the visible drama of decision-making to the invisible shaping of what people believe is possible. And it is most completely exercised when it prevents challenges from arising rather than defeating them after they emerge.

The most serious objection to a structural account of power is that it understates the role of human agency. Leaders make choices. Movements take shape because particular people decide to organize them. Reforms happen because someone chose to draft, propose, and fight for them. This is true and important. The structural account does not deny it. It denies that agency operates in a vacuum. The leader chooses among options the structure makes available. The movement organizes within constraints the structure imposes. The reformer drafts language that the structure will accept and rejects language it will not. Agency is real. It is also nested inside structure, which is why two leaders facing similar conditions tend to produce similar outcomes despite their personal differences. The structure does not eliminate the person. It explains why the person's range of effective action is narrower than the person believes.

These are the conceptual tools we carry through the rest of this book. They are not abstractions. They are lenses for examining how human societies have organized control over the past several thousand years. Every chapter that follows—from sacred power to military force, from economic leverage to cultural influence, from institutional persistence to popular revolt—returns to these fundamentals. Power is a system, not an event. Understanding it requires seeing the system, not just the moments when it becomes visible. The moments are dramatic. The system is what produces them. This book is about the system.

Three terms anchor the rest of the book: power as control over outcomes, authority as self-enforcing compliance, and legitimacy as the mechanism that makes self-enforcement possible. The chapters ahead vary the form. The fundamentals do not.

A note on usage. This book uses the word power in several related but not identical senses, and it is worth flagging this at the outset rather than letting the inconsistency accumulate. Sometimes power refers to a relation—what one party can get another to do, in the classic formulation. Sometimes it refers to a substance that converts between forms, the way capital converts between physical, financial, and cultural varieties. Sometimes it refers to a systemic property—the way arrangements produce outcomes that no individual decided and no individual can be held responsible for. Each of these is a real and useful sense of the word, and the philosophical literature has spent a century arguing about which is primary. This book treats the family resemblance among them as the unit of analysis, on the grounds that the dynamics it describes—accumulation, conversion, legitimation, normalization, resistance—operate across all three senses, and that requiring conceptual purity at this level would foreclose the cross-domain pattern recognition that is the project. Steven Lukes, in Power: A Radical View, distinguishes three faces of power that map roughly onto these three senses, and a reader who wants the philosophical apparatus should start there. This book is interested in the patterns rather than the philosophy.

2

VISIBLE AND INVISIBLE POWER

*"The best rulers are scarcely known. When their work
is done, the people say: 'We did it ourselves."*

Lao Tzu, Tao Te Ching
Ch. 17 (c. 6th c. BCE)

THE PREVIOUS CHAPTER DEFINED power as control over outcomes and traced the basic mechanics of authority, coercion, and legitimacy. What that chapter did not address—and what shapes everything in the chapters that follow—is that power does not appear in a single form. It operates on multiple levels at once, and the level that matters most is almost never the one being looked at.

The political theorist Steven Lukes formalized this layered structure as the three faces of power. The first face is decisions made openly in observable conflict — votes, laws, court rulings, the ordinary public business of governance. The second face is decisions kept off the agenda entirely — the issues that never become issues, because the conditions for raising them have been foreclosed before anyone can speak. The third face is preferences shaped by power before any conflict arises, so that the people most disadvantaged by an arrangement are the most likely to defend it. The framework has organized political-science thinking about power for fifty years, and it is the implicit organizing schema for this chapter and for the chapters on hidden power and structural influence later in the book. The visible-invisible-hidden distinction this book uses is a translation of Lukes's framework into language closer to ordinary speech.

The visible exercise of power is a small fraction of the total. The vote is counted. The contract is signed. The order is given. These are the moments when power becomes legible, and they are also the moments when power has the least at stake. The decisive work has already happened: in the selection of which candidates were on the ballot, in the drafting of the contract's standard terms, in the establishment of the chain of command that made the order obey-able. By the time power is visible, the contest has usually been settled by forces operating elsewhere.

This chapter examines those forces. It introduces the conceptual distinction between visible and invisible power, surveys the three dimensions on which power operates, and confronts the methodological problem that follows from accepting the distinction: how do you measure something that is most effective when it cannot be seen? The answer, it turns out, is that you accept you cannot measure it precisely, and you adjust your expectations accordingly. The chapter then turns to a present-day case—the modern corporation—that will reappear throughout the rest of the book as the running example of how visible and invisible power operate together in a single institutional form.

The Architecture of Power

Power operates on multiple levels simultaneously, and the most consequential level is usually the one nobody is watching. Political theorist Steven Lukes identified three dimensions of power, and the framework has proven durable because it distinguishes between power that announces itself and power that operates by determining what choices seem available in the first place. These distinctions are essential to understanding how control actually works in practice and why the people subject to it so rarely recognize its full extent.

The first dimension is decision-making power—the ability to prevail in observable conflicts. When a legislature votes on a bill, when a court issues a ruling, when a general orders an advance, we are watching decision-making power in action. This is the dimension that dominates popular understanding because it produces identifiable events with clear winners and losers. News coverage, political commentary, and historical narrative focus overwhelmingly on this dimension for the same reason that sports coverage focuses on goals rather than training regimes: the visible moment is easier to narrate than the invisible process that produced it.

The second dimension is agenda-setting power—the ability to determine which decisions are made and which never reach the table. This is considerably more consequential than decision-making power and considerably less photogenic. If a corporation can ensure that the question of its tax obligations never reaches the legislative agenda, it has achieved a more complete victory than defeating a specific tax proposal in a floor vote—and achieved it without the inconvenience of a public fight. If a political party can define the boundaries of acceptable policy debate, it wins even on issues where it appears to lose, because the losing happens within a framework it established. Agenda-setting power is exercised in committee rooms, editorial meetings, donor conversations, and bureaucratic processes that never attract a camera crew. It is the power to define what counts as a realistic option and what is dismissed as impractical, radical, or not worth the time. The dismissal is the exercise. Everything that follows is negotiation within boundaries that someone else drew.

The third dimension is the deepest and the most difficult to see, which is precisely why it is the most effective. It is the power to shape preferences, beliefs, and perceptions so thoroughly that conflict never arises in the first place. If a population has been educated to believe that extreme inequality is natural and inevitable, no revolution will be necessary to maintain that inequality—the population will maintain it for you, free of charge. If workers believe their interests are aligned with their employer's, no coercion will be necessary to prevent labor organizing. If citizens believe the existing political options represent the full range of possibility, no repression will be necessary to prevent radical challenges. This dimension of power operates through culture, education, media, religion, and the accumulated weight of tradition. It shapes what people want, what they expect, and what they believe is possible. It is the most efficient form of power because it eliminates the need for either coercion or visible authority. The population does the work itself, and does not send an invoice.

These three dimensions do not operate independently. They reinforce one another with the reliability of compound interest. A regime that controls decision-making can use that control to shape agendas. Agenda-setting power, exercised over time, shapes beliefs. A ruling class that controls the education system shapes the beliefs of each new generation, which affects what agenda items are considered legitimate, which determines what decisions are available to be made. The cumulative effect is a system of power that appears natural—not because it is, but because the power to define what seems natural has been exercised so effectively that the exercise itself has become invisible. The system does not look like power. It looks like the world.

The pattern is easier to see in cases where the three dimensions can be reconstructed from the historical record. Consider the East India Company in the late eighteenth century. The visible dimension was straightforward: a private trading firm with a charter from Parliament, conducting commercial operations across the subcontinent, occasionally fielding troops to protect its assets. The agenda-setting dimension was less visible but already substantial: the Company's directors and shareholders included sitting members of Parliament, which meant that the legislative agenda affecting the Company's regulatory environment was largely determined inside the institution being regulated. The third dimension was the most consequential and the least documented: the conceptual framework within which all of this operated, in which an English commercial venture administering an entire subcontinent through private armies was understood as legitimate trade rather than as conquest. None of these dimensions was hidden in the literal sense. The Company's annual reports were public. Its parliamentary connections were known. Its administrative footprint was visible from London to Calcutta. What was hidden was the reframing that made the whole arrangement appear to be commerce. Once that reframing was in place, the question of whether a private corporation should be governing a hundred million people did not arise as a serious political question for nearly a century, because the language for asking it had not been assembled.

This invisibility isn't exclusive to authoritarian systems. Democracies exhibit the same pattern through different mechanisms. Electoral choice may be broad in theory but narrow in practice because campaign financing, media access, and party organization limit which candidates are viable before a vote is cast. The decisions reaching voters are shaped by processes most never see and few understand. The beliefs informing voter preferences are shaped by media ecosystems, educational institutions, and cultural narratives that are themselves products of power. None of this requires conspiracy—only that each level operates by its own logic while collectively favoring those who already hold disproportionate influence. Conspiracy requires coordination. Structure requires only design, and the design needn't be intentional to be effective.

MEASUREMENT PROBLEMS

If power is difficult to define precisely and often operates invisibly, it follows that measuring it is a project that should come with a warning label. Yet measurement matters. Claims about who has power, how much they have, and how it is distributed are central to political debate, policy-making, and historical analysis. When these claims rest on poor measurement, the conclusions drawn from them are unreliable. And unreliable conclusions about power tend to serve the interests of whoever the measurement failed to capture, which is usually the people who were most invested in not being measured.

The most common approach is to observe outcomes and attribute power to whoever appears to have won. If a bill passes that favors industry over environmental groups, industry had more power on that issue. If a war ends with territorial gains for one side, the victorious side was more powerful. The approach has the advantage of simplicity and the disadvantage of being frequently wrong. Outcomes are the product of many factors—including luck, timing, and the kind of miscalculation that produces results nobody intended. Attributing outcomes to power alone is reasoning backward from results to causes, which is the analytical equivalent of deciding that the rooster's crow caused the sunrise because one reliably precedes the other.

A more sophisticated approach attempts to measure power through resources—wealth, military capacity, institutional positions, social connections. This avoids the circularity problem by measuring inputs before outcomes are known. But it introduces a different problem: the conversion rate between resources and power is neither fixed nor predictable. A billionaire has enormous potential power but may exercise none of it, preferring to spend the money on yachts and anxiety. A small but well-organized activist group may exercise influence far beyond what its budget would suggest. Resources are necessary conditions for power but not sufficient ones. The capacity to convert resources into outcomes depends on organization, strategy, legitimacy, and a constellation of contextual factors that resist the kind of quantification that would make political science feel more like physics. It will not feel more like physics. The subject will not cooperate.

A third approach focuses on reputation—asking people who they believe is powerful. This captures information about perceptions, which matter in their own right because perceived power often functions as actual power. If everyone believes a particular official is the real decision-maker, people act accordingly, which may make it true regardless of the organizational chart. But reputational measures are biased toward visible power and miss the deeper dimensions entirely. The people who are most successfully exercising invisible power are precisely those whose influence is least likely to show up in a survey—which means the survey is systematically undercounting the power that matters most.

Each approach captures a piece of the picture. None captures the whole, and this is not a methodological failure that better techniques will resolve. It is a fundamental feature of the subject. Power is relational, contextual, multi-dimensional, and partly constituted by perception. It is the kind of phenomenon that resists reduction to a single number, and anyone who offers you a single number is selling something—usually a consulting contract. The honest approach is to use multiple measures, acknowledge their limitations, and remain skeptical of any claim that power has been definitively mapped. Maps of power are always incomplete. The incompleteness always favors somebody.

This does not mean nothing useful can be said. It means the useful things are structural observations rather than precise measurements. We can observe that certain institutional arrangements consistently produce concentrated power. We can observe that certain economic structures consistently translate wealth into political influence. We can observe that certain cultural conditions consistently legitimate existing hierarchies. These patterns are robust even if the precise degree of power at any given point is uncertain. The chapters that follow rely on this approach: identifying the structural conditions under which power is built, maintained, and lost, rather than attempting to assign it a number and a decimal point.

Take a present-day case. Suppose the question is who holds power in the technology sector. The decision-making approach would tabulate corporate executive votes, regulatory agency rulings, and Congressional outcomes. It would produce a list dominated by named individuals: CEOs, commissioners, committee chairs. The resource approach would tabulate market capitalization, lobbying expenditure, patent holdings, and engineering headcount. It would produce a different list, dominated by firms rather than people. The reputational approach would survey industry observers and produce a third list, in which firms and individuals are mixed together and the rankings track perceptions that may or may not correspond to either decision-making outcomes or resource bases. None of these lists would be wrong. None of them would be complete. The complete picture would also have to include the agenda-setting dimension—who determines which technical standards become defaults, which platforms become infrastructure, which ways of building software become professional norms—and the third dimension, which would have to account for the cultural production of the assumption that technological progress is largely autonomous, mostly beneficial, and the proper province of private firms rather than public institutions. That third dimension is exercised by hiring practices, business-school curricula, science-fiction novels, government-relations strategies, and the unwillingness of major news organizations to cover technology as a political subject rather than as a consumer one. None of these mechanisms shows up in any of the three measurement approaches, and the omission is not a flaw in the methods. It is a consequence of the subject. The most consequential power in this sector cannot be measured because it operates by determining what counts as a measurement.

One final problem deserves attention because it affects everything that follows. Power tends to be measured in terms of what it does—the decisions it makes, the resources it commands, the conflicts it wins. But some of the most consequential exercises of power involve things that do not happen. The strike that is never called because workers know it will fail. The legislation that is never proposed because its sponsors know it will be vetoed. The protest that never materializes because potential participants believe it will be futile or dangerous. These non-events are exercises of power in their purest form: cases where control over outcomes is so complete that resistance never becomes visible. They are also, by definition, the hardest form of power to study, because there is no event to observe. The absence of conflict is not the absence of power. It is often the most complete expression of it. The most successful exercise of control is the one that never has to be exercised at all.

How Power Hides in Plain Sight

The most reliable test of whether something is power is whether the people exercising it bother to defend it as power. The state defends its authority constantly—through speeches, through ceremonies, through the visible deployment of police, courts, and armies. The corporation, by contrast, almost never describes itself as exercising power at all. It describes itself as conducting business, serving customers, optimizing operations, creating value. The vocabulary is technical and procedural. The activity it describes is among the most consequential exercises of power in the modern world.

This is not a coincidence. It is the shape of how invisible power presents itself. The corporation does not need to claim authority because it does not need consent in the political sense. It needs only employment, supply, and a regulatory environment that does not interfere too aggressively—and it has acquired considerable capacity to shape all three. The Walmart store in a small town does not announce itself as a political actor. It nonetheless determines what wages the local labor market can sustain, which suppliers stay in business, which products are stocked, which products are not, and which civic norms are reinforced or undermined by the rhythm of life it imposes on the surrounding economy. None of this is voted on. None of it is legislated. None of it requires legitimacy, because none of it is being recognized as power.

The same pattern operates at scale. A large pharmaceutical firm does not need to legislate which diseases get researched. It only needs to set its R&D budget, and the diseases that fall outside the budget go untreated. A platform company does not need to censor speech. It only needs to design its recommendation algorithm, and the speech that the algorithm de-prioritizes effectively disappears. A consulting firm does not need to write public policy. It only needs to be hired to advise the agencies that do, and its frameworks become the assumptions inside which the policy is drafted. In each case, the visible activity—the budget, the algorithm, the consulting engagement—is procedural and unremarkable. The invisible consequence is the structure of choice for everyone downstream.

This is not a recent development. The corporation has functioned as a vehicle for invisible power for as long as it has existed in something like its modern form, and the older examples make the structural pattern legible in ways the current ones obscure. The chartered companies of the early modern period—the East India Company most spectacularly, but also the Dutch East India Company, the Hudson's Bay Company, the Royal African Company—exercised governmental power across continents while describing themselves as commercial firms. They issued currency, fielded armies, conducted diplomacy, administered courts, and fought wars. They did all of this under charters from states that had effectively delegated public functions to private actors and then failed, for decades or in some cases centuries, to recognize what they had delegated. The fiction that these were trading companies rather than governments was sustained by the legal vocabulary of incorporation, by the accounting conventions that classified administrative expenditures as operating costs, and by the political theorists of the period who treated commerce and governance as separable spheres long after the separation had ceased to describe any actual institution. The historical pattern is suggestive. When power is exercised by an institution that nobody is calling a government, the absence of the word does most of the structural work. The institution does not have to hide. It only has to be miscategorized.

The corporation is also instructive because it makes the three-dimensional model unusually legible. A board vote is decision-making power: a visible event, a recorded outcome, a clear winner and loser. The setting of the corporate strategy that defines what reaches the board agenda is agenda-setting power: less photogenic, more consequential, exercised in offsites and email threads that no shareholder will ever read. The training of executives, the curation of business-school curricula, the financial-press conventions about what constitutes a successful company—these are the third dimension, the shaping of preferences and beliefs at a level so foundational that the people operating within them experience the framework as objective reality rather than as one possible framework among many. The MBA who has internalized that quarterly earnings are the primary measure of corporate success is not being coerced into that belief. The belief was installed during education, reinforced by professional culture, and ratified by the financial markets that pay for compliance with it. By the time the MBA is making decisions, the dimension of power that matters most has already exercised itself, and it has done so without ever appearing in any minutes.

This invisibility is also the corporation's most durable defense. A government that exercises power must justify itself in the language of legitimacy—must claim consent, or divine right, or constitutional authority, or some other ground for the population's compliance. A corporation has no equivalent burden. Its activity is described as economic rather than political, and the description is largely accepted, which means the question of legitimacy never has to be answered in public. The political theorist who suggests that the corporation exercises political power on the scale of a small state is dismissed as a polemicist; the financial analyst who reports that the same corporation has captured 80 percent of its market is reporting business news. The two statements describe the same fact. The framing determines which one feels controversial.

The defense is durable but not absolute. Corporate invisibility breaks down under specific conditions: when the firm's actions are sufficiently visible that the activity-as-business framing becomes implausible (a chemical spill, a financial collapse, a labor practice that crosses into open scandal); when a competing institutional actor with sufficient legitimacy points at the corporation and reframes its activity as power (a state, a movement, occasionally a court); or when the firm itself, through internal failure or external miscalculation, is forced to describe its own behavior in language that exposes what was previously procedural as discretionary. These breakdowns are real, and they sometimes produce reform. They do not, in most cases, produce structural change. The firm is sanctioned, the practice is adjusted, the language returns to procedure, and the underlying mechanics resume. The visibility that briefly forced the corporation to defend itself fades, and with it the political pressure that the visibility had generated. The pattern of invisibility-disruption-restoration is one of the most consistent dynamics in the modern political record, and the chapters ahead will return to it whenever a structural form of power is briefly exposed and then resumes its operations under a slightly modified vocabulary. The vocabulary does most of the work.

The corporation will return as the running example throughout this book. Sacred power will reappear in the rituals of corporate culture and the legitimacy-generating function of mission statements. Political power will reappear in the bureaucratic structure of corporate administration and the regulatory environments corporations help to design. Economic power will reappear in the most direct way of all, since the corporation is the principal vehicle through which economic power is currently exercised. Institutional power will reappear in the corporation's outliving of its founders. Knowledge power will reappear in the platform corporation's monopoly over data. Hidden power will reappear in the corporation's capacity to set agendas and shape preferences without ever appearing as a coercive actor. The point is not that the corporation is uniquely powerful. The point is that it is the institution in which the structural mechanics of power are presently most concentrated, most visible to the analyst, and most invisible to the public—which makes it the cleanest available case for watching the dynamics this book describes operate in real time.

The chapters that follow examine power as it has manifested across history—sacred, military, political, economic, imperial, institutional, cultural, technological, popular. Each of those forms operates in both registers, the visible and the invisible. The visible register is the one the historical record mostly preserves: the battle, the decree, the coronation, the strike. The invisible register is what determined whether the visible register would matter—the assumptions inside which the battle was fought, the legitimacy that authorized the decree, the cosmology that anointed the king, the framework within which the strike was understood as legitimate or as criminal. To see only the visible register is to read the photograph and miss the negative. The book's argument, in the chapters ahead, is that the negative is where the structural action mostly is.

3
POWER BEFORE STATES

B EFORE THERE WERE KINGS, before there were laws, before there were borders drawn on maps or taxes collected in ledgers, there was power. It looked nothing like the forms we recognize today—no thrones, no bureaucracies, no written constitutions, no organizational charts laminated and hung in lobbies. But power was present in every human group that has ever existed, because every human group has faced the same fundamental problem: how to coordinate action, resolve disputes, and distribute resources among individuals whose interests do not naturally align. The solutions that early human societies developed for these problems created the first structures of power, and those structures cast shadows that reach into the present. The shadows are longer than most people realize.

TRIBAL HIERARCHY AND KINSHIP AUTHORITY

The earliest human social groups were small bands of perhaps twenty to fifty individuals, rarely exceeding a hundred and fifty. At this scale, power operated through mechanisms that are almost unrecognizable to anyone accustomed to thinking about states and institutions. There were no offices to hold, no laws to enforce, no armies to command. What there was, universally and without exception, was hierarchy. Even the most egalitarian foraging bands that anthropologists have studied exhibit patterns of differential influence. Some individuals consistently shape group decisions more than others. Some voices carry more weight in discussions. Some people eat first. Egalitarianism, it turns out, is a matter of degree rather than kind, and the degree has never been zero.

Anthropologist Elman Service's classification of human political organization—from bands to tribes to chiefdoms to states—provides a useful framework for understanding this progression, though the chapter that follows treats the categories as ideal types rather than rigid stages. The primary organizing principle of these early hierarchies was kinship. Blood relationships and marriage alliances determined who owed what to whom, who could command loyalty, and who could call on others for support in a dispute. Kinship was not merely a social convention. It was the operating system of pre-state power—the framework on which everything else ran. In the absence of formal institutions, kinship networks provided the only reliable mechanism for establishing obligations, resolving conflicts, and organizing collective action. Your brother was obligated to fight alongside you not because a law required it but because the kinship bond carried an expectation of mutual support that was enforced by the entire community. Violating kinship obligations meant social death—exclusion from the network of reciprocal aid that made survival possible. There was no appeals process.

Kinship-based authority had distinctive properties that set it apart from every form of power that followed. It was deeply personal. Authority resided not in a position but in a relationship. A respected elder did not hold an office that could be transferred to a successor the way a modern CEO transfers a corner office. The elder's influence was a function of specific personal relationships, accumulated reputation, and demonstrated competence. When the elder died, the influence died with them. It had to be rebuilt from scratch by whoever came next, using their own relationships and their own track record. Every transition was a reset. Every generation started the negotiation over.

Kinship authority was also inherently limited in scale. The web of blood relationships and marriage alliances that sustained it could only extend so far before it became too thin to bear weight. Anthropologist Robin Dunbar estimated the cognitive limit at roughly a hundred and fifty stable relationships—the number of people a human brain can maintain meaningful social bonds with simultaneously. Beyond that number, strangers appeared. People who were neither relatives nor affines had to be dealt with, and kinship had no protocol for dealing with them. This limit created a ceiling on the size and complexity of kinship-based societies, and breaking through that ceiling would eventually require entirely new foundations for power. But for the overwhelming majority of human history, the ceiling was never reached. Most people lived and died knowing everyone who mattered, and kinship was the grammar in which every obligation was expressed.

The authority of kinship operated through obligation and shame rather than through command and punishment. An elder who wanted the group to move camp did not issue an order. The elder expressed a preference, made an argument, invoked shared experiences, and relied on the accumulated weight of past good judgment to carry the group along. If the elder's judgment had been consistently poor, no amount of seniority would compensate—a principle that many modern institutions would benefit from rediscovering. If a younger member had demonstrated superior skill in reading the landscape or tracking game, that person's opinion might carry more weight on that specific question regardless of age or genealogical position. Authority in these settings was task-specific and reputation-dependent. It bore almost no resemblance to the generalized, transferable, all-purpose authority that would emerge later and that we now treat as the default meaning of the word.

Physical Dominance and Resource Control

Kinship was the dominant framework for pre-state authority, but it was not the only one. Running alongside it—sometimes reinforcing it, sometimes competing with it—was a more primal basis for hierarchy: physical dominance. The capacity for violence, or more precisely the perceived capacity for violence, has been a source of power in every human society ever documented. In pre-state groups, where formal mechanisms for restraining aggression were weak or nonexistent, the individual who could fight most effectively held a form of influence that no amount of genealogical disadvantage could entirely negate. Blood ties matter. So does blood.

This was not the cartoonish vision of a muscular brute terrorizing a cowering group into submission. Physical dominance in small-scale societies was mediated by coalition dynamics. A single strong individual could be overcome by three or four cooperating weaker ones, and the cooperating weaker ones knew it. The anthropological and primatological evidence consistently shows that physical dominance in social species is not about individual strength alone. It is about the ability to form and maintain alliances. The most dominant individuals in pre-state groups were typically those who combined physical capability with social intelligence—the capacity to build coalitions, reward supporters, and isolate rivals. Raw strength without social skill produced bullies who were eventually brought down by collective action. Social skill without physical credibility produced advisors and mediators—influential but not dominant. The combination produced leaders. The pattern has not changed as much as we like to think.

Resource control represented a third axis of pre-state power, distinct from both kinship and physical capacity. In environments where critical resources—water sources, productive hunting grounds, stands of fruit-bearing trees, deposits of tool-quality stone—were unevenly distributed, individuals or groups who controlled access to those resources held leverage over everyone else. This leverage could be exercised through sharing, which created obligation, or through restriction, which created dependency. In either case, resource control translated into social power. The person who controlled the water did not need to be the strongest or the best connected. They needed to be standing next to the water.

The dynamics of resource control in pre-state societies prefigured patterns that would recur throughout the rest of human history with the reliability of a recurring decimal. Generosity was a tool of power. In many documented foraging and horticultural societies, the most influential individuals were not those who accumulated the most but those who gave away the most. The potlatch ceremonies of the Pacific Northwest, the feast-giving traditions of Melanesian big men, the meat-sharing norms of African foraging bands—all represent variations on the same underlying logic. By distributing resources, the generous individual created a web of social debts. Those debts could be called in when the individual needed support, labor, or political backing. The gift was never free. It was an investment in social capital that would yield returns in the currency of influence. Philanthropy, in its structural essence, was invented roughly forty thousand years before the word was.

This pattern is worth dwelling on because it inverts the assumption that power flows from hoarding. In many pre-state societies, aggressive accumulation was not just ineffective as a power strategy—it was actively dangerous. Hoarding marked an individual as a threat to the group's survival and could trigger collective punishment ranging from ridicule to ostracism to execution, a progression that escalated with impressive speed when the group felt its norms were being violated. The anthropologist Christopher Boehm documented extensive evidence of what he called reverse dominance hierarchies—social systems in which the group collectively suppressed any individual's attempt to dominate. Gossip, mockery, refusal to cooperate, and ultimately violence were deployed against would-be tyrants. These leveling mechanisms did not eliminate hierarchy. They kept it within bounds that the group could tolerate. They represented an early and enduring form of popular power—one that would echo in later revolutionary movements and democratic institutions, though the later versions would replace the mockery with constitutions and the executions with term limits. The structural impulse is the same.

The interplay of kinship, physical dominance, and resource control created pre-state power systems of considerable complexity. A successful leader in such a system needed to be embedded in a strong kinship network, physically credible or allied with those who were, and generous enough with resources to maintain a coalition of supporters. Failure on any one dimension could be compensated by strength on the others, but failure on all three was fatal to any ambition for influence. This multi-dimensional quality of pre-state power is important to recognize because it contradicts the simplistic narrative that early human hierarchy was purely about the strongest individual taking charge. It was never that simple. Power has never been that simple. The people who describe it as simple are usually selling a version that benefits them.

CONSENSUS GOVERNANCE AND ITS LIMITS

One of the most persistent myths about pre-state societies is that they were either anarchic—each individual doing as they pleased in a state of noble or ignoble savagery—or despotic—a single leader dictating to everyone else through superior violence. The ethnographic evidence supports neither picture. What it reveals instead is a third model: consensus governance. Decisions in most small-scale societies were made through extended discussion, negotiation, and the gradual emergence of agreement. This was not democracy in any formal sense. There were no votes, no constitutions, no minority protections. But there was a process by which the views of group members were heard, debated, and reconciled into a decision that most could accept. It was messy, slow, and remarkably effective within its operating parameters.

Consensus governance worked because it had to. In a group of fifty people who depended on one another for survival, imposing a decision over strong objections was not merely unjust. It was dangerous. A disgruntled minority could withdraw cooperation at the worst possible moment—during a hunt, a migration, a conflict with a neighboring group. Worse, they could leave. In an environment where group size was a critical survival variable, losing members to dissatisfaction was a threat no leader could afford to ignore. The need to maintain group cohesion imposed a structural constraint on the exercise of power that made consensus not an ideal but a practical necessity. The leader who failed to build consensus did not lose an election. The leader lost people, which in a band of forty meant losing the ability to defend a water source or bring down large game. Democracy's roots are not in philosophy. They are in arithmetic.

The mechanics of consensus governance varied across cultures, but certain patterns recurred. Discussion was typically led by senior or respected individuals, but leadership in discussion did not equate to decision-making authority. A skilled consensus leader guided conversation toward agreement without appearing to impose a preferred outcome—a talent that required enormous social intelligence and the patience of someone who had internalized the understanding that being seen to lead was the fastest way to lose the ability to lead. The best consensus leaders were, in effect, skilled politicians operating without any of the formal apparatus of politics. They managed egos, brokered compromises, and reframed disagreements in terms both sides could accept. The skills are identical to those required in any modern negotiation. The setting was different. The competence was not.

Consensus governance had genuine strengths. It produced decisions the entire group could support, which meant implementation was rarely a problem—a feature that modern legislatures, with their elaborate enforcement mechanisms for laws that half the population resents, might contemplate with some envy. It distributed information widely, since the discussion process required sharing knowledge and perspectives. It provided a check on individual ambition. And it generated legitimacy in its purest form: people complied with decisions because they had participated in making them.

But consensus governance also had severe limitations, and understanding these limitations is essential to understanding why states eventually emerged. The first was speed. Consensus takes time. When a decision needed to be made immediately—whether to flee from a predator, how to respond to a surprise attack, where to move when a water source dried up overnight—the slow process of discussion and negotiation was a liability that could be measured in bodies. Groups that could make fast decisions in emergencies had a survival advantage over groups that could not. This created pressure for leadership roles that could override consensus in moments of crisis—war chiefs, hunt leaders, individuals empowered to make binding decisions in specific, urgent circumstances. These emergency roles were the seeds from which permanent leadership positions would eventually grow. Temporary authority has a structural tendency to forget the temporary part.

The second limitation was scale. Consensus governance worked in groups where everyone knew everyone else, where the full range of opinions could be canvassed in a single gathering, and where social pressure could enforce compliance. As groups grew larger, these conditions eroded. With two hundred people, not everyone's voice could be heard. With five hundred, the full group could not practically assemble. With a thousand, consensus was physically impossible. Larger groups required delegation, representation, and hierarchy—mechanisms that were fundamentally incompatible with the intimate, face-to-face process of consensus building. The transition from consensus to hierarchy was not a moral failure. It was a scaling problem, and scaling problems do not care about your values.

The third limitation was inter-group relations. Consensus governance could manage internal disputes effectively, but it was poorly suited to managing relations with outsiders. Negotiation with other groups required representatives empowered to make commitments on the group's behalf—commitments that might not reflect the consensus view. Warfare required command structures that could coordinate action without pausing for a show of hands. Trade with distant partners required individuals who could make deals and enforce them. Each of these external pressures created demand for concentrated authority that consensus governance could not supply without ceasing to be consensus governance. Over time, the groups that developed mechanisms for concentrating authority in external affairs gained advantages over those that did not. And authority concentrated for external purposes has a persistent, well-documented, and entirely predictable tendency to expand into internal affairs. The general who wins the war rarely goes back to asking permission.

THE TRANSITION FROM PERSONAL TO INSTITUTIONAL POWER

The shift from personal power to institutional power is arguably the single most important transition in the entire history of human organization. It is the transition that made states possible, that enabled societies to scale beyond the limits of personal relationships, and that created the world we inhabit today. It is also the transition that most people have never heard of, because it happened gradually, over centuries, without a dramatic moment that could be assigned a date and commemorated with a monument. The most consequential changes rarely come with commemorative dates. They come with invoices that arrive generations later.

Personal power is power that resides in an individual. It depends on that individual's relationships, reputation, skills, and physical presence. When the individual dies or departs, the power dissolves. Every group must then negotiate a new power arrangement from scratch—a process that was often contentious, sometimes violent, and always uncertain. This is the mode that characterized human societies for tens of thousands of years. It worked, but it imposed a ceiling on social complexity. No structure built on personal power could outlast the person who built it. No organization larger than the reach of personal relationships could be sustained. The system had a lifespan problem, and the lifespan was one generation.

Institutional power is power that resides in a position, a role, a structure. It persists regardless of who occupies the position. When a chief dies, the chieftainship continues. When a priest retires, the priesthood endures. When a judge is replaced, the court remains. The power is attached to the role, not the person, and the role has an existence independent of any particular individual. This seemingly simple conceptual shift—from person to position—represents one of the great innovations in human social technology, comparable in its consequences to the invention of agriculture or writing. It is less celebrated than either, because it lacks a compelling origin story and because the people who benefited most from it had every incentive to make it appear natural rather than invented.

The transition did not happen overnight, and it did not happen in a single step. The ethnographic record suggests a gradual process in which personal authority became increasingly formalized and eventually detached from specific individuals. The first stage was the recognition of recurring leadership roles—the war chief, the ritual specialist, the dispute mediator. These roles were initially filled by whoever happened to be most capable, and they carried no authority outside their specific domain. The war chief led in battle but had no special standing in decisions about camp location or food distribution. The role was a hat you wore for a specific occasion and took off when the occasion passed.

The second stage was hereditary transmission. Once a leadership position began to pass from parent to child, the position itself took on an existence independent of any individual's personal qualities. A chief's son might be mediocre—might, in fact, be the kind of person the group would never have selected on merit—but he was still the chief's son, and the position carried expectations and deference regardless of whether they were earned. Hereditary succession was not inevitable. Many societies resisted it, and some continue to select leaders by merit or consensus. But where it took hold, it represented a decisive step toward institutional power. The position now had continuity. It could accumulate resources, obligations, and prestige across generations in a way that no individual lifetime could match. The institution was learning to outlive its occupants.

The third stage was the development of supporting structures—retainers, advisors, specialized functionaries who owed their status to the institution rather than to personal relationships with whoever happened to be leading at the moment. Once a chief had a permanent retinue—warriors fed from the chief's stores, priests performing rituals on the chief's behalf, craftsmen producing prestige goods for the chief's distribution—the institution had developed a constituency with a vested interest in its perpetuation. The retainers needed the chieftainship to continue because their own status depended on it. The institution had acquired the capacity for self-preservation, which is the moment any institution becomes genuinely dangerous and genuinely durable. An institution that can preserve itself has crossed a threshold that most individuals never cross. It has made its own survival someone else's problem.

The fourth stage, which overlapped with the third, was ideological justification. Personal authority required constant demonstration—the leader had to keep proving their worth through wise decisions, successful hunts, and generous distribution. Institutional authority required a different kind of justification: an explanation of why the position itself was legitimate, regardless of who occupied it. This is where sacred power entered the picture. Divine sanction, ancestral mandate, cosmological necessity: these frameworks provided the justification that institutional power needed to sustain itself without the inconvenience of constant personal demonstration. The leader no longer needed to be good. The leader needed to be anointed. The difference was the difference between earning authority and inheriting it, and the inheritance model scaled considerably better.

The transition from personal to institutional power was not clean, and it was not complete. Even in the most thoroughly institutionalized modern states, personal power persists alongside institutional authority. A charismatic president exercises influence beyond what the office formally grants. A well-connected bureaucrat wields power beyond what the organizational chart would suggest. Personal networks, individual reputation, and face-to-face relationships continue to shape outcomes even within elaborately institutional frameworks. The transition created a new layer of power. It did not replace the old one. Understanding any real-world power system requires attending to both layers simultaneously, which is why the simple versions are always wrong and the accurate versions are never simple.

Nor was the transition universally welcomed or irreversible. Many societies resisted the institutionalization of power, maintaining egalitarian or consensus-based systems for centuries after their neighbors had adopted hierarchical institutions. The history of this resistance is poorly documented—the people who successfully resisted state formation did not, by definition, develop the bureaucracies that produce written records. But the archaeological and ethnographic evidence suggests that the transition was contested at every stage. People who had lived under consensus governance did not voluntarily embrace hereditary authority. The transition required inducement, coercion, or the overwhelming pressure of competition with groups that had already made the shift. The state was not adopted. It was, in most cases, imposed—sometimes by conquest, sometimes by competitive necessity, and sometimes by the slow gravitational pull of an organizational model that was simply better at winning wars and collecting grain.

The pre-state period was not a primitive prelude to the real history of power. It was the laboratory in which the fundamental dynamics were established. Hierarchy emerged not from the imposition of the strong upon the weak but from the complex interplay of kinship, physical capacity, resource control, and social skill. Consensus governance demonstrated that power could be exercised collectively but also revealed the limits of collective decision-making at scale. The transition from personal to institutional authority created the scaffolding on which all subsequent structures of power would be built.

The patterns established in this period recur throughout the rest of this book. The tension between personal charisma and institutional continuity. The role of generosity in building coalitions. The structural pressure that competition places on egalitarian arrangements. The tendency of emergency authority to become permanent. The resistance of populations to concentrated power and the mechanisms by which that resistance is overcome. These are not ancient history. They are the permanent dynamics of human power, visible in every boardroom, legislature, and military command that exists today. The costumes have changed. The choreography has not.

A reasonable objection here is that pre-state societies often functioned with genuinely distributed authority and that imposing the language of "power" on them flattens the very real differences between coercive and consensual arrangements. The objection has merit. Many small-scale societies operated through deliberation, kinship obligation, and reciprocal influence rather than command. But this does not mean power was absent. It means power took forms that did not centralize, and the absence of centralization is itself a structural feature worth naming. The dynamics described in this chapter—how authority accumulates, how scale strains consensus, how temporary leadership becomes permanent—operated even in societies that prized equality, which is why those societies so reliably failed to remain equal once they grew.

What changed with the emergence of states was not the fundamental nature of power but the scale at which it operated and the tools available for exercising it. The next chapter examines the first and perhaps most powerful of those tools: the claim that authority comes not from human relationships but from the divine. It was an extraordinary claim. It worked extraordinarily well.

Pre-state power established three enduring truths: authority begins in relationship, scale strains consensus, and emergency power tends to become permanent. The state did not invent any of these. It industrialized them.

4

SACRED POWER

*"The various modes of worship which prevailed in the
Ro-man world were all considered by the people as
equally true; by the philosopher as equally false; and by
the magistrate as equally useful."*

Edward Gibbon
The Decline and Fall of the Roman Empire (1776)

T HIS CHAPTER TREATS RELIGION not as truth or falsehood, but
as a historical mechanism of legitimacy, coordination, and social
reproduction. The first person who claimed to speak for God solved a
problem that had been plaguing leaders since leadership existed: how to
make people obey without having to watch them constantly. Physical
dominance required presence. Kinship authority required relationship.
Resource control required generosity. Each method worked, but each
demanded ongoing effort from the person exercising it. Divine authority
demanded almost nothing—except that people believe the claim. Once
they did, the work was largely done.

Sacred power is the oldest force multiplier in the history of human
organization, and by a considerable margin, the most efficient. It does
not require the largest army. It does not require the fullest treasury.
It requires a population willing to accept that certain individuals have
access to forces beyond human comprehension, and that defying those
individuals means defying those forces. The leap from "I am stronger
than you" to "God wants you to do what I say" is not a small one. It
is arguably the single most consequential innovation in the technology
of control. Everything that follows in this book—military power, political power, institutional power—owes a structural debt to the moment

someone figured out that invisible authority is cheaper than visible force.

DIVINE KINGSHIP AND PRIESTLY AUTHORITY

The concept of the divine king—a ruler whose authority derives not from conquest or election but from a direct relationship with the supernatural—appeared independently in nearly every early civilization. Egypt had it. Mesopotamia had it. China had it. Mesoamerica had it. The Polynesian islands had it. These societies had no contact with one another, no shared religious tradition, no common ancestry that would explain the convergence. They arrived at the same solution because they faced the same problem: how to govern populations too large for personal authority and too dispersed for constant coercion. The divine king was the answer, and it worked so well that it became the default mode of rulership for most of recorded history.

The logic was elegant in its simplicity. The king was not merely a political figure. The king was a cosmic necessity. Egyptologist Jan Assmann's analysis of divine kingship illuminates this dynamic particularly well. In Egypt, the pharaoh was the living embodiment of Horus and the intermediary between the human world and the divine order, or Ma'at. If the pharaoh failed, the Nile might not flood, the harvests might fail, and chaos would consume the land. This was not metaphor. It was theology, and it carried the force of absolute conviction. Opposing the pharaoh was not a political act. It was an assault on the structure of reality itself. That framing made rebellion not just dangerous but cosmically irresponsible, which is a considerably higher barrier to action than the threat of imprisonment.

Mesopotamian kings operated with a slightly different model but identical results. The king ruled as the appointed agent of the gods, chosen to maintain order among humans the way the gods maintained order among cosmic forces. The appointment could be revoked—Mesopotamian theology allowed for divine displeasure in ways Egyptian theology generally did not—but the revocation came from the gods, not from the people. Citizens who disliked their king had no legitimate mechanism for removal. They could only hope the gods agreed with them, which is a remarkably convenient arrangement for the king.

China's Mandate of Heaven offered a variation that introduced something genuinely novel: a built-in accountability mechanism, at least in theory. The emperor ruled because heaven had granted the mandate, but heaven could withdraw it if the emperor governed poorly. Natural disasters, famines, and rebellions were interpreted as signs that the mandate had been lost. This sounds like an early form of political accountability until you notice the circularity: the mandate was lost when the dynasty fell, and the dynasty fell because the mandate was lost. The proof was always retrospective. No one could claim the mandate had been revoked while the emperor was still comfortably on the throne. The mechanism that appeared to limit power functioned, in practice, as another justification for it.

Alongside divine kings, and sometimes in competition with them, stood the priestly class—individuals whose authority derived not from political position but from specialized knowledge of the sacred. Priests knew the rituals. Priests interpreted the signs. Priests maintained the relationship between the community and its gods through ceremonies that no one else was qualified to perform. This specialization created a monopoly, and monopolies create leverage. A king who offended the priestly class risked losing access to the rituals that legitimized his rule. A population that ignored the priests risked divine punishment—or at least the priests said they did, which amounted to the same thing (The picture of the Mesopotamian priest-king as fully centralized despot is itself contested in recent scholarship — Norman Yoffee and Mario Liverani have argued for more fragmented, more contested early polities than the standard textbook image suggests. The structural mechanism described here — sacred authority overlaid onto resource control — operated, but in a more decentralized institutional landscape than the despotic-priest-king image implies.).

The relationship between kings and priests was the first great power-sharing arrangement in human history, and it was exactly as cooperative and contentious as every power-sharing arrangement since. When interests aligned, the partnership was formidable: the king provided military protection and material resources, the priests provided ideological legitimacy and social control. When interests diverged—over land, over tax revenue, over whose authority took precedence in ambiguous situations—the conflicts could be spectacular. The history of ancient Egypt includes multiple periods where priestly power rivaled or exceeded royal authority, particularly during the late New Kingdom when the priests of Amun at Thebes accumulated enough wealth and influence to effectively govern Upper Egypt independently. The pharaoh was still divine. He was just no longer the only one claiming a direct line to the divine, which complicated things considerably.

Ritual as Compliance Mechanism

Ritual is the technology that makes sacred power operational. Without ritual, divine authority is just a claim. With ritual, it becomes an experience—something people participate in, internalize, and reproduce. The claim that the king speaks for God is abstract. The ceremony in which the king is anointed with sacred oil, crowned in a consecrated temple, and presented to the people amid chanting and incense is visceral. It engages the senses, triggers emotion, and creates shared memory. Abstract claims can be doubted. Shared experiences are much harder to dismiss.

Every major system of sacred power developed elaborate rituals, and the elaboration was not decorative. It was functional. The more complex the ritual, the more specialized knowledge it required, which meant the more firmly the priestly class controlled access to it. A simple prayer that anyone could recite posed no barrier to entry. A three-day ceremony involving specific chants in a dead language, precise astronomical timing, animal sacrifice performed in a prescribed sequence, and purification procedures known only to initiated priests—that was a barrier. The complexity was the point. It created dependency. The community needed the priests because only the priests knew how to perform the rituals correctly, and incorrect performance risked catastrophe. Whether that catastrophe was real was beside the point. The belief in its possibility was sufficient.

Rituals also served as compliance mechanisms in a more direct sense: they required participation, and participation reinforced commitment. Attendance at religious ceremonies was rarely optional in early societies. The community gathered, performed the prescribed actions, and reaffirmed its relationship with the divine order collectively. Each repetition strengthened the framework. Each ceremony made the next one feel more natural. After generations of participation, the rituals stopped feeling like imposed obligations and started feeling like the way things had always been done. This is the quiet genius of ritual as a tool of power. It transforms external compliance into internal commitment without the subject ever noticing the transition.

Consider the practical implications. A king who relied on coercion needed enforcers on every corner, watching for disobedience and punishing it when found. A king who relied on sacred ritual needed the population to show up at the temple periodically and participate in ceremonies that reminded everyone—including the king himself—that the existing order was divinely sanctioned. The temple ceremony was cheaper than the enforcer on the corner. It was also more effective, because the enforcer generated resentment while the ceremony generated belief. People left the temple feeling that the social order was correct. People left an encounter with an enforcer feeling that the social order was oppressive. Both produced compliance. Only one produced legitimacy.

The calendar itself became a tool of ritual power. Sacred calendars determined when communities planted, harvested, celebrated, mourned, and rested. The priests who controlled the calendar controlled the rhythm of daily life. In Mesoamerica, the ritual calendar was so central to social organization that political decisions, military campaigns, and economic activities were timed to align with ceremonial cycles. The priests did not merely interpret the calendar—they owned it. Controlling time turned out to be one of the most effective forms of controlling people, a principle that factory owners would rediscover several thousand years later with considerably less theological justification.

Religion Stabilizing Hierarchy

Sacred power did not merely legitimize individual rulers. It legitimized entire social structures. The hierarchy itself—the arrangement of classes, castes, roles, and obligations—was presented as divinely ordained, which meant that one's position in the hierarchy was not the result of political accident or economic exploitation but of cosmic design. The farmer was a farmer because the gods had ordered society that way. The priest was a priest for the same reason. The slave was a slave because, well, the gods apparently had opinions about that too.

This is religion performing its most structurally important function: making inequality feel inevitable. If the social order is the product of human decisions, then human decisions can change it. If the social order is the product of divine will, then changing it requires defying the divine, which is a significantly heavier lift. The Hindu caste system, formalized through religious texts and reinforced through ritual practice, persisted for millennia in part because it framed social position not as an injustice to be remedied but as a spiritual condition to be navigated. One's caste was the result of karma accumulated over previous lifetimes. Challenging the system was not merely rebellious—it was spiritually ignorant. The suffering was the curriculum.

Medieval European Christianity performed a similar function with different theology but identical structural consequences. The feudal hierarchy—king, nobility, clergy, peasantry—was presented as God's intended order. Each person had a station, and that station carried obligations both upward and downward. The peasant owed labor and obedience to the lord. The lord owed protection and justice to the peasant. The arrangement was framed as reciprocal, which made it easier to accept, even when the reciprocity was largely theoretical and the protection somewhat intermittent. The Church taught that earthly suffering was temporary and that the true reward awaited in heaven. This is an extraordinarily effective message for maintaining social order. It acknowledges that the current arrangement is painful and then explains why enduring the pain is the correct response. Rebellion is not just futile—it jeopardizes your eternal soul. That is a compliance mechanism of remarkable durability.

The stabilizing function of religion extended beyond ideology into practical infrastructure. Religious institutions provided the social services that secular governments either could not or did not: hospitals, schools, poor relief, dispute resolution. The medieval Church operated the closest thing to a welfare state that existed in Europe for centuries. This created dependency that reinforced legitimacy. Communities that relied on the Church for education, healthcare, and charity had powerful practical reasons to maintain their relationship with it, entirely independent of theological conviction. The priest who educated your children, tended your sick, and mediated your disputes held a form of power that no amount of theological skepticism could easily dislodge. Sacred power was sustained not only by faith but by function.

Religious institutions also provided something that purely political institutions struggled to offer: continuity across generations. Kingdoms rose and fell. Dynasties were overthrown. Borders shifted. But the Church endured, providing a stable framework of meaning, community, and social organization that persisted regardless of who sat on the throne. The papacy outlasted the Western Roman Empire by more than a thousand years and is still operating. This longevity was not accidental. Religious institutions invested heavily in self-perpetuation—training successors, codifying doctrine, building physical infrastructure designed to last centuries, and creating governance structures that could survive the death of any individual leader. The institutional technology of self-preservation that we will examine in later chapters was pioneered, in large part, by religious organizations that understood something fundamental: gods are immortal, and the institutions that claim to represent them had better act like it.

SECULAR ECHOES OF SACRED AUTHORITY

Here is the part that tends to make people uncomfortable: sacred power did not disappear when societies secularized. It changed costumes. The structural logic of divine authority—the appeal to forces beyond human challenge, the use of ritual to generate compliance, the framing of hierarchy as natural or inevitable—persists in institutions that would never describe themselves as religious. The mechanisms survived. The theology was optional.

Modern nationalism borrowed heavily from the toolkit of sacred power, and it did so openly enough that the parallels are difficult to miss. The nation replaced the deity as the object of ultimate loyalty. National anthems replaced hymns. Flags replaced icons. Monuments replaced temples. Patriotic holidays replaced feast days. Military sacrifice was described in language indistinguishable from religious martyrdom—the fallen soldier "gave his life" for the nation the way the saint gave hers for the faith. The emotional architecture was identical. Only the object of devotion changed.

The rituals of the modern state—inaugurations, state funerals, military parades, the swearing of oaths on sacred or constitutional texts—perform precisely the same function as the rituals of ancient sacred power. They create shared experience. They generate emotional commitment. They transform abstract authority into visceral reality. A president who simply assumed office by filing paperwork would hold legal authority but would lack the emotional legitimacy that comes from the public ceremony, the oath, the hand on the Bible or Constitution, the crowd, the pomp. The ceremony is not a formality. It is a legitimacy machine. Removing it would not change the legal reality, but it would change the felt reality, and in politics, felt reality is the one that matters.

Legal systems carry their own secular sacredness. Courts operate with rituals—robes, gavels, prescribed forms of address, the requirement to rise when the judge enters—that serve no practical function but serve an enormous symbolic one. They signal that what happens in this room is different from what happens outside it. The judge's authority derives not from personal qualities but from the institution, just as the priest's authority derived not from personal holiness but from ordination. The robe is the vestment. The bench is the altar. The verdict is the pronouncement. Strip away the ritual, and the legal system still has enforcement mechanisms—police, prisons, fines. But enforcement mechanisms without the aura of legitimacy are just organized coercion, and organized coercion, as we established in the first chapter, is expensive and fragile.

Even corporations, those most pragmatic of modern institutions, deploy the logic of sacred power when they build cultures of devotion around their brands. The tech company that describes its mission as "changing the world," that holds all-hands meetings with the fervor of revival gatherings, that expects employees to demonstrate commitment beyond what any employment contract could reasonably demand—this is sacred power wearing a hoodie and speaking in keynote presentations. The founder is the prophet. The product is the gospel. The campus is the compound. The stock options are the promise of future reward for present sacrifice. The language is secular. The structure is ancient.

The persistence of sacred forms in secular contexts is not hypocrisy. It is evidence that the underlying mechanism works. Humans respond to ritual, to symbolic authority, to narratives that frame their participation in something larger than individual self-interest. These responses are not artifacts of primitive thinking that education will eliminate. They are features of how human groups generate cohesion and compliance. The clothing changes. The cut is the same.

Sacred power, then, is not a chapter in the history of human control. It is the template. Every subsequent form of power—military, political, economic, cultural—borrowed its methods, adapted its rituals, and relied on its fundamental insight: the most efficient way to control people is to make them believe that the control is not merely necessary but right. Force can compel obedience. Only belief can compel enthusiasm. And enthusiasm, it turns out, is far more useful than obedience when you are trying to build something that lasts.

Sacred power solved the scalability problem that consensus governance could not. It allowed societies to grow beyond the limits of personal relationships by providing a shared framework of meaning that did not require face-to-face contact to operate. You did not need to know the pharaoh personally to accept his authority. You needed to believe that the gods had chosen him, and that belief could travel across distances that personal charisma could not. The temple in your village connected you to the same divine order that the temple in the capital served. Sacred power was, in this sense, the first network technology—a system for transmitting authority across space and time without the signal degrading.

A reader committed to religious tradition may object that this chapter reduces faith to a mechanism of social control, ignoring its theological substance, its consolations, and its capacity to inspire genuine moral reform. The objection is fair, and the structural account is not a complete account of religion. Religion is also belief, community, ethics, and meaning. What this chapter argues is narrower: that whatever else religion does, it has been used—repeatedly, deliberately, and effectively—as a legitimacy technology by political authorities who needed compliance at scale. Recognizing this function does not deny the others. It does explain why even traditions that began as critiques of power have, with remarkable consistency, found themselves underwriting it within a few centuries of their founding.

The cost of this efficiency was rigidity. Sacred systems that derived their authority from eternal, divine truths could not easily adapt to changing circumstances without undermining the premise of their own authority. If the social order is God's will, then changing the social order implies either that God changed his mind or that the priests got the message wrong. Neither option is attractive to the people running the system. This tension between the stability that sacred authority provides and the adaptability that changing conditions demand is one of the recurring themes of this book. Power that cannot adapt eventually breaks. Power that adapts too readily loses the appearance of permanence that legitimized it in the first place.

Sacred power proved that invisible authority is cheaper than visible force. Once people believe a ruler speaks for the gods, the ruler no longer needs to be present, generous, or even competent—only legitimate. Every later form of power, from the bureaucratic to the corporate, inherits this trick: outsource enforcement to belief, and the system runs itself.

5
MILITARY POWER

Thucydides
The Peloponnesian War, Book V (c. 400 BCE)

V IOLENCE IS THE SIMPLEST form of power and the most expensive to maintain. It requires no ideology, no legitimacy, no consent. A man with a sword does not need you to agree with his worldview. He needs you to notice the sword. This directness is military power's greatest advantage and its most fundamental limitation. It can take a city in an afternoon and lose it over a decade. It can compel obedience from everyone within reach and from no one beyond it. Military power is fast, dramatic, and visible, which is why it dominates the history books—but it is also brittle in ways that less exciting forms of power are not.

Organized Violence and State Formation

States did not emerge because people sat around a fire one evening and decided that centralized governance sounded like a good idea. States emerged, in most cases, because someone with an organized capacity for violence found it more profitable to govern a population than to keep raiding it. The sociologist Charles Tilly compressed this insight into a sentence that has haunted political scientists ever since: 'war made the state, and the state made war'. The thesis is influential but not unchallenged: comparative historians of Latin America (Miguel Ángel Centeno) and of the early modern state system (Hendrik Spruyt) have shown that war did not produce the territorial nation-state everywhere it operated, and that the European trajectory Tilly described was one possible outcome of state-formation pressures rather than the inevitable one. The Tilly account remains the best general-purpose framework for European state-formation; it travels less reliably than the framework's universalism implies. The relationship was not incidental. It was constitutive. States are, at their historical origin, protection rackets that developed administrative ambitions.

The logic worked like this. In a landscape of competing groups, the group that could organize violence most effectively dominated its neighbors. Domination created territory. Territory required administration—someone had to collect tribute, resolve disputes among the conquered, and maintain the infrastructure that made the territory worth holding. Administration required revenue. Revenue required taxation. Taxation required records, enforcers, and a bureaucratic apparatus that could distinguish between subjects who had paid and those who had not. Each step in this chain moved further from the original act of violence and closer to what we would recognize as governance. The warlord became a king not through a change in character but through a change in operating requirements. The people being subjected to this process experienced it not as an elegant sequence of institutional development but as homes burned, families separated, harvests seized, and the permanent threat that resistance meant death.

This process was neither clean nor linear. Many attempts at state formation failed. Warlords who could conquer could not govern. Territories that could be seized could not be held. Revenue that could be extracted through plunder could not be sustained through taxation without some degree of cooperation from the taxed. The transition from raiding to ruling required a fundamental shift in orientation—from treating a population as a resource to be consumed to treating it as a resource to be maintained. Not every military leader made that shift. The ones who did built states. The ones who did not built legends, which is historically more romantic and structurally less useful.

The earliest states that left clear archaeological and documentary evidence—in Mesopotamia, Egypt, China, and the Indus Valley—all show the marks of this military origin. Fortifications, weapons caches, administrative records tracking military obligations, artistic depictions of rulers as warriors and conquerors. The king was, first and foremost, a military commander. His other roles—priest, judge, administrator—were additions to the core function, not replacements for it. The palace grew around the garrison, not the other way around. Understanding this sequence matters because it explains a pattern that persists into the modern era: the state's monopoly on legitimate violence is not a philosophical principle that preceded state formation. It is a description of what happened when one armed group eliminated or absorbed all the others.

The relationship between military organization and state complexity was self-reinforcing. Larger armies required more sophisticated logistics, which required larger bureaucracies, which required more revenue, which required more territory, which required larger armies. The cycle ratcheted upward, producing increasingly complex political structures at each turn. Societies that entered this cycle early—because of geographic advantages, population density, or competitive pressure from neighbors—developed state institutions earlier. Societies that faced less military pressure retained simpler organizational forms longer. The presence or absence of external military threat is one of the strongest predictors of how quickly a society developed centralized institutions. Peace, in this reading, was not the product of state formation. It was the luxury that state formation occasionally produced, briefly, before the next round of competition began.

STANDING ARMIES AND LOYALTY ENGINEERING

The creation of standing armies—permanent military forces maintained in peacetime—was one of the most consequential organizational innovations in human history, and also one of the most dangerous to the people who created them. A standing army solved the immediate problem of military readiness. It eliminated the delays and uncertainties of mustering temporary forces when a threat appeared. Trained, equipped, and available at all times, a standing army gave its ruler a decisive advantage over rivals who relied on seasonal levies of farmers-turned-soldiers who would rather be home planting crops. The advantage was real and measurable, which is why every major power eventually adopted the model.

The problem was what to do with the army when it was not fighting. A standing army is a permanent concentration of organized violence under the nominal command of a political leader. The word "nominal" is doing considerable work in that sentence. Command is only as real as the loyalty of the commanded, and loyalty is not an automatic feature of employment. Soldiers follow orders for many reasons—pay, ideology, fear, habit, personal attachment to a leader—and those reasons do not always point in the same direction. A general who commands the loyalty of his troops commands, in practical terms, a rival power center within the state. History is littered with rulers who built armies to protect their thrones and then lost those thrones to the armies they built. The Praetorian Guard in Rome made and unmade emperors with the casual efficiency of a hiring committee that also handled terminations.

The challenge of maintaining military loyalty produced an entire discipline of what might be called loyalty engineering—the systematic design of institutions, incentives, and cultural practices aimed at ensuring that armed forces served the state rather than themselves. The solutions varied, but the underlying logic was consistent: divide, distribute, and bind.

Division meant ensuring that no single military commander controlled enough force to threaten the ruler. Roman legions were stationed far from their regions of recruitment. Ottoman janissaries were deliberately separated from their families and communities of origin. Chinese dynasties rotated regional military commanders to prevent them from building local power bases. The principle was identical in each case: familiarity breeds loyalty, and loyalty to a local commander is dangerous to a central ruler. The solution was to keep the army loyal to the institution rather than to any individual within it, which is easier to describe than to achieve.

Distribution meant spreading the rewards of military service widely enough to create a constituency for the existing order. Roman soldiers received land grants upon retirement. Medieval knights received fiefs.

Ottoman janissaries received salaries, housing, and social status that elevated them above the civilian population. In each case, the military class had a material stake in the continuation of the system. Rebellion meant risking not just their lives but their property, their status, and the future of their families. The calculation was deliberate: make soldiers prosperous enough that they have something to lose, and they will think twice before gambling it on a coup.

Binding meant creating emotional and ideological attachment to the institution. Oaths of loyalty, unit traditions, shared rituals, distinctive uniforms, regimental histories, songs, symbols—the paraphernalia of military culture served a functional purpose beyond morale. They created identity. A soldier who thought of himself primarily as a member of the Third Legion or the King's Own Regiment had internalized an institutional loyalty that transcended personal relationships. The unit became a social world, complete with its own norms, status hierarchies, and codes of behavior. Leaving was not just a career decision. It was a form of exile from the only community the soldier fully belonged to. This is sacred power applied to military organization, and it worked for the same reasons: ritual, repetition, and the creation of meaning that made compliance feel like belonging rather than submission.

WAR AS LEGITIMACY GENERATOR

War is terrible, wasteful, and destructive. It is also one of the most reliable generators of political legitimacy ever discovered. This is not a comfortable observation, but it is a consistent one. Leaders who win wars gain a form of authority that no peacetime achievement can match. Churchill was a polarizing political figure for decades. After 1940, he was a national icon. Augustus was a ruthless political operator who eliminated his rivals through proscription and civil war. After Actium, he was the savior of Rome. The mechanism is straightforward: victory in war demonstrates competence in the domain that matters most—survival—and competence in survival generates deference in everything else.

The legitimacy-generating function of war explains behavior that otherwise appears irrational. Leaders throughout history have started wars they did not need to fight, escalated conflicts that could have been resolved through negotiation, and sustained campaigns long after the strategic objectives had been achieved or abandoned. The standard explanation attributes this to ego, miscalculation, or the momentum of events. These factors are real, but they do not fully account for the pattern. The missing variable is legitimacy. A leader who needs to consolidate domestic authority, silence political rivals, or distract from internal failures has a powerful incentive to find an external enemy. The enemy does not need to be genuine. It needs to be convincing. The threat does not need to be existential. It needs to be narratable. War provides a story in which the leader is the protagonist, the nation is the cause, and dissent is treason. That story is worth more, politically, than most peacetime accomplishments.

The Roman triumph—the ceremonial procession through the city that celebrated a victorious general—was the most literal expression of war's legitimizing function. The general rode in a chariot through cheering crowds, displaying captured enemies and plundered wealth, while a slave held a laurel wreath above his head and whispered, according to tradition, "Remember, you are mortal." The ceremony converted military success into political capital with theatrical precision. The general entered the triumph as a commander. He emerged as a figure of semi-divine authority, his name etched into public memory and his political position enormously strengthened. The incentive structure was obvious. If victory in war produced this kind of reward, ambitious men would seek wars to win. And they did. Roman expansion was driven not only by strategic calculation but by the political economy of glory. Generals needed victories. Victories required enemies. Enemies, when unavailable, could be manufactured.

The modern equivalent is subtler but structurally identical. Wartime presidents enjoy higher approval ratings. Military action generates rally-round-the-flag effects that suppress domestic opposition. Leaders who are perceived as strong on defense gain electoral advantages regardless of their competence in other domains. The mechanism is so reliable that political strategists factor it into their calculations. Not every leader starts a war for domestic political reasons, but every leader who fights a war benefits domestically from its early stages. The political cost comes later, when the war drags on, the casualties mount, and the promised victory fails to materialize. But later is a problem for later. The immediate political reward is available now, and political incentives overwhelmingly favor the immediate.

There is a darker dimension to war's legitimizing function that deserves explicit attention. War creates a category—the enemy—that simplifies the political landscape in ways that benefit whoever controls the definition. Once a population is at war, the spectrum of acceptable opinion narrows dramatically. Questions that were legitimate in peacetime become suspicious in wartime. Dissent that was tolerated becomes betrayal. The social pressure to conform intensifies. This narrowing is not merely a side effect of war. It is one of its political utilities. A government that faces serious internal opposition has a structural incentive to maintain a state of external conflict, not necessarily because the conflict serves strategic purposes, but because the state of conflict itself disciplines the domestic population. Permanent war as a tool of permanent domestic control is not a dystopian fiction. It is a recurring historical pattern, observable in empires, republics, and modern states alike.

LIMITS OF FORCE-BASED CONTROL

For all its power, military force has a persistent and well-documented tendency to defeat itself. The pattern is so consistent that it deserves to be stated as a principle: the more a system relies on force, the more force it needs. Coercion generates resistance. Resistance requires suppression. Suppression generates more resistance. The cycle escalates until the cost of enforcement exceeds the value of what is being enforced, at which point the system either collapses or transitions to some other basis of control. This is not a theoretical prediction. It is a historical description of what has happened to every regime that relied primarily on military power without developing alternative sources of legitimacy.

The Assyrian Empire provides the clearest ancient example. The Assyrians were, by the standards of their time, the most effective military power in the Near East. Their army was large, well-organized, technologically advanced, and spectacularly brutal. They practiced deportation on a massive scale, relocated entire populations, and advertised their violence through artistic depictions of impalement, flaying, and execution that were designed to terrify potential opponents into submission. The strategy worked for roughly three centuries. Then it stopped working. The empire collapsed with a speed that stunned contemporaries, overwhelmed by a coalition of peoples who had been subjected to Assyrian brutality and were motivated, above all else, by the desire to never be subjected to it again. The violence that had sustained the empire became the fuel for the coalition that destroyed it. The instrument of control became the motive for resistance.

The same pattern recurs with mechanical regularity across different centuries and different continents. The Mongol Empire conquered more territory more quickly than any political entity before or since. It held that territory for a historically brief period before fragmenting into successor states that governed through progressively less violent means. The Spanish Empire conquered the Americas with breathtaking military efficiency and spent three centuries managing insurgencies, rebellions, and resistance movements that drained the treasury and exhausted the military. The British Empire governed a quarter of the world's population and discovered that the cost of governing through force exceeded the economic returns of the colonies being governed. Every colonial power learned this lesson eventually. Some learned it faster than others. France, to pick an example not entirely at random, learned it twice.

The limitation is not that force is ineffective. It is that force is unsustainable as a primary mechanism of governance. Armies need to be paid. Soldiers need to be fed, housed, equipped, and replaced when they die or desert. Garrisons need to be maintained. Supply lines need to be protected. Intelligence networks need to be operated. All of these costs are ongoing, and they increase in direct proportion to the level of resistance being suppressed. A population that has been conquered by force and continues to resist imposes costs that a population governing itself voluntarily does not. The mathematics are unforgiving. A military occupation costs more per capita than a legitimate government, generates less revenue per capita than a legitimate government, and produces worse economic outcomes than a legitimate government. Force-based control is a losing proposition over any time horizon longer than a generation, and often shorter.

This is why every successful military conquest in history has been followed by an effort to convert military control into some other form of authority. Roman legions conquered Gaul, and then Roman administrators built roads, aqueducts, courts, and temples to romanize the population into willing participants in the imperial system. The Norman conquest of England was accomplished by cavalry in 1066 and maintained by a legal and administrative system that eventually made Norman authority feel indigenous. The United States conquered the American West by military force and consolidated that conquest through railroads, homestead acts, public education, and the cultural absorption of successive generations. In each case, the military victory was the beginning of the process, not its completion. The hard work was converting conquest into legitimacy, and that work required tools that armies do not carry.

The most instructive failures are those where the conversion never happened. The Crusader states in the Levant held territory for roughly two centuries without ever establishing genuine legitimacy among the majority population. They remained, for the duration of their existence, military garrisons surrounded by populations that tolerated them at best and resisted them at worst. When military support from Europe waned, the states collapsed because there was nothing underneath the military structure to sustain them. The parallel with modern military occupations is not subtle. Any student of the Crusader states could have predicted, with reasonable accuracy, the trajectory of military occupations that attempted to hold territory without converting the population's compliance from coerced to voluntary. The prediction would not require expertise. It would require only the recognition that a pattern repeated across a thousand years of history might be worth taking seriously.

Military power is the most visible, most dramatic, and most intuitively understood form of control. It is also, paradoxically, the weakest over time. It builds states but cannot sustain them. It generates legitimacy but cannot maintain it. It compels obedience but cannot produce consent. Every successful exercise of military power in history has been followed by a transition to some less violent form of authority, because the cost of not making that transition eventually exceeds the cost of making it. The sword gets you through the door. It does not keep you in the room.

The strongest objection to treating military power as fundamentally limited is the long historical record of regimes that ruled for centuries through coercion, surveillance, and the credible threat of violence. The objection cannot be waved away. Some highly coercive systems have lasted a long time. But the persistence of these regimes typically depended on more than force alone—on legitimacy generated by external threat, on economic delivery, on cultural identification, or on the routinization of fear into something the population stopped noticing. The structural reading does not claim military power produces no durability. It claims that military power produces durability only when supplemented by the other forms examined in this book, and that regimes which rely on force as their primary instrument enter the diagnostic territory of the next several chapters.

The form of power that proved most effective at keeping rulers in the room—at converting the temporary advantage of military victory into the durable stability of ongoing governance—was political power:

the slow, unglamorous work of bureaucracy, law, and administration. It lacks the drama of a cavalry charge. It compensates by lasting centuries rather than afternoons.

6

POLITICAL POWER

"A prince never lacks legitimate reasons to break his promise."

Niccolò Machiavelli The
Prince (1532)

B UREAUCRACY IS NOT EXCITING. It does not ride into battle, does not deliver prophecies from mountaintops, and does not generate the kind of stories that make it into epic poetry. What it does is persist. Long after the general has died and the priest has lost his audience, the clerk is still at his desk, recording transactions, filing reports, and ensuring that the system functions tomorrow in approximately the same way it functioned today. This is political power in its purest form: the capacity to make decisions stick, not through charisma or coercion but through process. It is the least glamorous form of authority in human history, and by a wide margin the most durable.

Bureaucracy Replacing Personality

The fundamental problem with personal rule is that persons are unreliable. They get sick. They make impulsive decisions after bad meals. They play favorites. They die, often at inconvenient moments, leaving behind power vacuums that invite exactly the kind of chaos the original concentration of authority was meant to prevent. Every kingdom that depended on the judgment of a single ruler faced the same structural vulnerability: the system was only as good as the person at the top, and the person at the top was only as good as their health, temperament, and the quality of information their subordinates chose to share with them.

The historical sociologist Michael Mann distinguished two ways political power operates, and the distinction is worth making explicit because the rest of this chapter has been describing one of them without naming it. Despotic power is the state's ability to act against its population without negotiation — to round up dissidents, conscript soldiers, or seize property by decree. Infrastructural power is the state's ability to penetrate civil society and coordinate routine activity through bureaucratic capacity — to register every birth, tax every transaction, route emergency services to any address, and enforce contracts between strangers across the entire territory. The two forms vary independently. A modern democratic state has comparatively weak despotic power and enormous infrastructural power. A weak post-colonial state may have considerable despotic power in the capital and almost none in the countryside, where the state's writ does not reach. The form that matters for the structural account in this book is overwhelmingly the infrastructural form, because that is the form that produces the routine, distributed, taken-for-granted compliance that makes modern governance possible at all. Despotic power is what makes states frightening. Infrastructural power is what makes them durable.

Bureaucracy solved this problem by making the person at the top largely irrelevant to daily operations. That is not how any king would have described it, but it is what happened. The earliest bureaucracies—in Sumer, Egypt, and China—emerged to handle tasks that were too complex, too numerous, or too tedious for a ruler to manage personally. Tax collection, land surveys, census records, military logistics, temple inventories, irrigation schedules. Each task required specialized knowledge, consistent procedures, and the kind of sustained attention that no individual ruler could provide across an entire kingdom. The solution was delegation, and delegation required a class of professional administrators whose authority derived not from personal relationship with the ruler but from their position within an organizational structure.

Sociologist Max Weber analyzed this transition as the shift from charismatic to legal-rational authority—from power that resided in personalities to power that resided in positions and procedures. This was a conceptual revolution disguised as clerical work. When a scribe in Ur recorded grain deliveries to a temple storehouse in 2500 BCE, he was not merely keeping accounts. He was demonstrating that the system could function through procedure rather than personality. The scribe did not need to know the king. He did not need the king to know him. He needed to know the procedure, and the procedure existed independent of both of them. If the scribe died, another scribe could read his records and continue the work. If the king died, the records remained valid. The procedure had acquired an existence separate from any individual, which is the moment that institutional power becomes real.

China produced the most sophisticated early bureaucracy, and the sophistication was deliberate. The imperial examination system, formalized during the Sui and Tang dynasties but rooted in earlier practices, selected government officials through competitive testing rather than hereditary privilege or personal patronage. The exams were grueling, covering classical texts, policy analysis, and administrative competence. They were also, at least in principle, open to anyone regardless of social origin. The principle was more honored in aspiration than in practice—wealthy families could afford tutors and years of study that poor families could not—but the structural effect was profound. Government positions were filled by people who had demonstrated competence in a standardized assessment rather than people who happened to be born into the right family. The system produced administrators who owed their positions to the institution rather than to a patron, which meant their loyalty was institutional rather than personal. A bureaucrat selected by examination served the system. A bureaucrat selected by patronage served the patron. The difference determined whether governance survived the patron's death.

The Ottoman Empire achieved something similar through a mechanism that was considerably more unsettling. The devşirme system took Christian boys from conquered territories, converted them to Islam, and trained them as administrators and soldiers. Separated from their families, communities, and original identities, these men owed everything to the imperial system and nothing to local power networks. They could not build dynastic power because their children did not inherit their positions. They could not form regional alliances because they had no regional roots. They were, by design, perfectly institutional humans—loyal to the system because the system was the only world they had. The method was brutal. The administrative product was remarkably effective. The Ottoman bureaucracy functioned with a consistency that most European kingdoms of the same period could not approach, precisely because it had solved the loyalty problem through a solution that no modern society would tolerate.

LAW AS SYSTEMATIZED AUTHORITY

Before written law, disputes were resolved by whoever had the authority to resolve them, using whatever standards seemed appropriate at the time. This worked tolerably well when the authority figure was wise, fair, and familiar with the circumstances. It worked catastrophically when the authority figure was none of those things. The fundamental problem with personal adjudication is the same as the fundamental problem with personal rule: consistency depends on the person, and persons are variable. The merchant who won his case before a fair judge might lose an identical case before a corrupt one the following week. The farmer whose land rights were upheld by a reasonable chief might find them revoked by the chief's less reasonable successor. Without written standards, justice was not a system. It was a lottery with better branding.

The earliest known legal codes—Ur-Nammu in Sumer, Hammurabi in Babylon, the Twelve Tables in Rome—did not invent justice. They systematized it. They took decisions that had previously been made ad hoc and rendered them predictable. If a man destroyed another man's eye, the consequence was specified. If a builder constructed a house that collapsed and killed the owner, the penalty was written. The content of these early laws was often harsh by modern standards, but the innovation was not the content. It was the form. By writing the rules down, these societies accomplished something that oral tradition could not: they made authority impersonal. The law applied regardless of who was interpreting it, at least in theory. The judge's role shifted from deciding what was just to applying what was written, which reduced—though never eliminated—the influence of personal bias, bribery, and mood.

Written law also solved a problem of scale. A king who adjudicated disputes personally could handle perhaps a few dozen cases per day. A legal code that trained judges could apply independently allowed thousands of disputes to be resolved simultaneously across an entire kingdom, all producing roughly consistent outcomes. The law became a technology of governance—a way of projecting authority across distances that no individual could physically cover. The king did not need to be present in every village. His law was present, enforced by local officials who applied the written standard. This is delegation at its most powerful: not the delegation of authority to trusted individuals, but the delegation of authority to a text that could be copied, distributed, and applied by anyone literate enough to read it.

The Roman legal tradition, which would eventually underpin most of Western jurisprudence, demonstrated both the power and the limitations of law as a system of authority. Roman law was remarkably sophisticated—it distinguished between types of property, types of obligation, types of legal personality. It created frameworks for contract, inheritance, and liability that remain recognizable in modern legal systems two thousand years later. It was also, like every legal system, a reflection of the power relationships in the society that produced it. Roman law protected property rights with great vigor, which was enormously beneficial if you owned property and somewhat less beneficial if you were property. The law was systematic, consistent, and thoroughly enmeshed in the interests of the class that wrote it. This is not a flaw unique to Rome. It is a feature of legal systems generally. Law systematizes authority, but the authority it systematizes is the authority of whoever had enough power to write the law in the first place.

The lasting significance of written law is not that it produced justice—a claim that would require a generosity of interpretation that the historical record does not support—but that it produced continuity. Legal codes survived the rulers who commissioned them. Hammurabi's code outlasted Hammurabi. Roman law outlasted Rome. The Napoleonic Code outlasted Napoleon, which Napoleon himself would have found ironic given that outlasting things was rather his aspiration. The text endured because it was useful, because it provided a framework for resolving disputes that did not require starting from scratch each time a new ruler took power. Legal continuity became one of the strongest threads of institutional persistence in human history, connecting societies across centuries through shared frameworks that no single generation created and no single generation could easily discard.

Administrative Continuity

Kingdoms fall. Empires collapse. Dynasties are overthrown in blood and fire and dramatic speeches. And then, the following Monday, someone has to collect the taxes. This is the secret of administrative continuity: the people who run the system at the operational level are rarely affected by changes at the top, because the people at the top need the people at the operational level more than the reverse. A new king who dismissed every administrator in his kingdom would not have a kingdom by the end of the month. He would have a title, a crown, and a deepening awareness that he had no idea where the tax records were kept.

The persistence of administrative structures through political upheaval is one of the most consistent patterns in the history of governance, and one of the least appreciated. When the Mongols conquered China, they did not replace the Chinese bureaucracy. They could not have governed without it. When the Normans conquered England, the Anglo-Saxon administrative system—its sheriffs, its courts, its land records—continued operating under new management. When the Ottoman Empire absorbed territories across three continents, it frequently retained local administrative structures intact, layering Ottoman authority on top of existing systems rather than replacing them. The pattern is not universal, but it is dominant: conquerors conquer the political leadership and inherit the administrative apparatus, because destroying the apparatus would destroy the thing they conquered it to possess.

This creates a dynamic that is deeply counterintuitive. The administrators—the people with no army, no divine mandate, no popular following—hold a form of power that survives precisely because it is boring. No one writes songs about the continuity of provincial tax collection. No one stages a coup to seize control of the land registry. These functions are invisible in the way that plumbing is invisible: unnoticed when functioning, catastrophic when absent. The administrator's power lies in this indispensability. The king can replace the administrator, but only with another administrator who will perform the same functions using the same procedures. The position survives because the function must be performed, and the function must be performed in roughly the same way regardless of who performs it. This is institutional power in its most elemental form: power that persists because the alternative to its persistence is disorder.

The career of the administrative class across civilizations follows a remarkably similar trajectory. Initially, administrators serve at the pleasure of the ruler, holding positions that can be granted or revoked at will. Over time, the positions become more formalized, the qualifications more specific, the tenure more secure. Administrators develop professional identities, codes of conduct, and institutional loyalties that exist independent of any particular ruler. They begin to see themselves not as servants of the king but as servants of the state—a distinction that sounds philosophical but has enormous practical consequences. A servant of the king does what the king wants. A servant of the state does what the state requires, which may or may not align with what the king wants. The moment the bureaucracy developed this self-concept—the idea that its obligation was to the institution rather than to the individual who happened to occupy the throne—political power acquired a life independent of personal authority.

This independence was both the great strength of bureaucratic governance and its great vulnerability. A bureaucracy that served the institution rather than the ruler provided stability, continuity, and resistance to the whims of bad leaders. It also provided resistance to the initiatives of good leaders. A ruler who wanted to reform the system faced an administrative apparatus with its own interests, its own procedures, and its own deeply ingrained resistance to change. The bureaucracy that survived the transition from one dynasty to the next did so partly because it was useful and partly because it was immovable. The same inertia that protected the state from the damage a bad ruler might cause also protected the state from the improvements a good ruler might attempt. This is the bargain that administrative continuity offers: stability in exchange for adaptability. Most societies have taken the deal, not because it is ideal, but because the alternative—rebuilding the administrative apparatus with every change of leadership—is worse.

Institutional Inertia

There is a point in the life of every institution when it stops serving its original purpose and starts serving its own survival. The two objectives may overlap, but they are not identical, and the divergence between them explains a great deal about why institutions behave the way they do. A tax agency created to fund public services eventually becomes an institution with employees, buildings, procedures, and a budget of its own. The employees have mortgages. The buildings have maintenance contracts. The procedures have been codified into manuals that fill entire shelves. The budget has constituencies that depend on its continuation. At some point, the tax agency's primary function is no longer collecting taxes. Its primary function is being a tax agency. The collection of taxes is a means to that end, not the end itself. This is institutional inertia, and it is the most powerful force in political life that no one campaigns on.

Institutional inertia operates through several mechanisms, all of which reinforce one another. The first is procedural entrenchment. Once a procedure has been established, documented, and practiced, it becomes the default. Changing it requires effort—new documentation, new training, new consensus among the people who perform it—while maintaining it requires nothing. The status quo has a structural advantage not because it is good but because it is already there. Proposed changes must justify themselves. Existing procedures must merely continue to exist. This asymmetry favors stasis in every decision, and the cumulative effect of thousands of small decisions favoring stasis is an institution that moves with the urgency of a geological formation.

The second mechanism is stakeholder accumulation. Every institutional process creates beneficiaries—people whose jobs, income, status, or identity depend on the process continuing. These beneficiaries have powerful incentives to resist change and relatively weak incentives to support it, even when change would serve the institution's stated mission more effectively. A procurement process that takes six months and requires fourteen approvals is objectively inefficient. It is also the reason fourteen people have jobs. Proposing to streamline the process threatens those fourteen people, each of whom will resist the proposal with considerably more energy than the diffuse beneficiaries of efficiency will support it. Concentrated losses generate more political resistance than dispersed gains generate political support. This asymmetry is the engine of institutional inertia, and it operates identically in ancient empires and modern democracies.

The third mechanism is cultural normalization. Institutions develop internal cultures—shared assumptions, unwritten rules, informal hierarchies, collective memories of past successes and failures—that shape how their members perceive problems and evaluate solutions. These cultures are powerful precisely because they are invisible to the people embedded in them. An organization that has always done things a certain way does not perceive that way as a choice. It perceives it as reality. Alternative approaches are not merely different; they are wrong, impractical, or dangerous, not because of evidence but because of familiarity. Institutional culture filters information, shapes interpretation, and determines which ideas are taken seriously and which are dismissed before they receive a hearing. Changing an institution's culture is possible. It is also slow, contentious, and often requires replacing the people who carry the existing culture, which circles back to the stakeholder problem.

The result of these mechanisms operating simultaneously is institutions that are extraordinarily resistant to deliberate change and extraordinarily persistent across time. This is not always bad. Institutional inertia is the reason that a change in government does not produce a change in property rights, contract enforcement, or traffic laws. The stability that citizens rely on daily is a product of institutional inertia—the enormous difficulty of changing systems that have embedded themselves into the fabric of social life. But the same inertia that prevents harmful changes also prevents beneficial ones. Institutions that should be reformed resist reform. Procedures that should be updated resist updating. Organizations that have outlived their purpose resist dissolution. The institution's will to survive is indifferent to whether its survival serves anyone other than itself.

Political reformers throughout history have discovered this reality with varying degrees of surprise and frustration. A new ruler arrives with ambitious plans. The bureaucracy listens politely, nods at appropriate intervals, and continues doing what it was doing before the ruler arrived. The plans are not rejected. They are absorbed—studied by committees, analyzed in reports, pilot-tested in small programs, evaluated in follow-up studies, and gradually diluted until the original ambition is unrecognizable. The process looks like cooperation. It functions as resistance. The institution has survived another reformer, as it survived the one before, and the one before that, and will survive the one coming next. This is not conspiracy. It is physics. Objects at rest tend to stay at rest, and institutions at rest tend to stay at rest with a determination that would impress Isaac Newton.

Political power is the infrastructure beneath the spectacle. It is less visible than military power, less emotionally compelling than sacred power, and considerably less interesting at dinner parties. It is also the form of power that most directly determines how people actually live. The army decides who rules. The priest decides why the ruler is legitimate.

The bureaucrat decides whether the roads get maintained, the taxes get collected, the disputes get resolved, and the water keeps flowing. Of these three functions, the third is the one that matters most on any given Tuesday, which is to say, it matters most on most days.

A defender of strong leadership might argue that bureaucracy is the obstacle, not the achievement—that history's decisive moments were produced by individuals who cut through institutional inertia, and that romanticizing administration mistakes the supporting cast for the protagonist. There is something to this. Decisive leaders matter. Crises sometimes require executive action that bureaucracy cannot supply. But the same bureaucracies that frustrate the leader during the crisis are the bureaucracies that implemented the previous leader's reforms, are implementing the current leader's policies, and will outlast both. The leader's decisive moment is real. It is also one moment in a system that produces continuity across thousands of moments the leader never sees, which is why the leader receives the credit and the system gets the durability.

The shift from personal rule to administrative governance did not eliminate personal power. Kings, presidents, and prime ministers still exercise individual judgment, still make consequential decisions, still shape their nations through force of personality. But they do so within systems that constrain, channel, and frequently outlast them. The system is the power. The leader is the temporary occupant. Understanding this distinction is essential to understanding everything that follows in this book, because every subsequent form of power—economic, imperial, institutional, cultural—operates through and upon the political infrastructure.

7

ECONOMIC POWER

"People of the same trade seldom meet together, even for merriment and diversion, but the conversation ends in a conspiracy against the public, or in some contrivance to raise prices."

Adam Smith
The Wealth of Nations (1776)

MONEY DOES NOT TALK. Money instructs, and the instruction is followed because the alternative is poverty, which concentrates the mind in ways that sermons and swords cannot. The principal vehicle through which this instruction is delivered, in the contemporary world, is the corporation. The argument introduced in Chapter 2 returns here in concentrated form: the corporation does not have to claim political authority because its activity is described as economic, and the description holds despite the political consequences of every major decision the firm makes. The vocabulary is commercial. The substance is structural. Economic power is the quietest form of control and, over sufficiently long periods, the most decisive. It does not announce itself with armies or consecrate itself with rituals. It accumulates in ledgers, compounds through interest, and converts into political influence with an efficiency that would embarrass the most optimistic general. A king must conquer territory to expand his power. A merchant must only extend credit.

Wealth Converting into Influence

The conversion of wealth into political power is so consistent across civilizations that it might reasonably be considered a law of political physics. Wherever surplus wealth has existed, it has been used to acquire influence over collective decisions. The mechanisms vary—patronage, bribery, philanthropy, lobbying, campaign finance, marriage alliances, land acquisition, debt creation—but the underlying dynamic is identical. Wealth provides options. Options provide leverage. Leverage provides influence. Influence, exercised consistently over time, becomes indistinguishable from authority.

The process begins with surplus. In subsistence economies, where everyone produces roughly what they consume, economic power is minimal because there is nothing to accumulate. The emergence of agriculture changed this by creating the possibility of surplus—more food than the producer needed for survival. Surplus could be stored, traded, or distributed, and whoever controlled the surplus controlled something that everyone else needed. The temple granaries of ancient Mesopotamia were not merely storage facilities. They were power centers. The priests who managed the grain supply managed the community's survival, which gave them leverage over every other institution, including the palace. A king who offended the temple risked disruption to the food supply, which was a faster route to political crisis than any military threat.

As economies grew more complex, the mechanisms for converting wealth into influence grew more sophisticated. In classical Athens—the society most celebrated for its democratic ideals—political participation was formally open to all citizens but practically dominated by the wealthy. Public service was unpaid, which meant that only men with independent means could afford to hold office for extended periods. Military service required providing your own equipment, which meant that wealthier citizens served in more prestigious roles. Liturgies—mandatory public contributions for festivals, warships, and infrastructure—fell disproportionately on the rich, but the rich used these contributions to build public reputations that translated directly into political influence. The system was democratic in form and oligarchic in function, which is a combination that has proven remarkably durable across the centuries. Modern democracies would find the Athenian arrangement uncomfortably familiar if they examined it closely, which is perhaps why they generally do not.

Rome dispensed with the pretense more efficiently. The Roman Republic was explicitly structured around wealth. Citizens were organized into classes based on property holdings, and voting power was weighted accordingly. The wealthiest classes voted first, and elections were decided once a majority of voting units had been tallied, which meant that the poorer classes frequently never voted at all. The system did not hide the relationship between wealth and power. It formalized it, encoded it into constitutional structure, and called it the natural order. When the Republic collapsed into civil war and then autocracy, the wealth-power connection did not disappear. It simply operated through new channels—imperial patronage, senatorial estates, tax farming, and the enormous commercial networks that sustained the empire. The form changed. The function continued.

The medieval period introduced feudalism, which was, at bottom, an economic arrangement dressed in military clothing. The feudal lord held land. The peasant worked the land. The lord provided protection, which was necessary largely because of the existence of other lords. The peasant provided labor, surplus, and military service. The arrangement was described in terms of mutual obligation and sacred duty, but the operating logic was economic: the lord controlled the productive asset, and everyone who depended on that asset was, to varying degrees, under the lord's authority. Feudalism was property rights with a sword and a prayer attached. The sword ensured compliance. The prayer explained why compliance was virtuous. The property rights did the actual work.

OWNERSHIP STRUCTURES AND DEPENDENCY

Control over productive assets creates dependency, and dependency is power's most reliable raw material. This principle operates at every scale, from the landlord who controls a tenant's housing to the corporation that controls a region's employment to the nation that controls a critical commodity. The mechanism is identical in each case: the party that controls what others need can set terms, and the party that needs what others control must accept them. The terms may be negotiated, but the negotiation occurs on a field that is tilted by the underlying distribution of ownership. The landlord and the tenant are both free to walk away from the negotiation. Only one of them sleeps outside if they do.

Land ownership was the original and, for most of human history, the dominant form of economic power. In agrarian societies, land was not merely an asset. It was the asset—the source of food, the basis of wealth, the foundation of political authority. Controlling land meant controlling the people who worked it, because those people had nowhere else to go. The feudal system formalized this dependency into a legal and social structure, but the dependency existed wherever land ownership was concentrated, regardless of the legal framework. Ancient Rome's latifundia—vast agricultural estates worked by slaves and tenant farmers—created economic dependencies that persisted for centuries. The hacienda system in colonial Latin America replicated the pattern. The plantation system in the American South replicated it again. The specific arrangements varied. The structural logic—concentrated land ownership producing concentrated power—did not.

The transition from land-based to capital-based economies shifted the locus of dependency without eliminating it. In industrial economies, the critical productive asset was no longer land but capital—factories, machinery, infrastructure, financial reserves. Workers who had been dependent on landlords became dependent on factory owners, exchanging one form of subordination for another that offered higher wages and worse air quality. The factory owner controlled the means of production in precisely the way the feudal lord had controlled the land: as the asset without which the dependent party could not sustain themselves. Karl Marx built an entire theoretical framework around this observation, and while his prescriptions generated considerable debate, his description of the dependency relationship was difficult to dispute. The worker who owned nothing but labor had to sell that labor on whatever terms the market offered, and the market's terms were set, in practice, by the people who owned the capital.

Modern economies have added layers of complexity to this basic structure without fundamentally altering it. Stock ownership, intellectual property, platform access, data control—each represents a new form of productive asset that creates new dependencies. A software platform that mediates transactions between buyers and sellers controls the marketplace in the same structural sense that the medieval lord controlled the land. The participants can leave, in theory. In practice, the cost of leaving—lost customers, lost data, lost network effects—functions as a form of economic gravity that keeps them in orbit. The platform does not coerce. It does not need to. It controls the infrastructure, and infrastructure is harder to replace than a lord, a factory, or a king. It is the new land, and it belongs to a remarkably small number of people, which is a pattern that should feel familiar by now.

The concentration of ownership follows a dynamic that is sometimes described as natural and is more accurately described as self-reinforcing. Economist Thomas Piketty documented this pattern extensively: wealth generates returns, returns generate more wealth, and more wealth generates more returns. The process is exponential, which means that small initial advantages compound into large ones over time. The landowner who starts with a hundred acres and reinvests the surplus from each harvest will, within a few generations, own a thousand acres, provided nothing intervenes to break the cycle. The capitalist who starts with a modest factory and reinvests the profits will, within a few decades, own a conglomerate. The process does not require unusual talent, exceptional luck, or particular virtue. It requires only the ownership of a productive asset and the passage of time. This is why wealth concentrates. Not because the wealthy are smarter or harder-working, but because the mathematics of compounding are indifferent to merit and relentless in application.

FINANCIAL LEVERAGE AS CONTROL

Debt is the conversion of future labor into present obligation, and it is one of the most effective instruments of control ever devised. A person in debt is a person whose future decisions have been constrained by a past transaction. The debtor must work to repay. The debtor must accept terms to renegotiate. The debtor must maintain the creditor's goodwill or face consequences that range from higher interest rates to seizure of assets to imprisonment, depending on the era and the jurisdiction. Debt transforms a voluntary economic relationship into a compulsory one, and compulsory relationships are the basic currency of power.

Ancient societies understood this perfectly. Debt bondage—the practice of forcing debtors to work for their creditors until the debt was repaid—was widespread in Mesopotamia, Greece, Rome, and across Asia. The practice was so common and so destabilizing that multiple ancient rulers found it necessary to issue debt amnesties—mass cancellations of outstanding debts—to prevent the entire agricultural population from falling into permanent servitude. The Babylonian misharum edicts, the biblical Jubilee, Solon's seisachtheia in Athens—each represented a recognition that debt, left unchecked, would concentrate power so completely in the hands of creditors that the social order itself would collapse. The debt amnesty was not generosity. It was structural maintenance. The creditor class had to surrender some of its leverage to prevent the system from tearing itself apart, a dynamic that modern policymakers encounter with depressing regularity.

The development of banking and financial instruments multiplied the power of debt by orders of magnitude. A medieval moneylender could extend credit to a few dozen borrowers. A Florentine banking house could finance a war. The Medici did not rule Florence through military conquest or divine mandate. They ruled through banking. Their loans to popes, kings, and city-states created a web of obligation that translated directly into political influence. When the Medici wanted something—a favorable papal decision, a trade concession, a military alliance—they did not need to make threats. They needed to remind the relevant parties of the outstanding balance. The reminder was usually sufficient. A creditor does not need an army. A creditor needs a ledger and the willingness to use it.

The creation of sovereign debt—government borrowing from private lenders—inverted the traditional power relationship between states and merchants in ways that are still playing out. A king who borrowed from bankers to finance a war placed himself in the position of debtor, which is not a comfortable position for a sovereign to occupy. The banker could not command the king, but the banker could refuse to lend, and a king who could not borrow could not fight. The Fugger banking family of Augsburg financed the election of Charles V as Holy Roman Emperor, an investment that paid returns in mining concessions, trade privileges, and political access for generations. The relationship was not one of equals. It was a partnership of dependencies: the king needed money, the banker needed protection, and each controlled something the other required. But the partnership tilted over time toward the party with the money, because money is patient and kings are not.

Modern financial systems have extended this logic to a global scale. Sovereign debt markets allow governments to borrow from investors worldwide, but the borrowing comes with constraints that function as governance from outside the political system. A government whose bonds are downgraded by credit rating agencies faces higher borrowing costs, which constrains its policy options regardless of what its citizens voted for. An emerging economy that accepts loans from international financial institutions accepts conditions—structural adjustment programs, privatization requirements, fiscal austerity measures—that reshape its domestic policies according to the lender's priorities. The mechanism is gentler than military occupation. The effect on sovereignty is comparable. The debtor nation retains its flag, its anthem, and its seat at the United Nations. It surrenders a significant portion of its policy autonomy to creditors who never appear on a ballot and never face the population whose lives their conditions reshape. This is financial leverage operating as governance, and it is considerably more widespread than most citizens of debtor nations realize, or most citizens of creditor nations care to acknowledge.

Markets Shaping Governance

Markets are described in economic textbooks as mechanisms for allocating resources efficiently. This is true in the same sense that a river is a mechanism for moving water downhill. The description is accurate but incomplete. Rivers also carve canyons, redirect ecosystems, and determine where cities are built. Markets also allocate political power, shape social structures, and determine which forms of governance are viable. The market is not a neutral space in which economic activity occurs. It is a force that reshapes everything it touches, including the political systems that claim to regulate it.

The relationship between markets and governance has always been reciprocal and always been contested. States create the conditions under which markets function—property rights, contract enforcement, currency systems, infrastructure. Markets generate the revenue that states need to operate. The interdependence is genuine, but it is not symmetrical. The party with greater leverage at any given moment shapes the terms of the relationship, and the balance of leverage has shifted over time in ways that are worth tracing.

In the earliest market economies, political authority clearly dominated. Rulers set prices, controlled trade routes, determined what could be bought and sold, and extracted revenue from commercial activity through taxes, tariffs, and outright seizure. Merchants operated at the sufferance of political power and could be enriched or ruined by a single royal decision. The merchant class was wealthy but politically subordinate—tolerated, taxed, and occasionally scapegoated when economic conditions deteriorated. In many ancient and medieval societies, merchants occupied a paradoxical social position: economically powerful but socially marginal, wealthy but not respectable, necessary but not trusted. The contempt that warrior and priestly classes directed at merchants was not mere snobbery. It was the instinctive hostility of established power toward a rival that it could not fully control.

The balance began to shift in late medieval and early modern Europe, when the cost of warfare increased faster than the revenue from traditional sources. Kings who needed money to fight wars turned to merchants and bankers who had it, and those merchants and bankers extracted concessions in return. Parliaments—originally convened to approve tax increases—became forums in which the commercial class could negotiate the terms under which they would finance the state. The English Parliament's gradual acquisition of power over the crown was, at its foundation, an economic negotiation: the king needed revenue, the propertied classes controlled revenue, and the price of their cooperation was a share of political authority. The Glorious Revolution of 1688, celebrated as a triumph of constitutional liberty, was also and perhaps primarily a triumph of creditors over a king who could not be trusted to repay his debts. Constitutional government and reliable debt service turned out to be the same demand, phrased in different registers.

The Industrial Revolution accelerated this shift beyond recovery. Industrial capitalism produced concentrations of private wealth that rivaled and eventually exceeded the resources of many states. A railroad company that employed tens of thousands of workers, controlled thousands of miles of track, and generated revenue exceeding the budgets of several states combined was not a private enterprise in any meaningful sense. It was a governing institution that happened not to have a flag. Its decisions about routes, rates, and employment determined where towns prospered and where they died, which industries thrived and which collapsed, which regions developed and which were left behind. The company did not need to hold elections. It held something more useful: the infrastructure on which economic life depended.

The twentieth century introduced regulatory frameworks designed to reassert political authority over market power—antitrust laws, labor regulations, financial oversight, environmental standards. These frameworks represented genuine constraints and genuine achievements. They also represented a negotiation rather than a resolution. The market's influence on governance did not end because governments passed regulations. It adapted, finding new channels through lobbying, campaign finance, regulatory capture, and the revolving door between government agencies and the industries they nominally oversaw. The result, in most advanced economies, is not government control of markets or market control of government but an entanglement so thorough that distinguishing between the two requires a level of analytical precision that neither political discourse nor most political participants are equipped to provide. The market shapes governance. Governance shapes the market. The question of which is the senior partner depends on who is asking and what they are trying to sell.

Economic power operates on a longer time horizon than military power and through quieter channels than sacred or political power, but its effects are no less structural and no less durable. It shapes who governs by determining who can afford to compete for office. It shapes what governments do by determining what they can afford to fund. It shapes what citizens expect by determining what the economy delivers and to whom. It is the current beneath the surface of political life—invisible most of the time, irresistible when it shifts.

The objection most often raised against treating economic power as a structural force is that markets are voluntary—that nobody is forced to take a job, sign a lease, or accept a contract, and that describing these arrangements as "power" misuses the word. The objection has surface appeal and a long intellectual pedigree. It also depends on a definition of voluntariness that ignores the conditions under which choice occurs. A worker who can refuse this job but cannot refuse all jobs is not in a meaningfully voluntary relationship with employment as a category. A tenant who can choose this lease but cannot choose to live without one is not in a voluntary relationship with shelter. The structural reading does not deny that markets allow choice within a frame. It observes that the frame itself is rarely chosen, and that the people who set the frame exercise a form of power that is more consequential than any choice the frame permits.

The forms of economic power have changed enormously since the first grain merchant extended credit to a farmer who needed seed. The scale is different. The instruments are different. The speed of transactions is different. What has not changed is the fundamental dynamic: control over economic resources translates into control over political outcomes, and the translation requires no formal mechanism because it operates through the most powerful informal mechanism available—the universal need to eat, to shelter, to survive.

8

IMPERIAL POWER

"They make a desert and call it peace."

Tacitus
Agricola (98 CE)

EMPIRES ARE WHAT HAPPEN when a state looks at its borders and decides they are suggestions. The impulse is older than the word itself and more persistent than any particular empire has managed to be. Akkad tried it. Persia tried it. Rome tried it. The Mongols tried it on a scale that made everyone else's attempt look like a land dispute. Spain, Britain, France, and several others tried it with ships, flags, and an extraordinary confidence that people on other continents would benefit from being governed by strangers who had never seen their country and could not pronounce their names. The attempts varied in method, duration, and body count. The structural pattern was the same in every case: expand, extract, impose, and eventually discover that the costs of holding distant territory exceed the benefits of possessing it.

EXPANSION BEYOND SUSTAINABLE GOVERNANCE

Empires begin with a competitive advantage, economic, technological, organizational, that allows one state to dominate its neighbors. The advantage is real, and the early returns on expansion are genuine. Conquered territory provides resources: agricultural land, mineral wealth, labor, trade routes, strategic positions. These resources fund further expansion, which provides further resources, which funds further expansion. The cycle is intoxicating. Each conquest pays for the next. The empire grows because growing feels like winning, and winning is difficult to argue against, particularly when the people making the argument are the ones benefiting from the spoils.

The problem is that the costs of holding territory grow faster than the benefits of acquiring it. The first province conquered is typically adjacent, culturally similar, and relatively easy to integrate. The tenth province is distant, culturally alien, and resistant to absorption. The garrison required to hold it is larger. The administrative apparatus required to govern it is more complex. The communication lines connecting it to the center are longer and more vulnerable. The local population's willingness to cooperate is lower. Each additional unit of territory produces diminishing returns and increasing costs, but the diminishment is gradual and the costs are distributed across the system in ways that make them difficult to attribute to any single decision. No emperor ever conquered a province and received an invoice itemizing the long-term administrative burden. The costs arrived later, dispersed across decades and budget lines, by which point the decision to expand had been celebrated, the general had been promoted, and the structural problem had become someone else's inheritance.

Rome illustrates the pattern with textbook clarity. The Roman Republic expanded across Italy through a combination of military superiority and shrewd alliance-building. Each conquest strengthened the next by providing soldiers, revenue, and strategic depth. The expansion was self-financing and self-reinforcing. Then Rome crossed the Mediterranean. North Africa, Spain, Greece, the Near East—each acquisition brought wealth but also brought governance challenges that the Republic's institutions were not designed to handle. Provincial governors operated with minimal oversight across vast distances. Military commanders accumulated personal armies and personal loyalties that rivaled the state's. The wealth flowing in from the provinces destabilized the domestic political economy, concentrating resources in the hands of a senatorial class that used them to purchase political influence on a scale that the Republic's constitutional framework could not contain. The Republic did not fall because it stopped expanding. It fell because the consequences of expansion overwhelmed the institutions that had made expansion possible.

The British Empire repeated the pattern with steam engines and better record-keeping. At its peak, Britain governed roughly a quarter of the world's land surface and a quarter of its population. The administrative achievement was genuine and, by the standards of the era, remarkable. The costs were equally remarkable but distributed in ways that made them less visible. Maintaining the Indian garrison consumed a significant share of Indian tax revenue. Policing the sea lanes required a navy whose budget exceeded the GDP of most nations. Managing the political relationships between London and dozens of colonial administrations with competing interests, local grievances, and varying degrees of cooperation required a Foreign Office and Colonial Office staffed by people whose job was, essentially, to prevent the whole thing from catching fire simultaneously. The empire generated enormous wealth, but the wealth flowed unevenly, the costs fell disproportionately on the governed, and the administrative complexity grew faster than the administrative capacity to manage it. By the time two world wars had exhausted Britain's financial and military reserves, the gap between the cost of empire and the capacity to sustain it had become unbridgeable. Decolonization was not generosity. It was arithmetic.

TRIBUTE SYSTEMS AND EXTRACTION

The purpose of empire, stripped of its ideological decorations, is extraction. The extraction was experienced by millions not as an economic arrangement but as starvation during famines that could have been prevented, forced labor that killed those performing it, and the systematic erasure of languages, religions, and ways of life that had existed for centuries. Territory is acquired because it contains something valuable—resources, labor, markets, strategic position—and the mechanism for transferring that value from the periphery to the center is the tribute system. The specific form varies: direct taxation, forced labor, commodity requisitions, trade monopolies, unequal commercial arrangements. The structural function is identical in every case. Wealth flows from the governed to the governors in quantities that exceed what the governed would voluntarily choose to provide. The difference between what is taken and what would be given freely is the operating margin of empire.

Ancient empires were relatively transparent about this. The Assyrian Empire demanded tribute from conquered peoples and publicized the demands through inscriptions that listed, with evident satisfaction, the quantities of gold, silver, livestock, and humans extracted from subject populations. The Persian Empire under Darius I organized its territory into satrapies, each assigned a specific tribute obligation denominated in silver talents. The system was rationalized, recorded, and administered with a sophistication that earlier empires had not achieved. It was also, from the perspective of the taxed populations, a formalized extraction regime that transferred wealth from provinces to the imperial center on a permanent basis. The roads and postal system that Darius built were genuine public goods. They were also the infrastructure that made efficient extraction possible. The road that carried trade also carried the tax collector, and the tax collector used the road more reliably.

The Mongol Empire refined extraction to an art form, partly because the Mongols had no interest in governing the populations they conquered and every interest in profiting from them. The Mongol approach was pragmatic to the point of transparency: submit, pay tribute, and retain your local governance structures; resist, and be destroyed with a thoroughness that served as advertising for the first option. The system worked because the Mongols were credible in both their promises and their threats. Cities that submitted were taxed but not destroyed. Cities that resisted were annihilated so completely that the ruins served as warnings for decades. The Mongol tribute system was not sophisticated in the bureaucratic sense—it relied heavily on local administrators and existing tax structures—but it was extraordinarily effective in the economic sense. Wealth flowed from China, Persia, Russia, and Central Asia to the Mongol elite with minimal administrative overhead, because the Mongols outsourced the administration and kept the revenue.

European colonial empires developed extraction systems of considerably greater complexity and considerably greater hypocrisy. The rhetoric shifted from tribute to trade, from extraction to development, from domination to civilization. The economics remained extractive. The British East India Company did not establish itself in Bengal to improve

Bengali living standards. It established itself to redirect Bengali revenue to company shareholders, which it did with impressive efficiency, transforming one of the wealthiest regions in Asia into a source of raw materials for British industry within a few generations. The Dutch East India Company performed similar operations across Southeast Asia. The Spanish Crown extracted silver from the Americas on a scale that reshaped the global economy, funding European wars with metal mined by forced indigenous and African labor under conditions that the word "brutality" understates. In each case, the machinery of extraction was wrapped in legal frameworks, commercial structures, and civilizational narratives that obscured the fundamental transaction: wealth was being transferred from populations that produced it to populations that had the military capacity to take it.

Extraction systems grew more sophisticated, but the underlying dynamic remained unchanged. Modern economic imperialism—structural adjustment programs, trade agreements favoring industrialized economies, intellectual property regimes protecting wealthy nations' innovations while restricting poorer ones' options—operates through mechanisms gentler than a Mongol army and more durable than colonial administration. They don't require garrisons. They require signatures. The debtor nation signs because the alternative is exclusion from the global financial system—a modern version of the Mongol choice, submit or be destroyed, delivered in a conference room rather than on a battlefield. The conference room is more comfortable. The structural effect is comparable.

CULTURAL IMPOSITION

Every empire that lasted more than a generation discovered the same thing: military control is expensive and cultural absorption is cheap. If the conquered population can be persuaded to adopt the conqueror's language, religion, laws, and customs, the cost of governance drops dramatically because the population begins to police itself according to norms that serve the imperial interest. The Roman Empire did not station legions in every town in Gaul for four centuries. It romanized the Gallic elite, who then romanized their own populations, who then maintained Roman cultural norms without requiring legions to enforce them. The process took generations, but the result was a province that functioned as part of the empire not because it was compelled to but because it had internalized the empire's cultural framework. The garrison could be reduced because the culture was doing the garrison's job.

The mechanism of cultural imposition typically followed a predictable sequence. First, the imperial language was established as the language of administration, commerce, and social advancement. Learning the language became necessary for anyone who wanted to participate in the governing structure, trade with the imperial economy, or rise above their current social position. The language carried with it categories of thought, legal concepts, and cultural assumptions that gradually displaced local alternatives. Second, the imperial legal system replaced or overlaid local legal traditions, establishing a framework of rights, obligations, and dispute resolution that operated according to imperial norms. Third, the imperial religion or ideology was promoted through a combination of missionary activity, institutional support, and social incentive. Conversion—whether to Christianity, Islam, Roman civic religion, or the particular ideology of the imperial power—provided access to networks, status, and opportunities that non-conversion did not.

The British Empire executed this sequence with particular thoroughness and particular self-regard. English became the language of law, commerce, and education across colonies on every inhabited continent. British legal traditions were implanted in legal systems from India to Nigeria to Hong Kong. British educational institutions trained local elites in British cultural norms, producing a class of intermediaries who could administer the colony using the colonizer's conceptual framework. The system was described, by the British, as a civilizing mission—the generous extension of advanced culture to populations that would benefit from exposure to it. The description was self-serving but not entirely inaccurate in its structural analysis, if not its moral evaluation. Cultural imposition did create a shared framework. The framework served the empire's interests far more effectively than it served the interests of the populations being civilized, which was rather the point.

Cultural imposition also generated its own resistance, and the resistance often used the imposed culture as its weapon. Indian independence leaders were, overwhelmingly, educated in British institutions and fluent in British political philosophy. They used the language of British liberalism—rights, self-determination, consent of the governed—to argue against British rule, forcing the empire to confront the contradiction between its stated values and its actual practices. This pattern recurred across colonial empires. The tools of cultural imposition became the tools of anticolonial resistance, because the culture being imposed contained within it principles that, taken seriously, undermined the legitimacy of the imposition. The British taught their subjects about parliamentary democracy and individual rights and were then surprised when those subjects demanded parliamentary democracy and individual rights for themselves. The surprise was genuine, which tells you something about the depth of imperial self-awareness.

Empire's cultural legacy outlasts the empire itself, often by centuries. Former colonies operate legal systems, speak languages, practice religions, and maintain institutions inherited from colonizers long after independence. This persistence reflects institutional inertia—systems embedded and hard to replace—and genuine utility. English dominates international commerce not by vote but because using it provides access to unmatched networks. Roman law persists in Europe not from reverence but because it works tolerably well and replacing it costs more than maintaining it. Cultural imposition creates path dependencies that constrain choices long after coercion ends. The empire is gone. Its categories remain.

OVEREXTENSION DYNAMICS

Every empire in recorded history has overextended, and every empire that overextended has eventually contracted or collapsed. The pattern is so consistent that it qualifies as something close to a law. Historian Paul Kennedy analyzed this phenomenon as "imperial overstretch"—the condition in which strategic commitments grow faster than the resources needed to sustain them. The question is not whether overextension will occur but when, and the answer is always: later than it should have been recognized and earlier than anyone in charge expected.

Overextension is the condition in which the costs of maintaining an empire exceed the empire's capacity to sustain them. It manifests in predictable ways: military commitments that strain the treasury, administrative complexity that exceeds institutional capacity, peripheral territories that consume more resources than they contribute, and a core population that bears increasing burdens for decreasing returns. The symptoms are identifiable in advance. The diagnosis is routinely ignored, because the people in a position to act on it are the people who benefit most from the current arrangement and are therefore least inclined to acknowledge that the arrangement is unsustainable.

The Roman Empire's trajectory is the canonical example, not because it was unique but because it was exceptionally well documented. At its territorial peak under Trajan in 117 CE, Rome controlled the entire Mediterranean basin, most of Western Europe, significant portions of the Near East, and a strip of North Africa. The territory was impressive. The cost of defending it was staggering. The frontier stretched for thousands of miles across terrain that varied from dense forest to open desert, requiring garrisons, fortifications, and logistics chains that consumed an enormous share of imperial revenue. Rome's military expenditure rose continuously from the second century onward, not because the empire faced dramatically worse threats but because the frontier was simply too long and the territory behind it too vast to defend economically. The empire did not face a single catastrophic military defeat that ended it. It faced a chronic fiscal crisis in which the cost of defense gradually outpaced the revenue available to fund it. The barbarian invasions that finally dismembered the western empire succeeded not because the barbarians were stronger than Rome but because Rome could no longer afford to stop them everywhere simultaneously. Overextension killed Rome. The barbarians just filed the paperwork.

The Spanish Empire provides an instructive variation. Spain's acquisition of American silver in the sixteenth century produced a windfall that appeared to solve the resource problem permanently. For a time, it did. Spanish silver financed wars across Europe, maintained armies in the Netherlands, Italy, and North Africa, and funded a navy that projected power across the Atlantic and Pacific. But the silver created its own problems. It generated inflation that eroded the domestic economy. It financed military commitments that grew faster than even American silver could sustain. It created a dependency on extraction that discouraged the development of domestic economic capacity. When the silver supply diminished and the military commitments did not, Spain entered a decline that lasted centuries. The empire had mistaken a temporary resource windfall for a permanent solution to the overextension problem, which is the imperial equivalent of spending your inheritance as though it were a salary.

The Soviet Union demonstrated that overextension is not limited to territorial empires in the traditional sense. The Soviet commitment to maintaining a global ideological empire—satellite states in Eastern Europe, client regimes across the developing world, a military establishment designed to match the United States across every domain—consumed resources that the Soviet economy could not sustainably generate. The gap between commitments and capacity widened throughout the 1970s and 1980s, masked for a time by oil revenues and accounting practices that would have impressed a creative fiction writer. When oil prices fell and the accounting could no longer obscure the structural deficit, the system unraveled with a speed that stunned observers who had been analyzing Soviet power from the outside. It should not have been stunning. The pattern was identical to every previous case of imperial overextension. The costs exceeded the capacity. The commitments exceeded the resources. The system held together through inertia and coercion until it could no longer hold together at all, and then it did not hold together gradually. It collapsed.

The dynamics of overextension operate through a feedback loop that is maddeningly difficult to interrupt. Expansion creates commitments. Commitments generate costs. Costs require revenue. Revenue requires either expansion or extraction, both of which generate further commitments. Retreat from any single commitment threatens the credibility that sustains all the others, because imperial power depends in part on the perception that the empire can and will defend its interests everywhere. Abandoning one province invites challenges in others. The empire is trapped between the unsustainable cost of maintaining its commitments and the potentially catastrophic cost of abandoning them. Most empires choose to maintain until they cannot, which means they pay the cost of both maintenance and collapse rather than the cost of strategic retreat alone. The rational choice is to contract before the contraction becomes involuntary. The historical record suggests that this choice is almost never made, for the simple reason that the people who would have to make it are the same people whose power, status, and identity depend on the empire continuing to exist in its current form. Asking them to preside over deliberate contraction is asking them to preside over their own diminishment, and humans are not, as a general rule, enthusiastic about that.

Imperial power is the most spectacular form of control and the most reliably self-defeating. It demonstrates, at the largest possible scale, the tension between expansion and sustainability that runs through every form of power examined in this book. The empire grows because the incentives favor growth. It collapses because the growth eventually outpaces the capacity to sustain it. The lag between the moment of overextension and the moment of collapse can last decades or centuries, which is long enough for everyone involved to mistake a structural problem for a manageable challenge. By the time the problem is acknowledged, the options for addressing it have narrowed to the point where the only remaining question is how the contraction will occur—managed or chaotic, gradual or sudden, negotiated or imposed.

Some readers will object that the structural critique of empire underplays the genuine benefits empires sometimes delivered—infrastructure, legal systems, internal peace, economic integration—and that the moral ledger is more mixed than the language of "extraction" allows. The mixed ledger is real. Empires built things. Some of those things were used by the conquered to their own advantage after the empire was gone. But the existence of benefits does not change the structural logic. Roads were built because tribute had to move. Legal systems were imposed because disputes had to be resolved on terms favorable to the metropole. The byproducts were often valuable. The system was not designed to produce them, and where the byproducts conflicted with extraction, extraction won.

The structures that empires leave behind—legal systems, languages, trade networks, institutional templates, cultural frameworks—often prove more durable than the empires themselves. Rome's roads outlasted Rome. Britain's legal traditions outlasted Britain's empire. The Mongol trade routes outlasted the Mongol khans. Empire is, in this sense, a delivery mechanism for institutional models, spreading systems of governance and culture across territories that would not have adopted them voluntarily. Whether this constitutes a legacy or a wound depends on who is assessing it and what they inherited.

9
INSTITUTIONAL POWER

Frédéric Bastiat
The State (1848)

PEOPLE DIE. INSTITUTIONS DO not, or at least they do not die easily, and the difference between those two facts explains more about how power works than any theory of leadership, ideology, or revolution. A charismatic founder builds something remarkable—a church, a corporation, a court, a university—and then, inevitably, the founder dies. What happens next is the test that separates a movement from an institution. If the thing collapses, it was a personality cult with a mailing list. If it survives, adapts, and continues operating with recognizable continuity, it has become something considerably more durable: an organization whose power no longer depends on any single human being. This is institutional power, and it is the closest thing to immortality that human organization has produced.

ORGANIZATIONS OUTLIVING FOUNDERS

The transition from founder to institution is the most dangerous moment in any organization's life, and the organizations that survive it are the ones that have, consciously or accidentally, solved a specific problem: how to transfer authority from a person to a structure. The problem is harder than it sounds. A founder's authority is typically personal—rooted in vision, charisma, relationships, and the accumulated credibility of having built the thing in the first place. None of these qualities can be bequeathed. The founder's successor inherits the title, the office, and the organizational chart. The successor does not inherit the trust, the reputation, or the network of personal loyalties that made the founder effective. The organization must find a way to function without the qualities that made it function in the first place, which is the institutional equivalent of removing the engine from a moving car and hoping the momentum carries it forward.

Economic historian Douglass North analyzed how institutions persist through the creation of formal rules and informal constraints that outlive their creators—structures that reduce uncertainty and shape incentives across generations. The organizations that manage this transition successfully tend to share certain characteristics. They codify. They proceduralize. They build structures that do not require exceptional individuals to operate. The founder made decisions by instinct, by personal judgment, by reading the room. The institution replaces instinct with policy, personal judgment with standardized criteria, and reading the room with committee processes that produce decisions regardless of whether anyone in the room possesses the founder's gifts. The decisions may be worse. They will also be more consistent, more predictable, and more resistant to the catastrophic failures that occur when an organization built around one person encounters a successor who is not that person.

Christianity is the most consequential example of this transition in human history. Jesus of Nazareth was, by any structural analysis, a charismatic founder whose authority was entirely personal. He held no office, commanded no army, controlled no treasury, and operated no bureaucracy. His influence derived from his teaching, his presence, and the commitment of a small group of followers who believed he was the messiah. When he was executed, the movement faced the founder's dilemma in its most extreme form: the founder was not merely gone but publicly killed by the very authorities the movement challenged. By every reasonable prediction, the movement should have dissolved. It did the opposite. Within three centuries, it became the official religion of the empire that had executed its founder, and within two millennia, it became the largest religious organization on the planet. The transition from Jesus to the Church is the most successful founder-to-institution conversion in recorded history, and it succeeded because the early Church did exactly what successful institutions always do: it codified the founder's teachings into doctrine, established procedures for leadership succession, built organizational structures that could function without charismatic authority, and created rituals that transmitted the founder's legacy to each new generation without requiring each new generation to have met the founder personally.

The pattern is visible, at smaller scale, in every organization that survives its creator. Standard Oil outlived Rockefeller's direct management because its organizational structure—the trust, the holding company, the divisional hierarchy—could function without Rockefeller in the room. The United States outlived Washington because the Constitution created a framework for governance that did not require Washington's personal judgment to operate. Oxford University has outlived every person who has ever attended or taught there because its institutional structures—colleges, faculties, degree requirements, governance procedures—reproduce themselves across generations without any single generation being essential. The founder provides the initial energy. The institution converts that energy into structure, and structure is what persists.

The organizations that fail this transition are equally instructive. Alexander the Great built the largest empire the ancient world had seen and left behind no institutional framework for governing it. Within a decade of his death, the empire had fragmented into competing successor states run by his generals, each claiming a piece of what Alexander's personal authority had held together. Genghis Khan's empire followed a similar trajectory—vast, powerful, and dependent on a system of personal loyalty that could not survive the dilution of authority across subsequent generations. In each case, the founder's extraordinary personal capacity masked the absence of institutional depth. The empire was the founder. When the founder was gone, the empire was a territory with no operating system.

SELF-PRESERVATION MECHANISMS

Once an institution survives its founder, it develops something that resembles a survival instinct. This is not consciousness. Institutions do not think. But they behave as though they do, because the people within them are incentivized to act in ways that preserve the institution, and the cumulative effect of those individual incentives produces organizational behavior that looks remarkably like self-preservation. The bishop protects the Church not because the Church asked him to but because his identity, status, income, and social world are embedded in it. The corporate executive protects the company not out of abstract loyalty but because her career, reputation, and stock options depend on its continued existence. The judge protects the court because the court is the source of the judge's authority. Individual self-interest, aggregated across an institution's membership, produces institutional self-interest. The mechanism is automatic, requires no coordination, and is extremely difficult to override.

Institutions preserve themselves through several interlocking mechanisms, each of which reinforces the others. The first is control over membership. Institutions decide who gets in, which means they can select for individuals who are likely to perpetuate the institution's values, norms, and practices. The legal profession controls admission through bar examinations. Medical schools control admission through accreditation and licensing. Religious orders control admission through novitiate periods and vows. Academic departments control admission through hiring committees that evaluate candidates against criteria that the department itself established. In each case, the institution selects its own future members, which means it reproduces itself across generations with a fidelity that would impress a geneticist. People who might challenge the institution's fundamental assumptions are filtered out before they arrive. People who internalize those assumptions are welcomed, promoted, and eventually empowered to filter the next generation. The process is not conspiratorial. It is structural, which makes it considerably more effective than conspiracy because it requires no meetings, no coordination, and no awareness on the part of the participants that it is happening.

The second mechanism is control over narrative. Institutions write their own histories, and those histories are, with impressive consistency, stories of necessity and virtue. The institution was founded to address a genuine need. It has served that need faithfully. Its continued existence is essential to the public good. Alternative arrangements would be inferior. This narrative is not necessarily false—many institutions do serve genuine needs—but it is always self-serving, because the institution that writes its own history will never conclude that history with the sentence "and then we became unnecessary." The Catholic Church's official history does not include a chapter titled "Periods When We Were Primarily a Land Management Corporation." The United States Senate's institutional narrative does not prominently feature the decades when it functioned as a retirement home for railroad executives. Every institution curates its history to support its continued existence, and the curation is so universal and so effective that challenging it feels like challenging reality itself.

The third mechanism is control over resources. Institutions accumulate assets—money, property, intellectual capital, relationships, legal rights—that make them difficult to replace and expensive to dismantle. A university that owns a campus, employs thousands, holds an endowment, and possesses accreditation authority has created a web of dependencies that extends far beyond its educational mission. Alumni depend on the institution's continued prestige for the value of their degrees. Employees depend on it for their livelihoods. Local businesses depend on it for customers. Government agencies depend on it for research. Each dependency creates a stakeholder with an interest in the institution's survival, and the accumulation of stakeholders creates a constituency so large and so diverse that the institution becomes, in practical terms, impossible to eliminate. It may decline. It may become ineffective. It may cease to serve its original purpose entirely. But it will not disappear, because too many people need it to exist for reasons that have nothing to do with its mission statement.

The fourth mechanism is the most subtle and the most powerful: the institution's capacity to define the standards by which its performance is evaluated. A hospital that sets its own quality metrics will, unsurprisingly, perform well against those metrics. A regulatory agency that defines what constitutes compliance will, unsurprisingly, find that its regulatory framework produces compliance. A university that defines academic excellence will, unsurprisingly, find that its graduates are academically excellent by its own definition. This is not fraud. It is institutional logic operating as designed. The entity that controls the standards controls the evaluation, and the entity that controls the evaluation is insulated from external accountability in the most fundamental way possible: it has defined accountability on its own terms.

COURTS, CORPORATIONS, RELIGIOUS BODIES

The three institutional forms that have demonstrated the greatest historical durability are courts, corporations, and religious bodies. Each has developed distinct mechanisms for self-perpetuation, but they share a common feature: they have each found a way to make their continued existence feel inevitable rather than contingent. The court feels like a natural feature of governance. The corporation feels like a natural feature of economic life. The church feels like a natural feature of spiritual life. None of them are natural. All of them are constructed, maintained, and reproduced through deliberate institutional practices. The feeling of inevitability is itself the institution's most successful product.

Courts derive their power from the legal system's need for authoritative interpretation. Laws are written in language, and language is ambiguous. Someone must decide what the words mean when applied to specific cases, and that someone's decision must be treated as binding, or the legal system collapses into competing interpretations with no mechanism for resolution. Courts occupy this position of interpretive authority, and once established, the position is nearly impossible to dislodge because dislodging it means removing the only mechanism for resolving legal disputes. You cannot abolish the court without first creating an alternative institution to perform the court's function, and the alternative institution is, by definition, a court. The function creates the institution, and the institution perpetuates itself by being the only available performer of an indispensable function. It is a closed loop of remarkable elegance and remarkable imperviousness to reform.

The English common law system illustrates this dynamic across nearly a millennium. English courts have operated continuously since the twelfth century, surviving civil wars, revolutions, the execution of a king, the restoration of a monarchy, the expansion and contraction of an empire, two world wars, and the complete transformation of the society they serve. The legal principles they apply have evolved beyond recognition. The institutional form has remained stable. The courts adapted their content while preserving their structure, which is the institutional equivalent of rebuilding a ship one plank at a time while keeping it afloat. The ship that sails today shares no planks with the ship that launched in 1154. It is, nevertheless, recognizably the same ship, and that continuity is itself a source of authority. A court that has existed for eight hundred years carries a weight of precedent and tradition that a newly created court cannot match, regardless of how well the new court is designed. Age is an argument. Duration is a credential. The institution that has persisted for centuries can claim, with some justification, that its persistence is evidence of its value, even if a more rigorous analysis might suggest that its persistence is evidence primarily of its persistence.

Corporations achieved institutional durability through a legal innovation so powerful that it deserves to be ranked alongside writing and double-entry bookkeeping in the history of organizational technology: the concept of legal personhood. A corporation is, in law, a person—not a human person, but an entity with legal rights, obligations, and the capacity to own property, enter contracts, and sue and be sued. This legal fiction freed the organization from dependence on any particular human being. Shareholders could die. Executives could be replaced. Employees could leave. The corporation continued, because the corporation was not its people. It was a legal entity that existed independently of whoever happened to be associated with it at any given moment. The Sumitomo Group traces its origins to a Kyoto book and medicine shop founded in 1615 and is still operating. It has outlived its founder, the Tokugawa shogunate that licensed its copper-mining concessions, the samurai class that patronized it, the Meiji state that re-incorporated it under modern commercial law, the imperial system that fueled its expansion, and the postwar Allied occupation that ordered its dissolution. The institution survived all of these. It is not the oldest surviving business—Japan alone hosts older firms, some measured in millennia—but it is a vivid demonstration of what legal personhood, and its functional pre-modern analogues, makes possible: organizational immortality, achieved through a legal fiction that successive political orders have agreed, each in its turn, to treat as fact.

Religious bodies combine elements of both courts and corporations with an additional ingredient that neither possesses: a claim to transcendent authority. A court's authority derives from the legal system. A corporation's authority derives from the market. A religious institution's authority derives from God, or the gods, or the cosmic order, or whatever framework of ultimate reality the institution claims to represent. This is an extraordinarily powerful basis for self-perpetuation because it places the institution's justification beyond the reach of human challenge. You can argue with a court's interpretation of law. You can challenge a corporation's business practices. Arguing with God is a less productive exercise, and institutions that claim to speak for God benefit from the difficulty. The Catholic Church has operated continuously for roughly two thousand years, surviving schisms, corruption scandals, military assaults, the rise of secular science, the Reformation, the Enlightenment, and the emergence of societies that have largely abandoned the theological framework on which the Church's authority nominally rests. It has survived because it possesses all the standard institutional self-preservation mechanisms—control over membership, narrative, resources, and evaluation standards—plus the additional advantage of representing something that, by its own account, cannot fail. An institution that claims to represent eternal truth has a built-in answer to every challenge: temporary difficulties do not invalidate eternal truths. The argument is circular, but circularity, it turns out, is structurally robust.

LEGITIMACY RECYCLING

Institutions do not merely preserve their power. They recycle it—transforming old forms of legitimacy into new ones as conditions change, without ever acknowledging that the transformation has occurred. This process of legitimacy recycling is one of the most important and least visible dynamics in institutional life, and it explains how organizations maintain authority across periods of radical social change that should, logically, have rendered them obsolete.

The process works like this. An institution is established on the basis of a particular claim to legitimacy—divine mandate, royal charter, democratic authorization, revolutionary achievement. Over time, the original basis for that claim erodes. The divine mandate is questioned by secularism. The royal charter becomes irrelevant after the monarchy falls. The revolutionary achievement fades from living memory. At this point, the institution faces a choice: defend the original claim, which is increasingly untenable, or quietly replace it with a new claim while maintaining the appearance of continuity. Successful institutions invariably choose the second option, and they execute it so smoothly that most observers never notice the substitution.

The British monarchy is a masterclass in legitimacy recycling. The original claim—divine right of kings—was formally abandoned after the Glorious Revolution of 1688 and effectively abandoned long before that. The replacement claim was constitutional authority: the monarchy ruled because the constitutional arrangement authorized it. When constitutional authority began to feel insufficient in an age of democratic expectation, the claim shifted again—to tradition, national identity, and the ceremonial embodiment of historical continuity. The monarchy no longer claims to rule by God's will or by constitutional necessity. It claims to represent the nation's heritage, to embody its continuity, to provide a focus for national identity that transcends partisan politics. The function has changed entirely. The institution remains. The transition from divine sovereign to constitutional monarch to national symbol occurred across three centuries without the institution ever acknowledging that it had fundamentally reinvented its purpose. Each iteration presented itself as the natural continuation of what came before, and the public largely accepted the presentation, because the alternative—recognizing that the institution's current justification bears no relationship to its original one—would require a conversation that neither the institution nor the public particularly wants to have.

Universities have performed a similar act of legitimacy recycling with comparable success. Medieval universities derived their authority from the Church, which chartered them, and from the scholastic tradition, which defined their intellectual framework. When the Church's authority declined and the scholastic tradition was superseded by empirical science, universities did not disappear. They adopted the new intellectual framework, claimed it as their own, and presented the transition as natural intellectual evolution rather than institutional reinvention. The modern research university bears almost no intellectual resemblance to its medieval predecessor. It teaches different subjects, employs different methods, pursues different goals, and operates under a fundamentally different epistemological framework. But it carries the same name, occupies the same buildings, maintains the same degree structures, and claims an unbroken lineage that suggests continuity where the reality is closer to metamorphosis. The institution recycled its legitimacy so effectively that the recycling is invisible, which is, of course, the measure of success.

Legitimacy recycling is not deception, though it involves a form of strategic amnesia. The institution does not lie about its past. It selectively remembers, emphasizing the elements that support the current claim and allowing the elements that contradict it to fade from institutional memory. This selective memory is maintained not through censorship but through institutional culture—the stories that are told and retold, the achievements that are commemorated, the figures who are celebrated. Over time, the curated version of history becomes the accepted version, and the accepted version becomes the only version anyone remembers. The institution's past has been revised not by altering the record but by choosing which parts of the record to keep in circulation. The effect is identical: the institution appears to have always been what it currently is, and the question of what it used to be becomes a matter of academic interest rather than institutional relevance.

The strongest objection to celebrating institutional persistence is that the same persistence that stabilizes good arrangements stabilizes bad ones, and that institutions designed to extract, exclude, or oppress are precisely as durable as the institutions designed to protect, distribute, or include. The objection is correct, and it is not actually an objection to the chapter's argument—it is a confirmation of it. Institutional power is structurally indifferent to the moral content of what it sustains. That indifference is the source of its durability and the source of the difficulty in reforming it. The institutions that have outlasted empires include some that should have, and several that should not have, and the structural mechanism that protects them is the same in either case.

Institutional power is the most patient form of authority in human experience. It does not seize. It accumulates. It does not conquer. It persists. It does not inspire the kind of loyalty that sacred power generates or the kind of fear that military power produces. It inspires something less dramatic and more useful: habit. People interact with institutions not because they are awed or terrified but because the institution is there, has always been there, and the effort of imagining an alternative exceeds the effort of continuing to participate. This is not a stirring endorsement, but it is an extraordinarily effective one. Empires last centuries. Institutions last millennia. The difference is that empires require active maintenance while institutions, once established, require only the absence of a compelling reason to dismantle them, and compelling reasons are harder to produce than most reformers appreciate.

10
KNOWLEDGE AS POWER

"Knowledge itself is power."

Francis Bacon
Meditationes Sacrae (1597)

THE PERSON WHO KNOWS something you do not has power over you, and the power increases in direct proportion to how badly you need the information and how difficult it is to obtain elsewhere. This principle is so elementary that it barely qualifies as an insight, yet it has underwritten more systems of control than any army, any treasury, or any throne. Priests who could read when no one else could. Physicians, who understood the body when patients understood only pain. Lawyers who knew the law when clients knew only that they were in trouble. Programmers who understood the machine when users understood only the interface. In every case, the asymmetry between those who possessed knowledge and those who needed it created a dependency as reliable as any produced by land ownership or military force. The dependency was less visible, which made it more durable. You can see the landlord's estate. You can see the general's army. You cannot see what someone knows that you do not, which means you cannot easily assess the terms of the exchange or determine whether you are being charged a fair price.

LITERACY MONOPOLIES

For most of human history, the ability to read and write was not a basic skill. It was a technology controlled by a small class of specialists, and the control was not accidental. Literacy required years of training in writing systems that were, in many early civilizations, deliberately complex. Sumerian cuneiform involved hundreds of symbols. Egyptian hieroglyphics involved hundreds more. Chinese characters required memorizing thousands. The complexity was partly a function of the writing systems' origins and partly a function of nobody having a strong incentive to simplify them. The scribal class that controlled literacy benefited from complexity the way a locksmith benefits from complicated locks. Simplification would have broadened access, and broadened access would have diluted the advantage.

In ancient Egypt, the scribal class occupied a privileged position precisely because they possessed a skill that the rest of society lacked. Scribes recorded harvests, managed temple accounts, drafted legal documents, composed royal correspondence, and maintained the bureaucratic records on which the entire administrative system depended. A pharaoh who could not read—and many could not, or at least relied heavily on scribes for interpretation—was dependent on his scribes for information about his own kingdom. The scribe who prepared the grain report determined what the pharaoh knew about the grain supply. The scribe who drafted the treaty determined what the foreign king understood the terms to be. The scribe who maintained the tax records knew who had paid and who had not, information that was valuable to the state and potentially more valuable to the person who might want to adjust the records. Scribes did not hold formal political power. They held something more useful: the infrastructure through which political power operated.

The relationship between literacy and religious authority was even more direct. In societies where sacred texts defined moral law, social norms, and cosmological truth, the ability to read those texts was the ability to control their interpretation. Medieval European Christianity concentrated literacy overwhelmingly within the clergy, who read and interpreted the Bible in Latin—a language the vast majority of the population did not speak, much less read. The arrangement was not a conspiracy, though it functioned like one. It was a structural consequence of an educational system controlled by the Church, which trained clerics in Latin because Latin was the language of the Church, which conducted its business in Latin because Latin was the language that clerics were trained in. The circularity was self-sustaining. The population received scripture through priestly interpretation, which meant the population received whatever the priest said scripture contained. Challenging the interpretation required literacy in Latin, which required education from the Church, which was unlikely to train people who would challenge its interpretations. The monopoly was elegant in its completeness.

The printing press broke this monopoly, and the consequences were so dramatic that they deserve to be taken seriously rather than recited as a familiar fact. When Gutenberg's press made it possible to produce books in large quantities at reduced cost, it did not merely make information more available. It made information uncontrollable. Martin Luther's Ninety-Five Theses were not revolutionary because of their theological content—scholars had raised similar critiques before. They were revolutionary because the printing press distributed them across Europe faster than any institution could respond. The Church's information monopoly was broken not by a more powerful institution but by a machine that made monopoly impossible. Luther understood this. He was, among his other accomplishments, one of history's most effective users of a new media technology, publishing pamphlets at a rate that overwhelmed the Church's ability to counter them. The Reformation was a theological event. It was also an information event, and the information dimension is what gave the theological dimension its reach.

The pattern—literacy monopoly sustaining authority, new technology breaking the monopoly, authority scrambling to adapt—has repeated with every major advance in information technology. The telegraph compressed information transmission from weeks to seconds, disrupting diplomatic and commercial networks that had depended on time delays. Radio broadcast information to mass audiences without requiring literacy, bypassing the gatekeepers of print media. Television added visual immediacy that transformed political communication. The internet made publication free and universal, eliminating the scarcity that had given institutional publishers their leverage. Each technology expanded the circle of people who could access and distribute information, and each expansion reduced the power of whoever had previously controlled access. The specific incumbents change. The dynamic does not: information monopolies are powerful, and they are fragile, because every new communication technology is a potential solvent.

Expertise Gatekeeping

When literacy ceased to be a monopoly, expertise became the replacement. The modern professions—medicine, law, engineering, finance, academia—are, in structural terms, the successors of the scribal class. They control access to specialized knowledge that others need, and they maintain that control through mechanisms that are considerably more sophisticated than writing in a difficult script. Licensing requirements, educational prerequisites, professional certifications, ethical codes, disciplinary procedures, and jargon so dense that outsiders cannot participate in the conversation without years of specialized training—these are the tools of expertise gatekeeping, and they serve a dual function. They ensure competence, which is the stated purpose, and they restrict supply, which is the structural effect. Both functions operate simultaneously, and disentangling them is considerably more difficult than the professions themselves would like to acknowledge.

Medicine provides the clearest example. The modern medical profession controls access to medical practice through licensing systems that require years of education, supervised training, and examination. The system produces physicians who are, on average, highly competent. It also produces an artificial scarcity of physicians that drives up compensation, limits access to care, and concentrates the power to make life-and-death decisions in a relatively small number of hands. The American Medical Association has spent a century carefully managing the supply of physicians through its influence over medical school accreditation, residency positions, and licensing standards. The quality argument is genuine—you do not want unqualified people performing surgery. The supply argument is also genuine—the deliberate restriction of physician supply has kept physician incomes among the highest of any profession and has contributed to healthcare access problems that a larger physician workforce might alleviate. The two arguments coexist uncomfortably, and the profession has no incentive to resolve the tension because the tension is the source of its leverage.

The legal profession operates on identical logic. Access to legal practice requires a law degree, bar passage, and continuing education—requirements that ensure minimum competence and also ensure that the supply of legal practitioners remains limited relative to demand. Legal language is notoriously opaque, not because clarity is impossible but because opacity is useful. A contract that any literate person could understand would not require a lawyer to interpret, which would reduce demand for lawyers. A tax code that a competent accountant could navigate without legal guidance would not generate the legal industry that currently thrives on its complexity. The complexity is partly inherent in the subject matter and partly a feature that the profession has limited motivation to reduce. Simplification is discussed, occasionally attempted, and never achieved in any way that significantly reduces the public's dependence on legal professionals. The pattern is not unique to law. It is present in every profession that benefits from the gap between what it knows and what its clients do not.

Academic expertise presents a variation that is worth examining separately because it demonstrates how knowledge gatekeeping extends beyond commercial self-interest into the domain of authority over truth itself. The university system controls access to academic credentials, which function as certificates of intellectual legitimacy. A person with a PhD in economics is authorized to speak on economic matters in ways that a person without one is not, regardless of how much the uncredentialed person may know. The credential is a license to be taken seriously, and the institution that grants the license controls who receives it. This is not merely a matter of professional access. It is a matter of epistemic authority—the power to determine what counts as knowledge, what counts as evidence, and whose claims deserve the weight of expert endorsement. The peer review process, the tenure system, the hierarchy of academic journals—each is a gatekeeping mechanism that determines which ideas enter the mainstream of accepted knowledge and which remain on the margins. The system is not without merit. It filters out a great deal of nonsense. It also filters out a certain amount of legitimate but inconvenient insight, and the distinction between filtering nonsense and filtering inconvenience is made by the same people whose positions depend on the current arrangement, which is a conflict of interest so fundamental that the profession has agreed to not discuss it in those terms.

INFORMATION ASYMMETRY

Information asymmetry—the condition in which one party to a transaction knows more than the other—is not a market imperfection. It is a power relationship. The party with superior information can set terms, time decisions, and exploit the other party's ignorance in ways that range from mildly advantageous to spectacularly predatory. The used car dealer who knows the vehicle's history and the buyer who does not. The insurance company that has actuarial tables and the policyholder who has a vague sense that bad things sometimes happen. The employer who knows the salary range and the applicant who knows only what they need. In each case, the information advantage translates directly into economic advantage, and the economic advantage compounds over time because the party with better information makes better decisions, which generates more resources, which funds the acquisition of more information, which produces better decisions. The rich get richer in part because the informed get more informed, and the two categories overlap with suspicious regularity.

Political scientist James C. Scott documented how states have systematically used information collection—censuses, surveys, cadastral maps, standardized measurements—to make populations "legible" and therefore governable. States have always understood this dynamic and have exploited it with varying degrees of sophistication. The census—an instrument so ancient that it appears in both the Bible and Chinese records from the third millennium BCE—was not created out of demographic curiosity. It was created so that rulers could know how many people they governed, where those people lived, what they produced, and how much they could be taxed. The Domesday Book, compiled for William the Conqueror in 1086, was the most comprehensive survey of English wealth and landholding ever attempted, and its purpose was entirely practical: William wanted to know exactly what he had conquered and how much revenue it could produce. The information asymmetry between the king who possessed the Domesday Book and the subjects recorded in it was not incidental to governance. It was governance. Knowing more about your population than your population knows about itself is the foundational advantage of the modern state, and it has been the foundational advantage of every state since record-keeping began.

The commercial exploitation of information asymmetry is older than capitalism but reached its full expression within it. Financial markets are, in theory, mechanisms for aggregating information and producing efficient prices. In practice, they are arenas in which participants with superior information extract value from participants with inferior information. Insider trading—the use of non-public information to make investment decisions—is illegal in most jurisdictions not because it is unusual but because it is the purest expression of a dynamic that pervades all market activity. The investment bank that advises a company on its merger while simultaneously trading in the company's stock. The commodity trader who knows the harvest report before the farmers do. The hedge fund that processes satellite imagery of parking lots to estimate retail sales before the earnings announcement. Each represents information asymmetry converted into profit, and the legality of each varies depending on where exactly the line between research and exploitation has been drawn, a line that moves with the lobbying budget of whoever wants it moved.

The intelligence services of modern states represent information asymmetry elevated to the level of national strategy. Espionage—the systematic acquisition of information that another party is trying to keep secret—is as old as organized conflict and as current as yesterday's headline. But the scale of modern intelligence operations has transformed a tactical advantage into a structural one. A state that can monitor the communications of foreign leaders, track the movements of military assets in real time, intercept financial transactions, and analyze the social media activity of millions of individuals possesses an information advantage that fundamentally alters the balance of power. The advantage is not that this information enables perfect decision-making—intelligence failures are a permanent feature of intelligence history. The advantage is that imperfect information is still dramatically better than no information, and the state that possesses it operates in a different strategic reality than the state that does not.

DATA REPLACING INTUITION

Something happened in the early twenty-first century that altered the dynamics of information power more fundamentally than any development since the printing press, and it happened so gradually that most people experienced it as convenience rather than as a restructuring of the relationship between individuals and institutions. The change was this: institutions began to know more about individuals than individuals knew about themselves. Not in the limited, census-and-tax-record way that states had always known about their populations. In a granular, behavioral, predictive way that no previous system of information gathering had approached.

The mechanism was data collection at scale. Every digital transaction—every search query, every purchase, every location ping, every social media interaction, every streaming choice, every click and scroll and pause—generated a record. Individually, these records were trivial. Collectively, analyzed by algorithms designed to detect patterns, they produced behavioral profiles of extraordinary specificity. The platform that tracked your purchases knew your income bracket, your dietary preferences, your health concerns, and the approximate date your running shoes would wear out. The platform that tracked your searches knew what you were worried about, what you were curious about, and what you wanted but had not yet purchased. The platform that tracked your social media knew your political orientation, your emotional state, your relationship status, and which advertisements you were most likely to respond to at which time of day. None of this required anyone reading your diary. It required only that your behavior be recorded and analyzed by systems designed to find patterns in behavioral data, which they did with an accuracy that consistently surprised the people being analyzed and rarely surprised the people doing the analyzing.

This represented a qualitative shift in the information asymmetry between institutions and individuals. Previous systems of surveillance—the secret police, the informant network, the census bureau—required human labor at scale and produced information that was incomplete, often inaccurate, and available only to the state. The new systems required minimal human labor, produced information of startling accuracy, and were available to any commercial entity willing to pay for them. The state still collected intelligence. But the most detailed behavioral profiles in human history were compiled not by governments but by advertising companies, which assembled them for the purpose of selling targeted advertisements and then discovered that the data was useful for a great many other things as well. The surveillance apparatus that earlier generations had feared as a tool of totalitarian government arrived instead as a tool of consumer marketing, which was somehow less alarming despite being, in many respects, more comprehensive.

The power implications of data-driven knowledge are still unfolding, but several patterns are already visible. First, data advantage compounds. Organizations that collect more data build better predictive models, which attract more users, which generate more data, which build better models. The cycle produces market concentration with the same reliability that capital accumulation produces wealth concentration, and for the same structural reason: the advantage feeds itself. Second, data creates asymmetry that individuals cannot overcome through individual effort. A person can educate themselves about medicine to reduce their dependence on physicians. A person cannot meaningfully reduce the information asymmetry between themselves and a platform that has processed the behavioral data of two billion users. The scale is incommensurable. Third, data-driven systems make decisions that affect individuals without the individuals understanding how those decisions were made. The algorithm that determines your insurance premium, your credit score, your job application ranking, or the news stories you see operates on logic that is proprietary, complex, and in many cases not fully understood even by the engineers who built it. The individual affected by the decision cannot challenge the reasoning because the reasoning is not disclosed, not because of malice but because disclosure would compromise the competitive advantage that the data represents.

The result is a form of power that is historically unprecedented in its scope and historically familiar in its structure. An institution that knows more about you than you know about yourself, that uses that knowledge to predict and influence your behavior, and that operates through mechanisms you cannot observe or challenge—this is not a new kind of power. It is the oldest kind of power, the priestly monopoly on sacred knowledge, updated with servers and machine learning. The priest knew what God wanted. The algorithm knows what you want. Both claims carry authority that the subject cannot independently verify, and both create dependencies that the subject cannot easily escape. The technology is different. The structural relationship is identical: asymmetric knowledge producing asymmetric power, maintained by the difficulty of accessing the knowledge on which the asymmetry depends. The platform corporation, returning here from Chapter 2, is the sharpest contemporary instance. The platform does not censor in the visible sense. It ranks, recommends, demonetizes, throttles, and defaults—a set of actions that is technically procedural, legally distinguishable from censorship, and structurally indistinguishable from it for the speaker whose audience the platform has decided to deny. The platform is also not legislating. It is updating its terms of service, which is a contractual matter, except that the contract is between several billion users and a private firm whose decisions shape the conditions of public discourse globally. The category mismatch—procedural action with political consequence, private contract with public effect—is the corporate form of invisible power operating at planetary scale.

A natural objection is that the internet has dismantled the knowledge monopolies described in this chapter—that information is now abundant, accessible, and democratized in ways that previous gatekeepers cannot reverse. The objection captures something real and overstates it. Raw information has indeed become abundant. Curated information, expert interpretation, and the capacity to distinguish reliable signal from manufactured noise have not. The new gatekeepers are platforms, algorithms, and credentialing systems that shape which abundant information reaches whom and which information is treated as trustworthy. The monopoly has not ended. It has changed hands, and the new holders are less visible than the old, which is a structural feature worth noticing.

Knowledge is power not as a proverb but as a description of a mechanism that has operated continuously since the first scribe realized that being the only person who could read the grain records gave him leverage over everyone who needed to know what the grain records said. The forms of knowledge that confer power have changed—from literacy to expertise to data—but the structural dynamic has not. Whoever controls access to information that others need controls the terms on which that information is shared, and those terms consistently favor the party with the information. The monopoly is never permanent. New technologies break old monopolies with the regularity of tides. But each broken monopoly is replaced by a new one, organized around the new technology, controlled by whoever mastered it first, and sustained until the next disruption arrives.

11

CULTURAL POWER

*"Those who can make you believe absurdities can make
you commit atrocities."*

Voltaire
Questions sur les Miracles (1765)

T HE MOST EFFECTIVE FORM of control is the kind that nobody
recognizes as control. A soldier standing on a corner with a rifle is
visible power. A law requiring a permit is institutional power. A price
increase is economic power. But the reason you feel embarrassed when
you cannot name the right wine at dinner, the reason you assume a doctor's opinion outweighs your own experience of your body, the reason
you believe hard work leads to success despite abundant evidence that
it sometimes does not, that is cultural power. It operates not through
commands or incentives but through the slow, ambient shaping of what
people regard as normal, desirable, and obvious. It is the water the fish
does not notice, and it is doing more structural work than every institution examined in this book combined.

Norms Shaping Compliance

A norm is a rule that nobody wrote down, nobody voted on, and nobody can precisely articulate, yet everybody follows. This is an extraordinary achievement of social engineering, made more extraordinary by the fact that no engineer designed it. Norms emerge from the accumulated weight of repeated behavior, mutual observation, and the deeply human desire to not be the person doing the wrong thing in a room full of people doing the right thing. They are enforced not by police but by discomfort, the raised eyebrow, the awkward silence, the subtle withdrawal of social approval that signals you have crossed a line whose location you were expected to know without being told. The punishment for violating a law is formal and specified. The punishment for violating a norm is informal and devastating, because it attacks not your freedom or your wallet but your standing in the community of people whose opinion you need to survive.

Norms produce compliance at a cost that no formal system can match. A government that wanted to ensure that people bathed regularly would need inspectors, regulations, penalties, and an enforcement apparatus of staggering intrusiveness. Social norms accomplish the same result through the mechanism of nobody wanting to be the person in the office who smells. The compliance is voluntary in the sense that no one forces it and involuntary in the sense that the social consequences of non-compliance are severe enough to make the choice feel compulsory. This ambiguity, voluntary compliance driven by involuntary social pressure, is the defining feature of cultural power. It looks like freedom. It functions like governance. The distinction between the two is real but considerably narrower than most people would like to believe.

The norms that matter most for power are not the ones about hygiene or table manners, though these have their own structural significance. The norms that matter are the ones that define what is politically possible, economically acceptable, and socially thinkable. Antonio Gramsci analyzed this phenomenon as cultural hegemony—the process by which dominant groups make their interests appear as common sense, rendering alternative arrangements not just undesirable but unthinkable. In a society where the norm is that wealth indicates virtue, redistributive taxation will always face an uphill battle regardless of the economic arguments in its favor, because the proposal violates a cultural assumption that is deeper than any policy debate. In a society where the norm is that authority should be respected, challenges to institutional power will be perceived as disorder rather than accountability, regardless of how justified they may be. In a society where the norm is that individual achievement explains individual outcomes, structural explanations for inequality will be dismissed as excuse-making, regardless of the evidence. The norm does not argue. It does not need to. It has established the frame within which arguments occur, and the frame determines which arguments are taken seriously before the first word is spoken.

The Confucian examination system in imperial China demonstrates how a single norm—filial piety—sustained political hierarchy for more than a millennium. The examination tested candidates' knowledge of classical texts emphasizing duty to parents and, by extension, to the emperor as the father of the nation. The system selected officials not just for administrative competence but for internalization of a norm that made hierarchy feel natural. Challenging imperial authority meant violating filial piety, which meant violating the most fundamental social norm in Chinese culture. The norm did more to maintain the empire than any army could.

Victorian Britain deployed the code of respectability as a class-discipline mechanism with comparable effectiveness. The elaborate rules governing dress, speech, sexual behavior, and social interaction separated the respectable working class from the disreputable poor—a distinction that mattered more for social control than any legal category. Workers who aspired to respectability policed themselves and each other, suppressing behaviors that might mark them as unrespectable. The code required no enforcement apparatus because the punishment—social exclusion—was administered by peers. The middle class set the standard. The working class enforced it on themselves.

Postwar American homeownership norms illustrate how cultural assumptions shape political allegiance. The belief that owning a home was essential to the American Dream, promoted through policy and media, created a constituency invested in property values, mortgage tax deductions, and zoning restrictions. Homeowners became a political bloc whose interests aligned with preserving existing economic arrangements, not through conspiracy but through the structural consequences of a norm that made ownership feel like achievement rather than recognizing it as a wealth-building strategy available primarily to those who already had wealth.

The power of norms is most visible when they change, because the change reveals how much was being held in place by assumption rather than by argument or force. The speed with which attitudes toward same-sex marriage shifted in many Western countries in the early twenty-first century surprised observers on all sides. Within roughly a decade, a position that had been mainstream became marginal, and a position that had been marginal became mainstream. The legal changes followed the normative shift, not the reverse. Courts and legislatures ratified what the culture had already decided, because cultural change created the political conditions under which legal change became possible. The sequence is important: the norm moved first, the institution followed. This is the standard pattern. Institutions formalize what culture has already made thinkable. They rarely lead the process, because institutional power depends on legitimacy, and legitimacy depends on alignment with prevailing norms. An institution that gets too far ahead of its culture loses support. An institution that gets too far behind its culture loses relevance. The norm sets the pace. Everything else adjusts.

LANGUAGE AND IDENTITY

Language is not a neutral medium for transmitting information. It is a system of categories that determines what can be easily said and, by extension, what can be easily thought. A language that has twelve words for snow makes distinctions that a language with one word for snow does not, and speakers of the first language perceive a world that is, in a meaningful cognitive sense, different from the world perceived by speakers of the second. This is not mysticism. It is the practical consequence of the fact that language provides the categories through which experience is organized, and categories that are linguistically available are cognitively easier to use. The language you speak shapes the thoughts you think, not absolutely, humans are creative enough to think beyond their linguistic categories, but persistently, in the way that a road shapes the routes you drive. You can go off-road. Most of the time, you do not.

This makes language an instrument of power of the first order. Whoever controls the dominant language of a society controls the categories through which that society organizes its experience. Imperial powers understood this with varying degrees of explicitness. The Romans did not merely conquer Gaul. They latinized it, replacing local languages with Latin as the medium of administration, commerce, and eventually everyday life. The replacement was not instant, local languages persisted for centuries in rural areas, but it was thorough. By the time Gallic languages finally disappeared, the population had been thinking in Roman categories for so long that the original categories were irrecoverable. The conquest was military. The absorption was linguistic. The linguistic absorption outlasted the military conquest by more than a millennium, because you can withdraw an army but you cannot easily withdraw a language once it has become the medium through which people understand their own lives.

The construction of national identity relied heavily on linguistic standardization, and the process was rarely gentle. France's revolutionary and post-revolutionary governments pursued the elimination of regional languages, Breton, Occitan, Basque, Alsatian, with a determination that treated linguistic diversity as a threat to national unity, which, from the state's perspective, it was. A population that spoke the same language could be governed through a single administrative system, educated through a single curriculum, and mobilized through a single national narrative. A population that spoke a dozen different languages required a dozen different systems, which was expensive, inefficient, and incompatible with the centralized state that the revolution had created. The suppression of regional languages was cultural violence committed in the name of national coherence, and it was effective. Modern France speaks French, and the regional languages survive as cultural artifacts rather than living systems of thought. The categories through which French citizens understand their world are French categories, which is to say, Parisian categories, which is to say, the categories preferred by the people who designed the educational system.

Sociologist Pierre Bourdieu analyzed how cultural knowledge functions as capital—an asset that can be accumulated, inherited, and converted into social advantage. Bourdieu's framework went further than the cultural-capital insight, and it is worth surfacing the rest of it here because the book has been using his concepts without naming them. Three more tools matter. The habitus is the set of dispositions, tastes, and reflexes that a person acquires from their position in social space and then carries into every subsequent context, often unconsciously. The habitus is what makes cultural distinction self-reproducing: the working-class person who attends an upper-class dinner does not simply lack the right knowledge but inhabits the situation differently, and the inhabiting is more visible than the knowledge. The field is the social arena in which a particular form of capital is the relevant currency. Politics is a field; academia is a field; finance is a field; the rules of one do not transfer to another, and the reason elite networks are so durable is that they include people fluent across multiple fields at once. Symbolic violence is the capacity of the dominant group to make their categorizations of the world appear natural, neutral, and self-evident, and the corresponding self-doubt of the dominated group when their experience does not match the official categorization. Each of these has been operating in this book under different names. Habitus is what makes normalization, in the chapter on hidden power, work at the level of the individual. The field is what institutional power, mentioned in a previous chapter, describes when seen from outside. Symbolic violence is the mechanism by which hidden power becomes invisible to the people experiencing it. The chapter on hidden power will return to these questions; this chapter introduces the apparatus that makes them legible. The ability to speak the prestige language, reference the canonical texts, display the markers of educated taste—these are not merely skills. They are forms of wealth that open doors, signal belonging, and distinguish insiders from outsiders. A student from a family that discusses literature at dinner arrives at university with cultural capital that translates directly into academic advantage, not because they are more intelligent but because they already speak the language the institution values. The translation from cultural capital to institutional success is so smooth that it appears to be merit, which is precisely why the system reproduces itself so effectively across generations.

Identity is language's most powerful political product. The categories "French," "German," "American," "Chinese" are not natural kinds. They are cultural constructions, assembled over centuries through the deliberate promotion of shared language, shared narratives, shared symbols, and shared enemies. A peasant in eighteenth-century Provence did not think of himself as French. He thought of himself as Provençal, or Catholic, or a subject of the king, or a member of his village. The identity "French" was manufactured through public education, military conscription, national media, and the systematic suppression of alternative identities that competed with the national one. The manufacturing process was so successful that the product now feels natural, people speak of national identity as though it were an inherent quality rather than an engineered one, which is the surest sign that the engineering worked. When a construction feels like nature, the construction is complete.

The political utility of identity is that it creates loyalty without requiring transaction. A citizen who identifies as American will make sacrifices for America that no rational cost-benefit analysis would justify, paying taxes that fund programs they will never use, obeying laws they personally disagree with, and in the extreme case, dying in wars whose strategic rationale they may not understand. Identity converts the abstract obligation of citizenship into a personal commitment that feels like self-expression rather than submission. The state does not need to coerce the patriot. The patriot coerces himself, and does so with enthusiasm, because the coercion has been reframed as devotion. This is cultural power at its most refined: compliance that feels like authenticity, obligation that feels like choice, governance that feels like belonging.

MEDIA INFLUENCE

Media is the distribution system for cultural power. It determines which stories are told, which images are seen, which voices are heard, and, crucially, which stories, images, and voices are absent. The significance of media is not primarily in what it says. It is in what it makes visible and what it leaves invisible, because visibility determines salience, and salience determines what people think about, which determines what people think. A newspaper that covers crime extensively and poverty rarely does not need to editorialize about the relative importance of the two topics. The coverage itself has established the hierarchy. The reader who absorbs thirty crime stories for every poverty story will, without any conscious deliberation, regard crime as a more significant problem than poverty, regardless of the statistical reality. The medium has done its work before the editorial page has said a word.

The history of media influence on power is substantially the history of who controls the means of cultural production. In oral societies, control rested with the storytellers, the bards, the priests, the elders who carried the community's narratives in their memories and delivered them in their voices. The storyteller's choices, which events to remember, which heroes to celebrate, which villains to condemn, shaped the community's understanding of its own history and, by extension, its own identity. This was cultural power in its most intimate form, exercised in person, adjusted to the audience, and limited by the reach of the human voice.

Print expanded the reach and centralized the control. A newspaper owner in the nineteenth century controlled the information environment of an entire city. The owner decided which events were news-worthy, which politicians deserved favorable coverage, which businesses merited attention. This was not abstract influence. It was direct po-litical power exercised through editorial decisions. William Randolph Hearst did not need to hold office to shape American politics. He needed printing presses and the willingness to use them, which he possessed in abundance. The press baron era demonstrated, with uncomfortable clarity, that media ownership was political power in a form that required no election, no appointment, and no accountability to anyone except the owner's creditors and the owner's ego, and the ego was rarely the constraining factor.

Radio and television concentrated media influence further by reduc-ing the number of channels through which information reached mass audiences. In the mid-twentieth century, a small number of broadcast networks shaped the information environment of entire nations. The American television news landscape was dominated by three networks whose editorial choices determined what roughly two hundred million people understood about the world. The anchors became authority figures not through expertise or election but through repetition, they appeared in living rooms every evening, their faces became familiar, their voices became trusted, and their framing of events became the default framing. Trust was a product of exposure. Authority was a product of trust. The mechanism was circular and self-reinforcing, and it produced a cultural consensus that was less a reflection of shared values than a reflection of shared information sources.

The internet fragmented this consensus without democratizing it, which is a distinction that matters enormously. The promise of digital media was that it would break the monopoly of centralized media in-stitutions by giving everyone the ability to publish, broadcast, and reach audiences without institutional gatekeeping. The promise was fulfilled in the literal sense, anyone can publish, and betrayed in the structural sense, because the platforms that mediate digital publishing exercise a form of editorial control that is more comprehensive than anything a newspaper baron ever achieved. The algorithm that determines which content appears in a user's feed is making editorial decisions at a scale of billions per day, and those decisions are shaped not by journalistic stan-dards or public interest but by engagement metrics that favor content producing strong emotional reactions, which is a polite way of saying that the most effective distribution system in the history of human communication is optimized for outrage. The result is not a marketplace of ideas. It is an attention economy in which the loudest, most provocative, and most emotionally manipulative content rises to the top, not because it is true or important but because it generates the clicks that generate the revenue that funds the platform that generates the clicks. The medium has always been the message. The message is now: whatever makes you angry enough to keep scrolling.

SOFT POWER DURABILITY

The term "soft power," coined by the political scientist Joseph Nye, describes the ability to shape the preferences of others through attraction rather than coercion or payment. The concept is useful but the label is misleading, because "soft" implies weakness, and cultural power is anything but weak. It is, by several important measures, the most durable form of power in human history. Military conquests are reversed. Economic advantages are competed away. Political institutions are overthrown. Cultural influence persists because it operates inside the minds of the influenced, and minds are harder to liberate than territories.

The durability of cultural power is a function of its invisibility. A military occupation is experienced as oppression. A cultural influence is experienced as preference. The occupied population resents the occupier and works to expel them. The culturally influenced population adopts the influencer's music, fashion, food, language, and values and experiences the adoption as free choice. The resistance that military and economic power reliably generate does not arise in response to cultural power, because cultural power does not feel like power. It feels like taste. Telling someone that their taste in music has been shaped by the cultural output of a hegemonic power is not a persuasive argument at parties, but it is a structurally accurate observation. The American entertainment industry has done more to spread American cultural norms globally than the American military has, and it has done so at a fraction of the cost, with none of the resistance, and with the enthusiastic cooperation of the people being influenced.

Hollywood is the most successful cultural export operation in human history, and it has never required a government directive to function as one. American films, television shows, and streaming content carry assumptions about individualism, consumer capitalism, the primacy of romantic love, the moral validity of personal ambition, and the general structure of a good life that are specific to American culture and are presented, through the medium of entertainment, as universal truths. The teenager in Jakarta who watches American films absorbs these assumptions not as ideology but as narrative convention. The assumptions are not argued for. They are built into the story structure, the hero pursues individual goals, overcomes institutional obstacles, and achieves personal fulfillment, and the structure is so familiar from thousands of hours of consumption that questioning it would feel like questioning the nature of storytelling itself. The cultural export succeeds because it does not present itself as an export. It presents itself as entertainment, and entertainment is the most effective vehicle for ideology ever discovered because it bypasses the critical faculties that ideology, presented as ideology, would activate.

The durability of cultural power is also a function of its generative quality. Military power is consumed in the exercise, every bullet fired, every soldier deployed, every campaign sustained costs resources that are not recovered. Cultural power generates returns. A popular film produces revenue that funds the next film. A fashion trend creates demand that funds the next collection. A language adopted for commerce creates a constituency that perpetuates the language. Each exercise of cultural influence creates the conditions for further influence, which is why cultural power compounds over time rather than depleting. The British Empire invested considerable resources in spreading English across its colonies. The investment paid returns long after the empire dissolved, because English became the language of international commerce, science, and diplomacy not because anyone mandated it but because enough people spoke it that learning it became rational regardless of one's feelings about British imperialism. The empire created the network. The network sustains itself. The power is self-perpetuating in a way that no army or treasury can match.

This self-perpetuating quality makes cultural power exceptionally difficult to challenge. You can defeat an army by building a bigger army. You can counter economic leverage by developing alternative economic relationships. You can reform political institutions by changing the rules. But how do you counter a cultural influence that the influenced population does not recognize as influence? How do you resist norms that feel like common sense? How do you challenge assumptions that are embedded so deeply in the way people think that they are not experienced as assumptions at all but as reality? The answer, historically, is that you do it slowly, unevenly, and usually by building an alternative culture rather than by arguing against the existing one. Counter-cultures, independence movements, religious revivals, each represents an attempt to replace one set of cultural assumptions with another, and the attempts succeed only when the alternative proves more compelling than the original. Compulsion does not work, because cultural power is immune to compulsion. Coercion can suppress a culture. It cannot replace it. Only a better story can do that, and better stories are not available on demand.

A skeptic might argue that attributing this much causal weight to culture risks circular reasoning—that "cultural power" becomes a residual category invoked to explain whatever other forms of power cannot, with no falsifiable content of its own. The concern is methodologically serious. Culture, broadly defined, can absorb any explanation. The defense is that the chapter does not invoke culture as a black box. It identifies specific mechanisms—norms, language, narrative, media—through which cultural power operates, and these mechanisms are observable, traceable, and sometimes deliberately manipulated. The fact that cultural power is hard to measure does not make it imaginary. It makes it harder to govern, which is one of the reasons it is so effective.

Cultural power is the atmosphere in which all other forms of power operate. It determines which exercises of military force are perceived as legitimate and which as aggressive. It determines which economic arrangements are accepted as fair and which as exploitative. It determines which political systems are regarded as democratic and which as authoritarian. It does not make these determinations through argument or evidence. It makes them through the accumulated weight of norms, narratives, language, and media that have shaped the perception of every person in the society before any specific argument or evidence is encountered. By the time a citizen evaluates a policy proposal, the cultural framework through which the evaluation occurs has already determined the range of likely conclusions. Cultural power sets the menu. Everything else is ordering.

12

TECHNOLOGICAL POWER

"Men have become the tools of their tools."

Henry David Thoreau
Walden (1854)

EVERY SIGNIFICANT SHIFT IN the distribution of power in human history can be traced, eventually, to a tool. Not to an idea, not to a leader, not to a movement—to a tool. The stirrup gave mounted cavalry an advantage that reshaped Eurasian warfare and the feudal systems built around it. The printing press broke information monopolies that had persisted for millennia. The cotton gin made slavery more profitable at the precise historical moment when moral arguments against it were gaining traction, which tells you something about the relationship between technology and ethics: the tool does not care about your principles. It reshapes the incentive structure, and the incentive structure reshapes everything else.

Tools Reshaping Hierarchy

The relationship between technology and hierarchy is bidirectional, which is what makes it so difficult to predict. Sometimes a new technology reinforces existing power structures by giving those already on top a better version of the advantages they already possessed. Sometimes it undermines existing structures by providing those at the bottom with capabilities that were previously monopolized at the top. The direction depends on the specific technology, the specific structure, and the specific moment—a combination of variables that has humbled every attempt at a general theory of technological determinism while leaving the basic observation intact: tools change who has power, and they do so whether anyone intended them to or not.

The domestication of the horse provides an early and vivid example. Before the horse, military power was essentially infantry power—large numbers of men on foot, equipped with whatever weapons their society could produce. The advantage went to the larger, better-organized force, which generally meant the wealthier, more densely populated society. The horse changed the equation. Mounted warriors could cover distances that infantry could not, strike with speed and withdraw before a response could be organized, and project force across territories that would have taken foot soldiers weeks to traverse. The horse gave steppe nomads—societies that were smaller, less urbanized, and less bureaucratically sophisticated than their agricultural neighbors—a military advantage that allowed them to dominate civilizations many times their size. The Hyksos in Egypt, the Huns in Europe, the Mongols across Eurasia—each represented a case in which a technological advantage inverted the existing power hierarchy. The settled civilization had the wealth, the population, and the administrative sophistication. The nomads had the horse. For extended periods, the horse won.

Gunpowder reversed this reversal. Firearms and artillery favored the society that could manufacture them in quantity, supply them with ammunition, and train soldiers to use them—which meant the society with the larger economy, the more developed metallurgy, and the more complex administrative apparatus. The mounted warrior who had dominated battlefields for centuries became vulnerable to a peasant with a musket and two weeks of training. The castle that had provided feudal lords with near-impregnable defensive positions became a target that a competent artillery crew could reduce to rubble in days. Gunpowder technology shifted the advantage back toward centralized states with the economic and industrial capacity to produce firearms at scale, which is why the gunpowder era coincided with the consolidation of centralized monarchies across Europe and the decline of the feudal aristocracies that had depended on mounted warfare and fortified positions for their power. The technology did not cause the political transition. It made the transition possible, profitable, and eventually inevitable.

The pattern is consistent: a new tool changes what is possible, and the change in possibility redistributes advantage among competing groups. The advantage does not always flow in the same direction. Some technologies are inherently centralizing—they require large capital investment, complex supply chains, and specialized expertise that only large organizations can provide. Nuclear weapons are the extreme example: only states with enormous industrial and scientific capacity can produce them, and possession confers an advantage so decisive that it restructures global power relations. Other technologies are inherently decentralizing—they are cheap, accessible, and enable small actors to do things that previously required large organizations. The personal computer, the smartphone, the internet—each put capabilities in the hands of individuals that had previously been available only to corporations or governments. The direction of technological power depends on the technology. The existence of technological power is constant.

INDUSTRIAL LEVERAGE

The Industrial Revolution was not merely an economic event. It was a power event—a wholesale reorganization of who controlled what and on what terms. Before industrialization, economic power was distributed across a relatively large class of agricultural landowners, artisans, and merchants, each of whom controlled some portion of the productive process. After industrialization, economic power concentrated in the hands of a much smaller class of factory owners and industrialists who controlled the machinery on which the entire economy depended. The redistribution was rapid, comprehensive, and accompanied by social upheaval on a scale that made most previous power transitions look like personnel changes.

The factory was the instrument of this redistribution, and its power derived from a simple but devastating principle: the machine was more productive than the hand. An artisan weaver could produce a finite amount of cloth per day using skill accumulated over years of apprenticeship. A power loom operated by an unskilled worker could produce many times that amount. The artisan's skill—which had been the basis of economic independence, social status, and bargaining power—became obsolete. The machine did not need the artisan. The artisan needed the machine, and the machine belonged to the factory owner. The dependency was total, rapid, and irreversible in any practical sense. You cannot un-invent the power loom. You can only adjust to a world in which it exists, and the terms of adjustment were set by the people who owned the looms.

The concentration of workers in factories created a new geography of power. Before industrialization, labor was dispersed across farms, workshops, and households. After industrialization, labor was concentrated in factory towns and urban centers, packed into working and living conditions that were, by any humane standard, appalling. But the concentration that made workers vulnerable also made them organizable. A dispersed rural population could not easily coordinate collective action. A factory floor housing hundreds of workers performing the same tasks under the same conditions, experiencing the same grievances, and seeing the same evidence of the gap between what they produced and what they received—that was an organizing environment. The labor movement did not emerge despite industrialization. It emerged because of industrialization, specifically because the factory system concentrated workers in conditions that made collective identity and collective action possible. The technology that created the power imbalance also created the conditions for resistance to it.

The industrialists understood this, which is why the history of industrial labor relations is largely a history of efforts to organize workers and efforts to prevent workers from organizing. Strikes, lockouts, union busting, labor legislation, collective bargaining—the entire apparatus of industrial labor conflict was a negotiation over the terms on which technological leverage would be shared. The negotiation was never between equals. The factory owner could survive a strike longer than the workers could survive without wages, a structural asymmetry that gave capital a permanent advantage in any confrontation. But the workers had numbers, and numbers had political consequences that even the most powerful industrialist could not entirely ignore. The democratic franchise, where it existed, gave workers a mechanism for translating numerical strength into political power, which produced labor legislation, safety regulations, minimum wages, and the other constraints on industrial leverage that industrialists fought and eventually, in most countries, accepted—not because they were persuaded but because the alternative was political instability that threatened their assets more than regulation did.

The global distribution of industrial capacity reshaped international power as thoroughly as it reshaped domestic power. Nations that industrialized early—Britain, France, Germany, the United States, Japan—acquired exponential advantages over those that didn't. An industrialized army with railroads, telegraphs, mass-produced rifles, and steel warships could project force across continents in ways pre-industrial armies couldn't match, regardless of size or courage. The colonial empires of the nineteenth century were the political expression of this advantage: European domination became militarily trivial and economically profitable. The scramble for Africa was not between African and European societies but among European powers for territories their industrial technology had made indefensible. The Maxim gun didn't cause imperialism—it made imperialism efficient, which was worse.

SURVEILLANCE CAPABILITIES

The capacity to watch people without their knowledge or consent has always been a source of power, but for most of history it was constrained by the same limitation that constrained all pre-industrial processes: it required human labor at scale. An informant network that covered a city required hundreds of informants, each of whom had to be recruited, managed, compensated, and evaluated for reliability. A secret police force that monitored a population of millions required tens of thousands of agents, each of whom consumed resources and produced information that had to be collected, analyzed, and acted upon by humans with limited time and limited attention. The East German Stasi, perhaps the most thorough surveillance apparatus of the pre-digital era, employed an estimated ninety thousand full-time agents and recruited roughly one informant for every sixty-three citizens. The effort was staggering. The results were incomplete. People found ways to evade, deceive, and subvert the system because the system, for all its resources, could not be everywhere at once. Human surveillance had a bandwidth problem, and the bandwidth problem set an upper limit on the power that surveillance could confer.

Digital technology eliminated the bandwidth problem. A network of cameras, sensors, and data collection systems can monitor a population continuously, automatically, and at a cost per person that falls with every improvement in processing power and storage capacity. The infrastructure required to surveil a city of ten million people in 1960 would have required an investment equivalent to a significant fraction of a national budget. The infrastructure required to surveil the same city today requires a municipal technology contract and a server farm. The cost reduction is not incremental. It is transformative, because it changes what is practically possible. When surveillance was expensive, only the most important targets could be monitored. When surveillance is cheap, everyone can be monitored, and the question shifts from "who should we watch" to "what should we do with everything we've recorded."

China's social credit system represents the most ambitious attempt to operationalize comprehensive surveillance as a governance tool. The system, still evolving and unevenly implemented, aims to assign citizens a score based on their behavior—financial reliability, legal compliance, social conduct, and, depending on the implementation, political loyalty. High scores bring benefits: easier access to credit, priority in government services, favorable treatment in various transactions. Low scores bring restrictions: denied access to certain transportation, reduced eligibility for jobs and education, public shaming. The system makes the connection between surveillance and social control explicit in a way that most surveillance systems prefer to leave implicit. It does not merely watch. It grades, and the grade has consequences that shape behavior as directly as any law and more continuously than any police force.

Western democracies have developed surveillance capabilities that are comparable in scope if different in stated purpose. The revelations of the early 2010s documented intelligence programs that collected communications data on a scale that previous generations of intelligence officials would have considered technically impossible and legally unimaginable. Phone metadata, email content, internet browsing history, location data—the collection was comprehensive, automated, and operated under legal frameworks that most citizens had never heard of and most legislators had not read carefully before approving. The stated purpose was counterterrorism, and the programs may well have served that purpose. They also created an infrastructure of surveillance that could be repurposed for other objectives by any future government with the inclination to do so, a possibility that the officials who built the infrastructure generally preferred not to discuss in detail.

The private sector's surveillance capabilities now exceed those of most governments, a development that would have struck observers in any previous century as deeply strange. Technology companies collect behavioral data on billions of users with a granularity that intelligence agencies envy, and they do so with the voluntary cooperation of the people being surveilled. The cooperation is not informed in any meaningful sense—nobody reads the terms of service, and the terms of service would not convey the full scope of the data collection even if they did—but it is technically voluntary, which provides legal cover that state surveillance lacks. The result is a dual surveillance architecture: government systems that monitor for security purposes under legal constraints of varying rigor, and commercial systems that monitor for profit under legal constraints of varying existence. The two systems are not separate. Governments purchase data from commercial providers. Commercial providers comply with government data requests. The boundary between public and private surveillance is, in practice, a polite fiction maintained for the comfort of people who prefer to believe that the watch is being kept by one entity rather than by all of them simultaneously.

AUTOMATION AND ASYMMETRY

Automation is the final turn of the screw. If industrial technology concentrated power by making labor dependent on machinery, automation concentrates power by making labor unnecessary. The factory owner needed workers. The automated factory owner needs technicians, and fewer of them, and the leverage that workers once derived from being needed evaporates when the need itself disappears. This is not a prediction about the future. It is a description of a process that has been underway for decades and is accelerating.

The first wave of automation eliminated routine physical tasks. Assembly lines that had required hundreds of workers were operated by robotic systems that required dozens of supervisors. The workers displaced by automation could, in principle, retrain for the supervisory roles, though in practice the retraining was expensive, time-consuming, and available to a fraction of the displaced workforce. The net effect was a reduction in the number of people required to produce a given output, which meant a reduction in labor's share of the value produced and a corresponding increase in capital's share. The factory still produced wealth. It distributed that wealth to fewer people. The owners' share grew. The workers' share shrank. The consumers' share fluctuated depending on whether the cost savings were passed through as lower prices or retained as higher profits, a decision made by the owners, which is to say, by the people whose share was already growing.

The second wave of automation is eliminating routine cognitive tasks, and its implications for power distribution are considerably more unsettling. Software that processes loan applications, analyzes legal documents, generates financial reports, writes marketing copy, diagnoses medical images, and performs dozens of other tasks that previously required educated professionals is not replacing assembly line workers. It is replacing the knowledge workers who were supposed to be automation-proof—the people who retrained, went to college, acquired expertise, and built careers on the assumption that cognitive work was safe from the forces that had disrupted manual labor. The assumption was reasonable for a time. It is no longer reasonable, and the adjustment is producing anxiety in a class of workers who had previously observed automation's effects from a comfortable distance.

The power implications of cognitive automation extend beyond labor markets. When decisions that affect people's lives—credit approvals, hiring selections, criminal sentencing recommendations, medical diagnoses, insurance pricing—are made by automated systems, the locus of power shifts from human decision-makers who can be questioned, appealed to, and held accountable, to algorithmic systems that are proprietary, opaque, and answerable to the organizations that built them rather than to the people affected by their outputs. A loan officer who denied your application could be asked to explain the decision and could, in principle, be persuaded to reconsider. An algorithm that denied your application cannot be asked anything, because it does not have reasons in the sense that humans have reasons. It has correlations, weighted by training data, producing outputs that are statistically justified but not explanatorily transparent. You can appeal the decision. You cannot argue with the logic, because the logic is a black box, and the box belongs to someone else.

The asymmetry that automation produces is not merely economic. It is epistemic. The organizations that build and deploy automated systems understand those systems—imperfectly, but far better than the people affected by them. The gap between the builder's understanding and the subject's understanding is a power gap, and it is widening. Each generation of automated systems is more complex, more capable, and less interpretable than the last. The trajectory points toward a world in which the most consequential decisions affecting individual lives are made by systems that no individual can fully understand, built by organizations that have no obligation to explain them, and governed by legal frameworks that were designed for a world in which decisions were made by humans who could be held accountable for their reasoning. The legal frameworks are catching up. They are catching up slowly, which is the normal speed at which law follows technology, and in the interim, the power asymmetry between those who build the systems and those who are subject to them grows with every deployment.

The concentration of technological power in the early twenty-first century mirrors, structurally, the concentration of industrial power in the late nineteenth. Five companies—Alphabet, Amazon, Apple, Meta, and Microsoft—control the platforms, the data, the algorithms, and the infrastructure on which an increasing share of economic and social life depends. Between them, they mediate how billions of people communicate, shop, access information, navigate physical space, and store their digital lives. The market capitalization of these five companies exceeds the GDP of all but a handful of nations. Amazon controls roughly 40 percent of U.S. e-commerce and a comparable share of cloud computing infrastructure. Google processes roughly nine in ten search queries in most markets. Meta's platforms host over three billion active users. Apple and Google's operating systems run on virtually every smartphone in circulation. Their founders and executives exercise influence over communications, commerce, information access, and social interaction at a scale that the most powerful industrialists of the Gilded Age would have found staggering. The parallels are not exact—technology companies do not employ armies of factory workers, and their products are less tangible than railroads and steel—but the structural position is comparable: control over infrastructure that everyone depends on, exercised by a small number of actors, constrained by regulatory frameworks that were designed for a different era and have not yet adapted to the current one. The Gilded Age produced antitrust law, labor regulation, and the progressive movement. Whether the current concentration produces comparable responses remains to be seen. The historical pattern suggests that it will, eventually, because concentrated power generates resistance, and resistance generates reform. The pattern also suggests that the reform will arrive later than it should, will be less comprehensive than it could be, and will be shaped as much by the interests of the powerful as by the interests of the public. This is not cynicism. It is the pattern.

A common objection is that technology is neutral—that the same tool can serve liberation or oppression depending on who uses it, and that treating technology as a power dynamic confuses the artifact with the politics surrounding it. This is partly right. The same encryption protocol can protect dissidents and shield criminals. The same surveillance camera can deter assault and enable a police state. But neutrality at the level of the artifact does not mean neutrality at the level of the system. Technologies are deployed within existing distributions of power, and the deployment consistently amplifies whoever was already advantaged. The tool is neutral. The terms of its adoption are not, and the terms are where the power lives.

Technology is the great redistributor. It does not create power. It moves it—from one group to another, from one institution to another, from one era's winners to the next era's. The redistribution is never neutral and never voluntary. Those who hold power under the existing technological arrangement resist changes that would diminish their position. Those who would gain power from a new arrangement push for its adoption. The contest between these forces determines the pace and direction of technological change, which is why technological progress is neither as smooth as optimists suggest nor as dangerous as pessimists fear. It is contested, political, and shaped by the same dynamics of interest, power, and resistance that shape every other domain examined in this book. In the contemporary world, the contest over which technologies are adopted, on what terms, and to whose benefit is conducted overwhelmingly through corporations. Public research labs still exist. State-directed industrial policy still operates. But the principal sites where new technologies are developed, deployed, and shaped into commercial form are private firms, which means that the political question of who benefits from a new tool is in the first instance a corporate question, decided in board rooms and product roadmaps long before any legislator hears the issue posed.

13
POPULAR POWER

"Power concedes nothing without a demand. It never did and it never will."

Frederick Douglass
Speech at Canandaigua, NY (1857)

REVOLUTIONS MAKE EXCELLENT STORIES and unreliable blueprints. The crowd storms the palace. The tyrant flees. The old order collapses. The new order announces itself with declarations, flags, and the intoxicating conviction that history has turned a corner. Then Monday arrives, and someone has to figure out how to run the water system. The gap between the drama of popular uprising and the tedium of what comes after is where most revolutions go to die, not because the people lacked courage or conviction but because overthrowing a system and replacing it are two entirely different skills, and the second one does not make for good murals.

COLLECTIVE ACTION DYNAMICS

The fundamental puzzle of collective action is not why it happens. It is why it does not happen more often. The conditions that produce popular uprising—inequality, exploitation, perceived injustice, the concentration of power in the hands of people who use it badly—are present in virtually every society at virtually every point in history. If grievance were sufficient to produce collective action, every society would be in a state of permanent revolution. They are not, which means something other than grievance is required to move a population from resentment to action. Understanding what that something is explains both the power and the fragility of popular movements.

The primary obstacle to collective action is the free-rider problem, which is less a problem of economics than a problem of human nature dressed in economic language. If a revolution succeeds, everyone benefits from the new order regardless of whether they participated. If a revolution fails, the participants bear the costs—imprisonment, execution, exile, loss of livelihood—while the non-participants bear none. The rational calculation for any individual is to let others take the risk and enjoy the benefits if they succeed. But if everyone makes this calculation, no one acts, and the revolution never happens. The free-rider problem is not a theory. The economist Mancur Olson formalized this logic in *The Logic of Collective Action*, demonstrating that rational individuals will not act to achieve their common goals unless there is coercion to make them do so, or unless some separate incentive distinct from the collective benefit is offered. The theory explains not why revolutions happen but why they are so rare despite the ubiquity of grievance. It is the reason most oppressed populations remain oppressed most of the time. Grievance is universal. Willingness to bear personal costs for collective benefit is not.

Collective action happens when something overrides the free-rider calculation. That something can take several forms. Social networks—dense webs of personal relationships in which trust exists and reputation matters—reduce the cost of coordination and increase the cost of non-participation. If your neighbors are marching and they know you stayed home, the social penalty may exceed the physical risk of joining. Ideology provides a framework that redefines the calculation by making participation a moral obligation rather than a strategic choice. The revolutionary who believes the cause is just does not weigh costs and benefits in the way the economist predicts, because the economist's model does not account for the weight of conviction. Focal points—dramatic events that crystallize diffuse grievances into concentrated outrage—provide the coordination signal that dispersed populations need to act simultaneously. The self-immolation of Mohamed Bouazizi in Tunisia did not create the conditions for the Arab Spring. The conditions had existed for decades. Bouazizi's act provided the focal point around which those conditions became actionable.

Collective action is the most visible form of popular power but not the most consistent. The political scientist James C. Scott argued that subordinate populations have always exercised power through what he called weapons of the weak—foot-dragging, dissimulation, false compliance, sabotage, gossip, the deliberate misunderstanding of orders. None of these produces dramatic political change. Each of them, distributed across a population over decades, modifies what the powerful can plausibly demand. The Polish workers under communism did not destroy the system through strikes; they destroyed its legitimacy through the relentless, low-grade refusal of the official categories—telling jokes, working slowly, hoarding, lying on official forms, treating the entire apparatus as something to be managed and gamed rather than believed. The cumulative effect was a state that no one inside or outside took seriously, and a state that no one takes seriously cannot collect compliance even when it can collect taxes. The cycle this chapter examines—mobilization, peak, dissipation, institutionalization—is one mode of popular power and the one most visible from outside. The Scott account is the other mode: continuous, distributed, deniable, never institutionalized because never officially acknowledged, and arguably more consequential over the long run than any single revolutionary moment.

The role of the focal point deserves emphasis because it explains why popular uprisings so often appear sudden and unpredictable. The underlying grievances are chronic. The triggering event is acute. Observers who focus on the trigger conclude that the uprising was spontaneous—an eruption of popular anger with no structural basis. Observers who focus on the grievances conclude that the uprising was inevitable—a pressure cooker that was always going to blow. Both are wrong. The grievances made the uprising possible. The focal point made it actual. Without the grievances, the focal point would have been a tragedy that inspired sympathy but not action. Without the focal point, the grievances would have remained what they had been for years: a chronic condition that everyone endured because no one could coordinate a response. Popular power emerges at the intersection of structural conditions and contingent events, which is why predicting it precisely is impossible and recognizing the conditions for it is not.

REVOLUTIONS AND MOBILIZATION LIMITS

Revolutions are popular power at its most concentrated and its most unstable. They represent moments when the normal constraints on collective action collapse and large numbers of people act simultaneously against the existing order. These moments are rare, dramatic, and almost always shorter than they feel to the participants. The French Revolution, the most analyzed popular uprising in Western history, lasted in its radical phase roughly five years—from the storming of the Bastille in 1789 to the fall of Robespierre in 1794. Five years to demolish a monarchy that had governed for centuries, reorganize a society of twenty-eight million people, and establish the principle that sovereign authority resided in the nation rather than the king. Also five years to produce a terror that executed tens of thousands, a civil war that killed hundreds of thousands, and a power vacuum that was eventually filled by a Corsican artillery officer who restored most of the authoritarian structures the revolution had dismantled. The revolution accomplished enormous things. It also demonstrated, with painful clarity, the limits of what popular power can achieve and the speed with which it can be captured by individuals and institutions that were not part of the original project.

The Russian Revolution of 1917 followed a structurally similar trajectory at higher speed and greater scale. A mass uprising fueled by war exhaustion, economic collapse, and decades of accumulated grievance toppled a three-hundred-year-old dynasty in a matter of weeks. The revolutionary energy was genuine, broad-based, and powered by convictions that the existing order was unjust and unsustainable. Within months, the broad-based movement had been captured by a disciplined minority—the Bolsheviks—who understood something that the broader movement did not: in a revolutionary moment, the group that controls the organizational apparatus controls the revolution. The Bolsheviks did not have majority support. They had organizational coherence, a clear theory of power, and the willingness to use force against their own allies when organizational control required it. The popular uprising produced the revolutionary moment. The organizational minority determined what the moment produced.

This pattern—popular energy creating an opening, organized minority filling it—recurs with such regularity that it might fairly be considered a law of revolutionary dynamics. The Iranian Revolution of 1979 was a broad coalition of secular liberals, leftists, students, workers, merchants, and clerics united by opposition to the Shah. The coalition that overthrew the Shah was genuinely popular. The regime that replaced him was the product of the most organized faction within that coalition—the clerical establishment—which outmaneuvered its secular allies by controlling the mosques, the religious networks, and the institutional infrastructure that provided organizational capacity when all other institutions had been disrupted. The Egyptian revolution of 2011 followed the same logic at accelerated pace. A popular uprising removed Mubarak in eighteen days. The military, the most organized institution in Egyptian society, managed the transition and eventually installed one of its own as president. The crowd provided the energy. The institution provided the outcome.

The limitation is structural, not moral. Popular movements are, by their nature, broad, loosely organized, and internally diverse. They must be, because breadth is the source of their power—a narrow movement does not generate the numbers required to challenge an entrenched system. But breadth comes at the cost of coherence. A movement that includes liberals, socialists, nationalists, religious conservatives, and apolitical citizens united only by opposition to the current regime will agree on what it opposes and disagree on everything else. The disagreement does not matter while the regime stands, because the shared enemy provides sufficient unity. The disagreement becomes decisive the moment the regime falls, because the coalition must now agree on what to build, and that agreement requires resolving the differences that the shared opposition had concealed. The revolution is a coalition of disagreements temporarily united by a common target. Remove the target, and the disagreements resurface with the intensity of disputes that have been deferred rather than resolved.

EMOTIONAL ENERGY CYCLES

Popular power runs on emotional energy, and emotional energy is a depletable resource. This is not a metaphor. It is a description of how human motivation works in collective action settings. The early phase of a popular movement is characterized by what sociologists call effervescence—a state of heightened collective emotion in which individual concerns are subsumed by group purpose, personal risk feels diminished, and the belief that change is possible reaches a pitch that makes sustained sacrifice tolerable. People march, organize, sacrifice sleep, risk arrest, and maintain commitment at levels that would be unsustainable under normal psychological conditions. The energy is real. It is also temporary, because human beings cannot sustain heightened emotional states indefinitely. The body rebels. The mind recalculates. The mundane demands of survival—rent, food, children, employment—reassert themselves with the quiet persistence of gravity.

The lifecycle of a popular movement's emotional energy follows a curve that is remarkably consistent across different movements, different cultures, and different centuries. The French Revolution demonstrates this cycle with brutal clarity. The emotional peak—roughly July 1789 through the summer of 1792—saw the storming of the Bastille, the Declaration of the Rights of Man, the abolition of feudalism, and mass popular participation in political clubs and assemblies. By 1793, the Terror had begun: the revolution devouring itself as Girondins, then Hébertists, then Dantonists went to the guillotine. The committees that had replaced the crowds executed not enemies of the revolution but fellow revolutionaries whose visions diverged. By 1794, when Robespierre himself was executed, revolutionary energy had exhausted itself through internal purges and external war. The Directory that followed was corrupt, unstable, and welcomed Napoleon's coup in 1799 as a relief from revolutionary chaos. From Bastille to Bonaparte: ten years in which France moved from absolute monarchy through radical popular sovereignty to military dictatorship, demonstrating both the power of revolutionary energy and its inability to sustain the institutional construction that follows demolition.

The initial phase is marked by rapid escalation—growing numbers, increasing boldness, expanding ambition, and the intoxicating sense that history is accelerating. The peak is a period of maximum participation and maximum belief, when the movement feels unstoppable and the existing order feels fragile. The decline is gradual at first and then accelerating, as participants who joined during the peak discover that the sustained effort required to achieve structural change is less exciting than the initial confrontation that drew them in. Meetings replace marches. Negotiations replace demands. Committees replace crowds. The work shifts from dramatic confrontation to tedious institution-building, and the people who were energized by confrontation are frequently not the same people who are energized by committees. The movement does not fail. It metabolizes, shedding participants who signed up for the revolution and did not realize they were also signing up for the budget meetings.

This emotional energy cycle creates a window of maximum effectiveness that is both narrower and more consequential than most movement participants realize. The window opens when collective energy is high enough to compel concessions from the existing power structure. It closes when the energy dissipates to the point where the power structure can wait the movement out. The critical question for any popular movement is what it achieves during that window, because what it achieves during the window is, in most cases, all it will ever achieve. Movements that extract institutional concessions during the peak—legislation, constitutional amendments, structural reforms embedded in law—lock in gains that survive the dissipation of the energy that produced them. Movements that spend the window on symbolic victories, internal debates, or escalating demands without securing institutional commitments find, when the energy fades, that they have nothing durable to show for the effort. The existing structure remains. The movement dissipates. And the participants are left with memories of a moment that felt transformative and produced nothing permanent.

The civil rights movement in the United States provides the clearest positive example of a movement that understood this dynamic and acted accordingly. The movement's emotional peak—roughly 1963 to 1965—produced the Civil Rights Act of 1964, the Voting Rights Act of 1965, and a series of judicial decisions that dismantled the legal architecture of segregation. These were institutional achievements, embedded in law and enforceable through courts, that persisted long after the marches ended and the movement's emotional energy dissipated. The movement did not achieve everything its participants wanted. It achieved what could be locked into institutional form during the window of maximum leverage, and that institutional achievement proved more durable than the emotional energy that produced it. The strategy was not accidental. King repeatedly emphasized that the goal was not catharsis but change, not demonstrations for their own sake but demonstrations that produced legislative outcomes. The 1963 Birmingham campaign was designed specifically to create a crisis that would force federal intervention—and it worked. The movement's leadership—King, the SCLC, the NAACP's legal team—understood that the window was finite and that what mattered was not the intensity of the mobilization but what the mobilization produced in the form of binding institutional change.

Three qualifications belong with this case. The legislative victories of 1964–65 captured what could be locked in during the window of maximum leverage; they did not capture King's later turn toward economic justice (the Poor People's Campaign, the Memphis sanitation strike, the broader argument of Where Do We Go From Here), which never produced legislation and barely survives in the public memory. The movement was internally divided—between the SCLC's nonviolent integrationism and the SNCC's increasing radicalism, between King's coalition strategy and the rising Black Power tradition—and the divisions are not visible in the legislative outcomes. The Cold War context produced a federal interest in civil rights as anti-Communist propaganda that does not appear in the standard story. And the institutional achievements have proven less durable than the immediate aftermath suggested: the 2013 Shelby County decision gutted the Voting Rights Act's preclearance regime, mass incarceration emerged as a racialized control mechanism that the legislative victories did not address, and voting-rights rollback continues. The structural achievement was real. It was also more partial, more contested, and more reversible than the standard narrative allows—which is itself an instance of the legitimacy-recycling and structural-resilience dynamics described elsewhere in this book.

INSTITUTIONAL ABSORPTION OF DISSENT

The most effective response that an established power structure can make to a popular challenge is not suppression. It is absorption. Suppression creates martyrs, galvanizes opposition, and validates the movement's narrative that the existing system is unjust. Absorption neutralizes the movement by incorporating its demands, its leaders, and its energy into the existing framework, satisfying enough of the grievance to defuse the mobilization while preserving the fundamental structure that produced the grievance in the first place. This is not cynicism on the part of the absorbing institution. It is structural competence. The institution that can absorb dissent survives. The institution that can only suppress it accumulates pressure until it breaks.

The mechanism of absorption operates at multiple levels simultaneously. At the most visible level, institutions make concessions—policy changes, legal reforms, symbolic recognitions—that address the movement's stated demands partially or fully. The concession is real and may represent genuine improvement. It also defuses the mobilization by providing participants with a tangible achievement that justifies demobilizing. The demand has been met, or met enough, and the emotional energy that sustained the mobilization finds its resolution in the satisfaction of partial victory. The fundamental distribution of power has not changed. But the specific grievance that animated the movement has been addressed, and without the specific grievance, the movement loses its focal point and its capacity to coordinate action.

At a deeper level, institutions absorb dissent by incorporating the movement's leaders into the existing structure. The activist becomes the legislator. The organizer becomes the administrator. The revolutionary becomes the minister. In each case, the individual's energy and legitimacy are transferred from the movement to the institution. The new official may retain their reformist convictions. They will also discover that institutional constraints—budgets, procedures, coalition politics, bureaucratic inertia—limit what any individual can achieve from the inside. The activist who was effective at organizing protests discovers that governing requires skills and compromises that protest did not prepare them for. The institution gains the activist's legitimacy. The activist gains the institution's constraints. The exchange is not equal, and it rarely favors the activist.

The most sophisticated form of absorption operates at the cultural level, where institutions adopt the movement's language, symbols, and values while draining them of operational content. A corporation that celebrates diversity in its marketing while maintaining homogeneity in its executive suite has absorbed the language of social justice without absorbing its demands. A government that declares a national holiday commemorating a revolutionary movement while preserving the power structures the movement opposed has absorbed the movement's symbolism while neutralizing its substance. The language of the movement becomes part of the institutional vocabulary. The demands of the movement become part of the institutional archive. The power that the movement challenged remains where it was, now dressed in the movement's clothing, which provides better camouflage than the previous outfit.

This pattern is depressing to movement participants and structurally logical to institutional analysts. Institutions survive by adapting, and adaptation includes absorbing the forces that threaten them. The labor movement demanded better conditions and got labor law, which improved conditions and also channeled labor activism into legal frameworks that the state controlled. The environmental movement demanded ecological protection and got environmental regulation, which provided genuine protections and also created regulatory processes that industry could influence through lobbying, litigation, and the staffing of regulatory agencies. The feminist movement demanded equality and got equal opportunity legislation, which expanded access and also redefined the struggle in legal terms that could be managed through courts and bureaucracies rather than through the kind of sustained mobilization that had produced the legislation in the first place. Each movement achieved real gains. Each movement's energy was channeled from the street into the institution, where it operated according to the institution's rules rather than the movement's. The institution did not defeat the movement. It domesticated it, which was more effective and considerably less photogenic.

The few movements that have resisted absorption—that have maintained their independence from existing institutions over extended periods—tend to share a common characteristic: they refused to accept the institution's framing of the problem. They defined the issue on their own terms, maintained their own organizational structures, and treated institutional concessions as partial victories rather than resolutions. This is extraordinarily difficult to sustain, because the pressure to accept partial victory and demobilize is intense, and the people offering partial victory are often sincere in their belief that it represents the best achievable outcome. The movement that holds out for more risks losing what has been offered. The movement that accepts what is offered risks losing the energy to demand more. The dilemma is genuine, and there is no formula for resolving it. What can be said is that the movements that produced the most durable structural change were the ones that maintained organized pressure longest, accepted institutional concessions as steps rather than destinations, and refused to cede organizational independence to the structures they were trying to reform. This is easier to describe than to do, which is why it happens less often than it should.

The most thoughtful objection to a structural account of popular power is that it underestimates the revolutionary moments where ordinary people genuinely have transformed the political order—the abolitions, the suffrages, the civil rights victories that no incumbent power voluntarily granted. The objection deserves a direct answer. Those victories happened. They were real, costly, and consequential. They also happened because organized popular action met institutional opportunity, because movements built durable structures rather than relying on energy alone, and because reforms were defended after the moment passed. The structural reading does not diminish what popular power has achieved. It explains why some movements achieved it and others, with equal moral urgency, did not.

Popular power is the necessary counterforce in every system of control, the reminder that legitimacy ultimately rests on the tolerance of the governed and that tolerance has limits. It is real, consequential, and historically decisive. It is also episodic, structurally disadvantaged, and persistently vulnerable to absorption by the systems it challenges. The crowd can overthrow a government. It cannot, by itself, build one. The movement can force concessions. It cannot, without institutional form, prevent those concessions from being eroded after the movement dissipates. Popular power is the spark. Institutional power is the furnace. The spark is necessary. The furnace determines the shape of what is produced.

14

POWER AND FEAR

"Fear is the foundation of most governments."

John Adams
Thoughts on Government (1776)

FEAR IS THE OLDEST management technique and the cheapest. It requires no complex ideology, no elaborate ritual, no sophisticated institutional apparatus. It requires only the credible promise that disobedience will be met with consequences severe enough to make compliance the preferred alternative. A severed head on a pike communicates this message with a clarity that no mission statement has ever achieved. The method is crude, the psychology is elementary, and the results are immediate, which is why every system of power in human history has relied on fear to some degree, including the ones that claim they do not.

PUNISHMENT SPECTACLE

Public punishment is not about the person being punished. It is about the people watching. This distinction is the key to understanding why states throughout history have invested extraordinary resources in making punishment visible, theatrical, and memorable. A quiet execution in a prison basement achieves the same result for the individual being executed. A public execution in a town square achieves something the basement cannot: it communicates to every witness that the state possesses the power to do this and the willingness to use it. The individual is eliminated. The audience is educated. The education is the point.

The Roman Empire understood this with characteristic thoroughness. Crucifixion was not merely a method of execution. It was a technology of communication. The condemned were displayed on roadsides, at city gates, along major thoroughfares—anywhere that maximum visibility could be achieved. The process was deliberately prolonged, sometimes lasting days, ensuring that passersby would encounter the display repeatedly. The message was not subtle: this is what happens to those who challenge Roman authority. The method was reserved primarily for slaves, pirates, and enemies of the state—categories that Rome considered beneath the dignity of a quicker death—which added a layer of social messaging to the political one. Crucifixion communicated not only the consequences of disobedience but the social status of those who disobeyed. The punishment degraded as it deterred, and the degradation was part of the deterrence.

Medieval and early modern Europe elaborated the punishment spectacle into an art form of baroque complexity. Public executions were staged events with formal procedures, assigned roles, and audiences that sometimes numbered in the thousands. The condemned were paraded through streets. The charges were read aloud. The execution itself was performed with a deliberation designed to maximize its psychological impact on spectators. Methods varied—hanging, burning, breaking on the wheel, drawing and quartering—but the variation was not random. The severity of the method was calibrated to the severity of the offense and, more importantly, to the severity of the message the state wished to send. Treason warranted the most extreme methods not because traitors suffered more than murderers in any moral calculus but because the threat to state authority was greater, and the deterrent message needed to be proportionally more dramatic.

Michel Foucault argued that the shift from public punishment to private incarceration in the eighteenth and nineteenth centuries represented a fundamental change in the nature of power—from the spectacle of sovereign violence to the discipline of institutional surveillance. The argument is influential and partially correct. The spectacle did recede. Public executions became less common, eventually disappearing from most Western societies. Prisons replaced scaffolds. The audience was removed from the punishment. But Foucault's account underestimates the degree to which the spectacle persisted in modified forms. Modern media—newspapers in the nineteenth century, television in the twentieth, social media in the twenty-first—restored the audience that the walls of the prison had excluded. The mugshot, the perp walk, the televised trial, the viral arrest video—each serves the same communicative function as the Roman roadside cross: it makes punishment visible and thereby extends its deterrent reach beyond the individual being punished to the population being governed. The scaffold was dismantled. The spectacle was relocated.

The persistence of punishment spectacle in democratic societies that pride themselves on humane criminal justice is worth noting because it reveals the structural function that spectacle serves regardless of the political system in which it operates. A democracy that publishes sex offender registries, mandates public notification of released prisoners, televises high-profile trials, and circulates arrest footage through news media is deploying the logic of visible punishment with different tools and a different self-narrative than the medieval kingdom that hanged criminals at crossroads, but the structural function is identical: making the consequences of transgression visible to the population in order to deter transgression. The democracy tells itself that transparency and public safety justify the visibility. The medieval kingdom told itself that divine justice and public order justified it. Both were correct in their own terms. Both were also, in structural terms, performing the same operation: using the punishment of the few to govern the behavior of the many.

DETERRENCE PSYCHOLOGY

Deterrence is fear systematized. Rather than reacting to disobedience after it occurs, deterrence aims to prevent disobedience before it begins by ensuring that potential transgressors understand the consequences of transgression and conclude that the costs exceed the benefits. The logic is simple. The execution is considerably more complex, because deterrence depends on a chain of psychological assumptions, each of which must hold for the system to function, and several of which are questionable under close examination.

The first assumption is that potential transgressors are rational—that they calculate costs and benefits before acting and choose the option that maximizes their expected utility. This assumption works tolerably well for premeditated crimes and strategic decisions. A tax evader who weighs the probability of audit against the savings from evasion is performing roughly the calculation that deterrence theory predicts. A corporate executive who weighs the fine for regulatory violation against the profit from violation is performing the same calculation. In these cases, increasing the severity or certainty of punishment does affect behavior, because the decision-maker is, in fact, calculating. The assumption works less well for crimes of passion, crimes of desperation, and crimes committed under the influence of substances that impair the calculating faculty. The person who kills in a moment of rage is not weighing sentencing guidelines. The person who steals to feed a family is not comparing the expected cost of imprisonment with the expected benefit of food. Deterrence theory assumes a rational actor. Much human behavior is not rational, a reality that deterrence theorists acknowledge in footnotes and ignore in policy recommendations.

The second assumption is that potential transgressors know the rules and the consequences. This assumption is so obviously problematic that it barely requires argument, yet entire criminal justice systems are built upon it. The legal fiction that ignorance of the law is no excuse presumes that citizens have read, understood, and internalized a body of law so vast that no single lawyer, much less any single citizen, has mastered it. In the United States, federal criminal law alone encompasses thousands of statutes, and regulatory offenses number in the hundreds of thousands. The notion that a citizen contemplating action consults this body of law and reaches a considered judgment about the risk of prosecution is not a description of human behavior. It is a legal premise that serves the system's need for a coherent framework rather than the citizen's actual experience of navigating a world of incomprehensible rules. Deterrence requires knowledge, and knowledge requires a legal system simple enough to be understood by the people it governs. No modern legal system meets this criterion, which means deterrence operates, at best, on a general awareness that bad things happen to people who get caught doing bad things—a level of precision that would embarrass any other field of applied psychology.

The third assumption is that the certainty and severity of punishment are perceptible to potential transgressors. Research consistently demonstrates that certainty of punishment deters more effectively than severity. A moderate penalty that is reliably imposed changes behavior more than a severe penalty that is rarely imposed. This finding is robust and widely replicated, and it is almost universally ignored by legislatures, which consistently prefer to increase severity—longer sentences, higher fines, more dramatic punishments—rather than invest in the detection and enforcement systems that would increase certainty. The preference for severity over certainty is not evidence-based. It is politically motivated. Passing a law that doubles the sentence for a particular offense is cheap, visible, and communicates toughness. Funding the investigative capacity to double the prosecution rate for that offense is expensive, invisible, and communicates nothing that fits on a campaign sign. The result is a deterrence architecture that is optimized for political messaging rather than behavioral effect, which produces systems that are simultaneously harsh and ineffective—a combination that satisfies the emotional demand for punishment without satisfying the strategic demand for deterrence.

Despite these limitations, deterrence works—not perfectly, not universally, but sufficiently to justify its place in every governance system that has ever existed. It works not because every potential transgressor makes a rational calculation but because enough of them do, or because the general atmosphere of consequence-awareness is sufficient to suppress a meaningful portion of the behavior that would otherwise occur. The bank that might be robbed less often because its security is visible. The border that might be crossed less frequently because the patrol is present. The regulation that might be violated less routinely because the auditor occasionally appears. None of these effects is total. All of them are real. Deterrence is an imperfect mechanism applied to imperfect actors in an imperfect information environment, and it still works well enough to be indispensable.

The failures of deterrence, when they occur, are often catastrophic precisely because they demonstrate the limits of fear as a governing mechanism. The British response to the Easter Rising of 1916 provides a textbook example. The Rising itself was militarily insignificant—a few hundred republicans holding central Dublin for less than a week before surrendering. The British response was textbook deterrence: mass arrests, court martials, and the execution of sixteen leaders over ten days. The logic was impeccable: make the consequences of rebellion so severe that no one would attempt it again. The result was the opposite. The executions, carried out with deliberate publicity, transformed marginal figures into martyrs and galvanized a nationalist movement that had been fractured and marginal. Within five years, the Irish Free State was established. The deterrence had failed not despite its severity but because of it—the punishment spectacle that was supposed to terrify instead legitimized the cause and delegitimized the authority imposing the punishment. The British had demonstrated their power. They had also demonstrated that their power rested on coercion rather than consent, and in doing so, they forfeited the legitimacy that makes deterrence work without escalation. The alternative—a governance system with no credible threat of consequences for transgression—has never been attempted, which is itself the strongest argument for deterrence's necessity, if not its sufficiency.

SECURITY NARRATIVES

Fear requires a threat, and when a genuine threat is unavailable, a narrative will serve. Security narratives—stories about dangers that justify the expansion or maintenance of state power—are among the most effective tools for translating fear into political authority. The narrative identifies an enemy. The enemy justifies a response. The response requires resources, powers, and permissions that the state might not otherwise possess. The sequence is so reliable and so well-documented that its recurrence should surprise no one, yet it retains its effectiveness because the fear it invokes is real even when the threat it describes is exaggerated, manufactured, or mischaracterized. People are afraid. The state offers protection. The price of protection is power. The transaction occurs at a speed that leaves little room for the careful evaluation of whether the threat warranted the price.

The Cold War provided the twentieth century's most durable security narrative and its most consequential expansion of state power justified by that narrative. The Soviet threat was real. Soviet nuclear weapons could destroy American cities. Soviet ideology was hostile to Western political systems. Soviet military capability was substantial and, at various points, appeared to be growing faster than the West's. None of this was fabricated. But the narrative that grew around the threat expanded well beyond what the threat itself could justify. The domino theory—the idea that the fall of one country to communism would trigger the fall of its neighbors in an unbroken chain—justified military interventions across Southeast Asia, Latin America, Africa, and the Middle East that had more to do with great power competition than with any realistic assessment of communist expansion dynamics. Domestic security programs surveilled, infiltrated, and disrupted political organizations whose connection to Soviet communism was tenuous at best and fictional at worst. The security narrative created a permission structure in which virtually any expansion of state power could be justified by invoking the threat, and the invocation was difficult to challenge because challenging it invited the accusation that the challenger was indifferent to the threat or sympathetic to the enemy. The narrative policed itself.

The War on Terror replicated the pattern with updated vocabulary and expanded technological capability. The September 11 attacks provided a genuine threat and a genuine trauma. The security narrative that grew around them produced the most significant expansion of surveillance authority, executive power, and military commitment in a generation. The PATRIOT Act was drafted before the political conditions for its passage existed and passed through Congress at a speed that precluded careful evaluation—not because legislators were coerced but because the security narrative had created an environment in which opposing the legislation felt politically impossible. The narrative framework was familiar: a threat demands a response, the response requires new powers, and questioning the powers means questioning the response, which means failing to take the threat seriously. The framework is self-sealing. Once the narrative is established, every objection to the expansion of power can be reframed as an objection to security itself, and no politician who values reelection wants to be positioned as objecting to security.

Security narratives are not limited to external threats. Domestic security narratives—crime waves, drug epidemics, immigration crises, moral panics—perform identical functions using domestic populations as the identified threat. The American war on drugs, launched in the early 1970s and escalated over the following decades, produced an expansion of law enforcement power, incarceration capacity, and surveillance authority that transformed the relationship between the state and significant portions of its own population. The narrative identified drug use as an existential threat to American society. The response justified mandatory minimum sentences, civil asset forfeiture, no-knock warrants, and incarceration rates that made the United States the world's largest jailer by a significant margin. Whether the threat warranted the response is a question that the narrative was designed to make unanswerable, because the narrative's function was not to produce accurate threat assessment but to produce political permission for the expansion of state power. The expansion occurred. The threat persisted. The narrative continued, because a security narrative that resolved its own threat would eliminate the justification for the powers it had authorized, and authorized powers are rarely surrendered voluntarily.

The structural pattern is consistent across eras and political systems: a threat—real, exaggerated, or constructed—is identified. The threat generates fear. Fear generates demand for protection. Protection requires expanded state power. Expanded state power, once established, persists beyond the duration of the threat because the institutional apparatus created to address the threat develops its own constituency, its own budget, and its own institutional interest in continuing to exist. The Department of Homeland Security was created in response to a specific threat. It is now a permanent fixture of the federal government with a budget exceeding fifty billion dollars and a workforce exceeding two hundred thousand employees. The specific threat may evolve. The institution does not shrink. Security narratives are ratchets: they expand state power in one direction and resist contraction in the other. The fear subsides. The apparatus remains.

FEAR AS STABILIZER

Fear is discussed most often as a tool of oppression, which it frequently is. But it also functions as a stabilizer—a mechanism that preserves social order by discouraging the disruptions that would occur if every grievance were acted upon and every impulse were followed. This stabilizing function is uncomfortable to acknowledge because it suggests that systems we find objectionable may persist not only because of the power of those who benefit from them but also because of the rational risk assessment of those who do not. Fear keeps people in line. Being kept in line is not always unjust. It is sometimes the alternative to chaos, and chaos is not distributed equally. The people who suffer most when social order breaks down are rarely the people who were on top when it was intact.

The stabilizing function of fear operates most effectively when it is internalized—when the external threat of punishment has been converted into the internal habit of compliance. A population that complies with laws because it fears the police is a policed population. A population that complies with laws because the habit of compliance has become second nature is a self-policing population. The conversion from external fear to internal habit is the same process described in the chapter on sacred power—the transformation of coerced compliance into normalized behavior—and it operates through the same mechanism: repetition. The child who is punished for stealing internalizes a prohibition against theft that persists long after the threat of punishment recedes. The citizen who obeys traffic laws does so not because a police officer is present at every intersection but because the habit of stopping at red lights has become automatic. The fear was the initial mechanism. The habit is the durable product. Fear plants the seed. Routine grows the tree.

This internalization is so complete in well-functioning societies that most citizens do not experience their compliance as fear-based. They experience it as normal. The law-abiding citizen does not feel afraid. The citizen feels that obeying the law is what one does, that the rules are reasonable, that the system is fair enough to warrant cooperation. This feeling is genuine. It is also the product of a socialization process that began with fear—parental discipline, school rules, legal consequences—and gradually replaced the fear with habit and the habit with identity. The person who does not steal does not think of themselves as someone deterred from stealing by the threat of punishment. They think of themselves as someone who does not steal, period. The fear has been so thoroughly internalized that it has disappeared from conscious awareness, which is the point at which it becomes maximally effective. Visible fear is expensive to maintain. Invisible fear—fear that has become identity—is free.

The danger arises when the stabilizing function of fear is invoked to justify the maintenance of systems that serve the interests of the powerful at the expense of everyone else. Every authoritarian regime in history has justified its coercive apparatus as necessary for stability, and some of them have been correct—in the narrow sense that removing the apparatus would produce disorder. The question is whether the stability being preserved is worth the cost of preserving it, and who bears that cost. A social order that is stable because a majority of the population has been terrorized into compliance is stable in the same sense that a prison is stable: the absence of disorder does not indicate the presence of justice. The confusion between stability and justice—the assumption that because things are orderly they are therefore acceptable—is one of the most persistent errors in political thought, and fear is the mechanism that makes the confusion possible. Fear produces compliance. Compliance produces order. Order is mistaken for legitimacy. And the system that should be challenged is instead preserved, because challenging it would be disorderly, and disorder is what everyone has been taught to fear.

The relationship between fear and legitimacy is, in this sense, circular and self-reinforcing. Fear produces compliance. Compliance produces stability. Stability is interpreted as evidence of legitimacy. Legitimacy justifies the system that produced the fear. The circle can rotate for generations without being disrupted, because disrupting it requires challenging the stability that fear has produced, and the fear that produced the stability is designed to prevent exactly that challenge. Breaking the circle requires either an external shock powerful enough to destabilize the system despite the fear, or an internal shift in perception—a collective recognition that the stability is not legitimate, that the order is not just, that the fear is a tool of control rather than a condition of civilization. Both have happened. Neither is easy. And the systems that rely on fear for their stability are, by design, the systems that make recognizing the reliance most difficult.

A reader might object that this chapter overgeneralizes—that many functioning democracies operate without producing meaningful fear in their citizens, and that treating fear as universal flattens the genuine difference between liberal and authoritarian systems. The objection is partly right. Democracies produce far less fear than authoritarian regimes, and the difference is not cosmetic—it is the largest single variable affecting daily life under one system or the other. But "less fear" is not "no fear." The fear of unemployment, eviction, medical bankruptcy, or social ruin is not produced by jackboots, but it is produced by the system, and it shapes behavior in ways that look remarkably similar to the more visible kind. The volume is lower. The function is preserved.

Fear is the low note in every power structure—present always, dominant sometimes, denied frequently. It operates beneath the more respectable forms of authority the way a foundation operates beneath a building: invisible when the structure is intact, exposed when the structure cracks. A government that is losing legitimacy increases its reliance on fear. An institution that is losing relevance increases its threats. A leader who is losing support increases the volume of warnings about what will happen if the leader is replaced. The escalation is diagnostic. When fear becomes the primary visible instrument of governance, it is evidence not of strength but of the erosion of every other basis for authority. The regime that governs primarily through fear has run out of better options.

15
POWER AND CONSENT

"It is on opinion only that government is founded."

David Hume
Of the First Principles of Government (1741)

CONSENT IS THE MOST flattering story that power tells about itself. The governed agree to be governed. The ruled accept the rules. The hierarchy persists not because those at the bottom are compelled but because they have chosen—freely, rationally, with full awareness of the alternatives—to participate. It is a beautiful idea. It is also, in its purest form, almost entirely fictional. No population in history has been presented with a genuine choice between being governed and not being governed, evaluated the options with full information, and selected governance on the merits. What populations have done is accommodate themselves to existing arrangements, internalize the norms those arrangements produce, and describe the result as consent because the alternative descriptions—habit, resignation, lack of viable options—are less flattering to everyone involved.

SOCIAL CONTRACT FICTIONS

The social contract is the foundational metaphor of modern political legitimacy, and it is worth noting at the outset that it is a metaphor. No contract was signed. No terms were negotiated. No party had the option to decline. Hobbes, Locke, and Rousseau each proposed versions of an original agreement in which individuals surrendered certain freedoms to a collective authority in exchange for security, property rights, or the general will. The proposals differed in their details and their conclusions, but they shared a structural feature that is more important than their disagreements: they were all hypothetical. The social contract describes what rational people would agree to if they were starting from scratch, which they never are. Every actual society is inherited, not chosen. The person born into a political system did not consent to it any more than they consented to the language they speak or the climate they inhabit. They found it there. They adapted to it. They may approve of it, tolerate it, or despise it, but none of these responses constitutes consent in the sense that the word carries in any other context.

Try applying the concept of consent as it operates in contract law to the social contract, and the difficulties become immediately apparent. A valid contract requires informed parties, voluntary agreement, consideration from both sides, and the option to decline. The social contract fails on every count. Citizens are not informed of the terms—the body of law that constitutes the "contract" is so vast that no individual has read it, much less understood it. Agreement is not voluntary—the alternative to accepting governance is not a return to the state of nature but exile, imprisonment, or death, depending on how vigorously one pursues the alternative. Consideration is asymmetric—the state provides services, but the citizen's obligation to pay taxes and obey laws is not contingent on the quality of those services. And the option to decline does not exist in any meaningful sense—one cannot opt out of the jurisdiction in which one was born without considerable cost, legal complexity, and the permission of the very authority one wishes to leave. If a commercial contract operated on these terms, it would be voided in any court in the developed world. As a political metaphor, it has sustained three centuries of political theory and shows no signs of retirement.

The durability of the social contract metaphor despite its obvious inadequacies tells us something important about the function it serves.

The social contract is not a description of how political legitimacy was established. It is a justification for political legitimacy as it currently exists. It works backward from the conclusion—this government is legitimate—to a premise that supports the conclusion—because rational people would have agreed to it. The reasoning is circular, but the circularity is a feature, not a bug. A justification that works backward from the desired conclusion is unfalsifiable, because any arrangement can be justified by constructing a hypothetical in which rational people would have chosen it. The social contract does not constrain power. It rationalizes whatever power arrangement happens to exist, provided the theorist is sufficiently creative in describing the hypothetical choice situation. This is why the social contract has been used to justify everything from absolute monarchy (Hobbes) to liberal democracy (Locke) to direct democracy (Rousseau). The metaphor is flexible enough to support any conclusion, which is what makes it useful and what makes it empty.

The practical function of the social contract in contemporary politics is not philosophical but rhetorical. When a government describes its authority as resting on the consent of the governed, it is making a claim that performs several useful operations simultaneously. It positions the government as the agent of the people rather than their master. It frames obedience as voluntary rather than compelled. It shifts the burden of justification from the government, which would otherwise need to explain why it possesses the authority to coerce, to the citizen, who must now explain why they refuse to honor an agreement they are deemed to have made. The rhetorical inversion is elegant: the government that claims to rule by consent is not asking permission. It is asserting that permission has already been granted, and that anyone who disagrees is not a dissenter but a contract-breaker. The language of consent is the language of freedom. The structure of consent, as actually practiced, is the structure of presumed obligation.

Manufacturing Consent

The phrase "manufacturing consent" entered the political vocabulary through Walter Lippmann, who used it approvingly, and Noam Chomsky, who used it as an indictment. The difference in their evaluations is less important than their agreement on the phenomenon itself: in complex societies, public opinion is not simply expressed. It is shaped, guided, and constructed by institutions that have the resources, the expertise, and the motivation to influence what people think. The media, the educational system, political parties, corporations, religious organizations, and the state itself all participate in this process, not through crude propaganda—though that exists too—but through the subtler mechanisms of framing, agenda-setting, and the selective presentation of information that determines which questions the public considers and which answers appear reasonable.

The mechanism operates through what communication scholars call framing. A frame is a conceptual structure that organizes information and determines its meaning. The same event—a strike, a war, a policy change—can be framed in multiple ways, and the choice of frame determines how the audience understands the event and what responses seem appropriate. A strike framed as workers exercising their rights produces a different public response than the same strike framed as economic disruption caused by union intransigence. A war framed as defense of national security produces a different response than the same war framed as a choice made by political leaders for strategic reasons. The frame is not a lie. It is a selection—an emphasis on certain aspects of reality and a de-emphasis of others—and the selection determines what the public consents to, because the public consents to what it understands, and what it understands is shaped by how the information is presented.

Agenda-setting is the complementary mechanism. If framing determines how people think about issues, agenda-setting determines which issues people think about. The issues that receive sustained media attention become the issues the public considers important. The issues that do not receive attention do not register as significant, regardless of their actual impact. A society in which media coverage focuses overwhelmingly on crime will produce a public that considers crime its primary concern, even if crime rates are declining. A society in which media coverage focuses on economic growth will produce a public that evaluates its government primarily on economic performance, even if other dimensions of governance—environmental policy, civil liberties, institutional integrity—are deteriorating. The agenda is not set by the public. It is set for the public, by institutions that have their own interests in determining which issues receive attention and which do not. The public then expresses opinions on the issues it has been given, and those opinions are described as public will, and public will is described as consent. The circle closes neatly.

The manufacturing of consent is most effective when it is least visible—when the people whose consent is being manufactured experience their opinions as independently formed rather than institutionally shaped. This is the crucial distinction between propaganda and manufactured consent. Propaganda is visible. It announces itself through its crudeness, its repetition, and its obvious connection to the interests of the propagandist. Manufactured consent is invisible. It operates through the selection of which facts are reported, which experts are quoted, which perspectives are represented, and which questions are asked—all of which occur within institutional processes that appear neutral, professional, and independent. The journalist who selects stories based on news values that favor conflict, novelty, and elite sources is not conspiring to manufacture consent. The journalist is doing their job within a professional framework that happens to produce coverage systematically favoring certain perspectives over others. The effect is the same as conspiracy without requiring anyone to conspire, which is considerably more sustainable.

The digital information environment has complicated the manufacturing of consent without eliminating it. The internet decentralized information production, broke the traditional media's gatekeeping monopoly, and gave individuals and non-institutional actors the ability to reach audiences that previously required corporate media infrastructure. This was celebrated, initially, as a democratization of information that would make manufactured consent impossible. The celebration was premature. What the internet produced was not the end of manufactured consent but its multiplication. Instead of consent being manufactured by a relatively small number of media institutions operating within shared professional norms, it is now manufactured by thousands of sources operating with no shared norms, no editorial accountability, and no commitment to the distinction between information and persuasion. The result is not an informed public making autonomous judgments. It is a fragmented public, each segment receiving information curated by algorithms designed to maximize engagement rather than accuracy, forming opinions within information environments so thoroughly filtered that exposure to challenging perspectives is not merely unlikely but architecturally prevented. Consent is still manufactured. The factory has been decentralized.

ELECTIONS AS LEGITIMATION RITUALS

Elections are the primary mechanism through which democratic societies produce consent, and they accomplish this with an effectiveness that deserves both admiration and scrutiny. The citizen enters a booth, marks a ballot, and participates in a process that determines who governs. The act is genuine. The choice is real, within boundaries. The outcome reflects, in some aggregated and mediated fashion, the preferences of the electorate. All of this is true. It is also true that elections function as legitimation rituals—structured performances that produce the consent of the governed regardless of which candidate wins, because the act of participating in the election constitutes acceptance of the system that produced it. The voter who marks a ballot has consented to be governed by whoever wins, including the candidate they voted against. The consent is produced not by the outcome but by the participation. The election is a machine for manufacturing legitimacy, and it operates every time a ballot is cast, regardless of what is written on it.

This observation is not a critique of elections. It is a description of their function, and the function is valuable precisely because alternatives to it—hereditary succession, military coup, revolutionary seizure—produce legitimacy deficits that elections resolve. A government that won an election can claim a mandate. A government that seized power can claim only that it has power, which is sufficient for coercion but insufficient for the kind of voluntary compliance that makes governance efficient. Elections produce voluntary compliance because the governed experience the outcome as, in some sense, their own doing. The difference between systems that hold competitive elections and systems that do not is real and consequential, and the difference is not merely symbolic. Electoral democracies produce peaceful transfers of power between competing factions—a mechanism for resolving succession disputes that historically required violence. They create institutional channels through which popular dissatisfaction can be expressed and partially addressed without destabilizing the entire system. They generate information about public preferences that non-electoral systems lack, information that even self-interested governments must take into account when calculating political risk. The consent produced by elections is constrained, manufactured, and shaped by forces beyond the voter's control. It is also more genuine than the 'consent' produced by authoritarian plebiscites where the outcome is predetermined, more accountable than hereditary succession where the governed have no voice, and more stable than revolutionary seizure where legitimacy rests on force alone. Elections do not produce pure consent any more than markets produce perfect competition. They produce a workable approximation that is both better than the alternatives and worse than the ideal. We elected this government. If it governs badly, we can elect a different one. The possibility of replacement is what makes the current arrangement tolerable, and the tolerability is what produces the consent. Elections do not guarantee good governance. They guarantee the perception that governance is accountable, and the perception is what produces legitimacy.

The boundaries within which electoral choice operates are worth examining because they define the limits of the consent that elections produce. Voters choose between candidates, but they do not choose the process that selected the candidates, the funding structures that determined which candidates were viable, the media environment that shaped public awareness of the candidates, or the institutional framework within which the elected candidate will govern. The menu is presented. The diner chooses from the menu. The diner did not design the menu, stock the kitchen, or set the prices. The choice is real within the constraints. The constraints are not chosen. A voter in a two-party system who finds both parties inadequate has the freedom to vote for either one—a freedom that is formally genuine and substantively limited. The consent produced by the election is consent to be governed by one of two options, neither of which the voter may have wanted, within a system whose fundamental parameters were established before the voter was born and will persist after the voter is dead.

The ritual dimension of elections becomes most visible when the election produces an outcome that challenges the system's legitimacy rather than reinforcing it. When a candidate who threatens institutional norms wins an election, the system faces a contradiction: the legitimation ritual has produced a result that undermines the institutions the ritual was designed to legitimate. The responses to this contradiction reveal the depth of the ritual's power. Defenders of the institutions argue that the election must be respected because democratic legitimacy requires accepting outcomes. Opponents of the winner argue that the institutions must be defended because democratic legitimacy requires more than electoral outcomes. Both arguments invoke consent. Neither can resolve the contradiction, because the contradiction is built into a system that treats elections as the source of legitimacy while also treating institutional constraints as the framework within which elections operate. When the election and the institutions point in different directions, the system has no mechanism for determining which form of consent takes priority, because both are genuine and both are limited. This is not a failure of democracy. It is its permanent structural tension, managed in practice through norms, negotiations, and the pragmatic calculations of people who understand that destroying the system's legitimacy to win a single contest is a bad trade regardless of which side makes it.

THE CONSENT SPECTRUM

The binary distinction between consent and coercion obscures more than it reveals. In practice, compliance with any power system exists on a spectrum that runs from enthusiastic endorsement through passive acceptance to grudging tolerance to active resistance, and most individuals occupy different positions on this spectrum at different times, for different aspects of the same system. The citizen who enthusiastically supports the national defense may grudgingly tolerate the tax system that funds it, passively accept the regulatory framework that governs their business, and actively resist the immigration policy they find objectionable. This citizen consents to the system as a whole while dissenting from specific components, cooperates on most dimensions while resisting on others, and describes their overall relationship with the state in terms that depend on which dimension of governance happens to be under discussion at the moment. The relationship is not consent or coercion. It is a complex, shifting mixture of both, and the mixture varies across individuals, across issues, and across time.

The concept of passive consent—consent inferred from the absence of active resistance—is the most structurally important and the most philosophically problematic form on the spectrum. Most citizens most of the time are passively consenting to most aspects of their governance. They are not marching in support of the tax code. They are not protesting against it either. They are filing their returns, paying their obligations, and directing their active political energy, if they have any, toward issues they care more about. The state interprets this compliance as consent, which is reasonable in the sense that the alternative interpretation—that the entire population is coerced into compliance with every law—is implausible. But passive consent is not the same as affirmative endorsement, and the gap between them is where a great deal of governance actually lives. The population complies because compliance is the path of least resistance, because the costs of resistance exceed the costs of compliance, and because the system works well enough—for enough people, on enough dimensions—to make active opposition seem disproportionate. This is not consent in any philosophically robust sense. It is acquiescence, and acquiescence is the operating system of most governance most of the time.

Acquiescence is stable as long as the gap between what the population tolerates and what the system demands does not exceed a threshold that varies by culture, by era, and by the availability of alternatives. When the system demands more than the population is willing to tolerate—higher taxes, greater restrictions, more visible corruption, more blatant inequality—acquiescence erodes, and the population's position on the consent spectrum shifts toward resistance. The shift is typically gradual, marked by declining trust, increasing cynicism, reduced participation in legitimation rituals like voting, and growing receptivity to narratives that challenge the system's legitimacy. The shift can also be sudden, triggered by focal events that crystallize diffuse dissatisfaction into concentrated outrage—the dynamic described in the chapter on popular power. In either case, the shift represents a withdrawal of the passive consent on which the system depends, and the withdrawal is dangerous precisely because the system has been operating as though passive consent were active endorsement. The government that mistakes acquiescence for approval discovers, when the acquiescence evaporates, that it has no reserve of genuine support to draw upon. The legitimacy was thinner than it appeared. The consent was quieter than it sounded.

The most sophisticated power systems maintain themselves by managing the consent spectrum—by ensuring that enough of the population remains in the zone between passive acceptance and enthusiastic endorsement to sustain the perception of legitimacy. This management involves a combination of genuine responsiveness to public concerns, strategic concessions that address the most politically dangerous grievances, symbolic gestures that communicate respect for the governed, and the careful cultivation of narratives that frame the existing arrangement as the best available option. The management is not total. Genuine dissent persists. Genuine resistance occurs. But the management is sufficient, most of the time, to keep the center of gravity within the range where the system can describe itself as resting on consent without the description being laughably inaccurate. The description is never entirely accurate either. It is approximately true, which is the most that any claim about consent can be and is, evidently, enough.

Liberal political theory raises a serious objection here: that distinguishing "real" consent from "constructed" consent threatens to dismiss the genuine preferences of ordinary citizens as false consciousness, and that the move is paternalistic in ways the chapter does not acknowledge. The concern is legitimate, and the chapter has tried to honor it. The argument is not that citizens are deceived about what they want. It is that the conditions under which preferences form are themselves shaped by power, and that ignoring those conditions produces an account of consent that mistakes the outcome of an institutional process for the spontaneous expression of free choice. People genuinely prefer the systems they endorse. The endorsement is real. The conditions that produced it are also real, and both deserve attention.

Consent is neither the fiction that radicals describe nor the reality that liberals celebrate. It is a constructed condition, produced by institutional processes, sustained by information environments, ratified by rituals, and experienced by most of the governed as something between voluntary agreement and resigned acceptance. It is real in the sense that people genuinely prefer the systems they endorse, genuinely participate in the processes they support, and genuinely experience their compliance as chosen rather than compelled. It is constructed in the sense that the preferences, the participation, and the experience are all shaped by systems that have an interest in producing consent and the institutional capacity to shape the conditions under which it is formed. The construction does not make the consent fake. It makes the consent contingent—dependent on conditions that are maintained rather than natural, managed rather than spontaneous, and vulnerable to disruption when the conditions change.

16
POWER IN DECLINE

"A dynasty rarely lasts beyond three generations."

Ibn Khaldun
Muqaddimah (1377)

DECLINE IS THE PART of the story that nobody inside the story recognizes while it is happening. This is not because the symptoms are subtle. They are, in retrospect, obvious—so obvious that historians writing after the fact invariably express puzzlement that contemporaries failed to notice what was directly in front of them. The treasury was emptying. The institutions were calcifying. The rhetoric was inflating in inverse proportion to the capacity it described. The gap between what the system claimed to be doing and what it was actually doing had widened to the point where maintaining the fiction required more energy than addressing the reality. And yet the people operating the system—the administrators, the politicians, the generals, the executives—continued operating as though the system were functioning, because the system had always functioned, and the assumption of continuity is the last assumption to die. It dies after the currency. It dies after the army. It sometimes dies after the state itself. People will stand in the ruins of an institution and describe it as undergoing temporary difficulties with a sincerity that would be admirable if it were not diagnostic.

OVERREACH INDICATORS

Overreach was examined in the context of empires, but it is not an exclusively imperial pathology. Every system of power—a corporation, a political party, a regulatory agency, a religious institution, a military alliance—can overreach, and the indicators are structurally identical regardless of the system's scale or domain. Overreach occurs when commitments exceed capacity, when the system takes on obligations it cannot sustain, and when the gap between ambition and resources is filled not by expanding resources but by borrowing against the future. The borrowing can be financial, institutional, or reputational. In every case, it produces the same result: a period of apparent strength that is actually a period of accelerating vulnerability, because the strength is being financed by resources that have not yet been earned and may never be.

The first indicator of overreach is the divergence between operational tempo and institutional capacity. A system that is doing more than its institutions were designed to support is a system that is compensating for structural inadequacy with individual effort—longer hours, faster decisions, reduced oversight, deferred maintenance. The compensation works in the short term, which is why it is adopted. It fails in the long term, because individual effort is a depletable resource and institutional capacity is what remains when individual effort is exhausted. The Roman Empire in the third century was not less competent than the empire in the first century. It was more committed—defending longer borders, managing more provinces, fighting more wars—with institutions that had not scaled to match the commitments. The individual emperors, generals, and administrators worked harder. The system worked worse. The divergence between effort and outcome is the earliest measurable symptom of overreach, and it is routinely misdiagnosed as a personnel problem. The leadership is not good enough. The workers are not dedicated enough. The solution is better people. The actual problem is that the system is demanding more than any people, however good, can deliver within the existing structure. Replacing the people changes the faces. It does not close the gap.

The second indicator is the proliferation of commitments that cannot be individually abandoned without threatening the credibility of the whole. This is the entanglement problem. A state that has guaranteed the security of thirty allies cannot abandon one without every other ally questioning whether their guarantee is next. A corporation that has promised growth to shareholders, stability to employees, innovation to customers, and responsibility to regulators cannot retract any single promise without undermining the credibility of the others. Each commitment is individually rational. Collectively, they create a rigidity that makes strategic adjustment impossible, because every adjustment threatens a relationship that the system depends on. The system becomes trapped by its own promises, unable to reduce its obligations because reduction in any one area signals weakness that compounds across all others. The result is a system that continues to honor every commitment at diminishing levels of quality rather than honoring fewer commitments well—a strategy that postpones the reckoning while ensuring that the reckoning, when it arrives, will be comprehensive rather than contained.

The third indicator is the substitution of narrative for performance. A system that is meeting its objectives does not need to explain, at length, why it is meeting its objectives. A system that is failing to meet its objectives needs to explain why the failure is temporary, why the metrics are misleading, why the critics are wrong, and why the trajectory is about to improve. The volume of explanation is inversely proportional to the quality of performance. This is observable at every scale. The corporation whose earnings call is dominated by forward-looking statements and strategic repositioning narratives is a corporation whose current performance does not speak for itself. The government whose public communications focus on enemies, conspiracies, and the inadequacy of its predecessors rather than on its own accomplishments is a government whose accomplishments are insufficient to sustain its legitimacy. The institution that spends more energy managing its reputation than managing its operations has, in structural terms, already begun to decline. The narrative is compensating for the performance, and the compensation is itself a cost—resources and attention directed toward explaining why things are fine rather than making things fine. The explanation becomes the activity. The activity it was supposed to explain atrophies beneath it.

The fourth indicator is the most difficult to detect from inside the system and the most obvious from outside: the system's increasing inability to tolerate honest assessment. A healthy system can absorb bad news because it has the capacity to respond to it. A declining system cannot absorb bad news because it lacks the capacity to respond, which means bad news is not information to be acted upon but a threat to be managed. The messenger is shot not out of malice but out of structural necessity—the system cannot process the message, so it eliminates the messenger. Internal critics are marginalized. External critics are dismissed. Data that contradicts the official narrative is reinterpreted, reclassified, or ignored. The process is rarely conscious. It operates through institutional incentives: the person who delivers good news is rewarded, the person who delivers bad news is not, and over time the information environment within the system becomes so thoroughly curated that the leadership is making decisions based on a version of reality that bears decreasing resemblance to the actual one. The system is flying blind and has disabled the instruments that would tell it so. This is not a failure of intelligence. It is a success of institutional self-protection, operating at the expense of institutional survival.

Loss of Credibility

Credibility is the currency of legitimacy, and like all currencies, it can be inflated to the point of worthlessness. A system that says what it means and does what it says accumulates credibility over time. A system that says one thing and does another spends credibility with every contradiction, and the spending is cumulative, irreversible in the short term, and eventually fatal to the system's capacity to govern through consent rather than coercion. The transition from consent-based governance to coercion-based governance is the structural definition of legitimacy collapse, and it is preceded, in every case, by a period of credibility erosion so gradual that the people presiding over it mistake each individual contradiction for a minor inconsistency rather than a contribution to a trend.

Credibility is lost in specific, identifiable ways, and the taxonomy is worth cataloging because the categories recur with monotonous regularity across different systems and different centuries. The first category is the promise-performance gap—the distance between what the system promises and what it delivers. Every system overpromises to some degree. The degree matters. A government that promises prosperity and delivers modest growth has a manageable credibility deficit. A government that promises prosperity and presides over economic contraction has a credibility crisis. The crisis is not proportional to the absolute level of performance. It is proportional to the gap between expectation and reality, which means a system that promised less and delivered modestly would retain more credibility than a system that promised extravagantly and delivered competently. The lesson is obvious. It is also systematically ignored, because the incentive structure of every competitive system—political, corporate, institutional—rewards the promise and defers accountability for delivery. The candidate who promises modestly loses to the candidate who promises extravagantly, and the extravagant promiser then governs with a credibility deficit that was baked into the campaign. The deficit is structural, not personal. The system selects for overpromising and then punishes the overpromisers for failing to deliver, which is a design flaw so consistent that calling it a flaw may be too generous. It may simply be how competitive systems work.

The second category is hypocrisy—the visible contradiction between the system's stated values and its actual behavior. Every institution is hypocritical to some degree, because institutions operate on principles and principles simplify reality in ways that create contradictions when applied to specific cases. The degree of hypocrisy matters less than its visibility. A church that preaches charity while accumulating wealth retains credibility as long as the accumulation is not widely known or as long as the explanation for it is accepted. The same church loses credibility catastrophically when the accumulation becomes visible and the explanation is rejected. The credibility was not lost when the behavior occurred. It was lost when the behavior became known. This distinction is important because it means credibility erosion is often a function of information availability rather than behavioral change—the institution did not become more hypocritical; the hypocrisy became more visible. The printing press, the newspaper, the television, and the internet each expanded the visibility of institutional hypocrisy, and each expansion produced a corresponding erosion of institutional credibility. The institutions did not change. The information environment changed around them, and the change exposed contradictions that had previously been invisible to most of the governed.

The third category is the credibility of competence—the belief that the system can do what it claims to be able to do. This form of credibility is lost not through moral failure but through operational failure, and it is in some ways more damaging because it cannot be repaired by apology, reform, or moral renewal. A government that fails to respond effectively to a natural disaster loses credibility not because it lied or betrayed its values but because it demonstrated, visibly and publicly, that it could not perform its basic function. A financial system that collapses loses credibility not because regulators were corrupt—though they may have been—but because the system failed to do the thing it existed to do: manage financial risk effectively. Competence credibility is earned slowly and lost quickly, because a thousand days of adequate performance are less visible than a single day of catastrophic failure. The failure becomes the defining data point, and no amount of subsequent competence fully restores the credibility that the failure destroyed. The institution remembers its successes. The public remembers its failures. The asymmetry is permanent.

Credibility loss compounds. Each instance makes the next instance more damaging, because each instance lowers the baseline of trust from which the system operates. A government with high credibility can survive a scandal because the public gives it the benefit of the doubt. A government with low credibility cannot survive the same scandal because the benefit of the doubt has been exhausted. The compounding is nonlinear—credibility erodes slowly at first, as individual contradictions are absorbed and explained, and then rapidly, as the accumulated weight of contradictions exceeds the public's capacity to rationalize them. The tipping point is difficult to identify in advance but unmistakable in retrospect: the moment when the public stops giving the system the benefit of the doubt and starts interpreting everything the system does through a lens of suspicion. Once that lens is adopted, credibility recovery becomes nearly impossible, because even genuine reforms are interpreted as strategic maneuvers, and even honest communications are received as sophisticated deceptions. The system that has lost the benefit of the doubt has lost the capacity to be believed, and a system that cannot be believed cannot govern through consent. What remains is coercion, and coercion, as this book has repeatedly observed, is the most expensive and least sustainable basis for power.

Administrative Decay

Administrative decay is the least dramatic and most consequential form of decline. It does not announce itself with crises, scandals, or military defeats. It announces itself with delays, errors, workarounds, and the quiet accumulation of dysfunction that degrades institutional performance so gradually that no single moment registers as a failure. The forms do not arrive on time. The database has not been updated. The regulation has not been enforced. The inspection was cursory. The training was abbreviated. The maintenance was deferred. Each individual lapse is minor. Collectively, they constitute the progressive erosion of the institutional capacity on which the entire power system depends. A government that cannot collect taxes efficiently, deliver services reliably, or enforce regulations consistently is a government that is losing the operational basis for its authority, regardless of how effectively it manages its political messaging or how enthusiastically it conducts its legitimation rituals.

The mechanisms of administrative decay are mundane, which is why they receive less attention than they deserve. The first mechanism is talent attrition. Effective administration requires competent people, and competent people have options. When an institution's compensation, prestige, or working conditions decline relative to alternatives, competent people leave and are replaced by less competent people who have fewer alternatives. The process is incremental. No single departure is catastrophic. But the cumulative effect—a gradual decline in the average capability of the institution's workforce—degrades performance in ways that compound over time. The experienced official who understood the system's intricacies is replaced by a novice who follows procedures without understanding their purpose. The procedures work well enough in normal conditions. In abnormal conditions—the crisis, the edge case, the situation that requires judgment rather than procedure—the absence of experienced judgment produces failures that the procedure was not designed to prevent. The institution appears functional until it is tested, at which point the talent deficit becomes visible and the test becomes a crisis.

The second mechanism is procedural ossification. Institutions create procedures to ensure consistency, reduce error, and preserve institutional knowledge. Over time, the procedures accumulate. New procedures are added to address new problems. Old procedures are rarely removed because removing a procedure requires someone to take responsibility for the consequences of its absence, and taking responsibility for absence is riskier than maintaining a procedure that may no longer be necessary. The result is a procedural environment of increasing complexity, decreasing efficiency, and decreasing comprehensibility. The new employee confronted with the procedure manual finds a document that is hundreds of pages long, internally contradictory in places, and organized according to a logic that reflects the sequence in which procedures were added rather than the sequence in which they are needed. Compliance with the procedures becomes an end in itself—the institutional equivalent of a cargo cult, in which the forms of effective governance are maintained without the substance. The report is filed. The box is checked. The outcome is not examined because the procedure did not require examining the outcome. It required filing the report and checking the box.

The third mechanism is resource diversion. Every institution diverts some portion of its resources from its stated mission to the maintenance of the institution itself—overhead, administration, self-promotion, internal politics. In a healthy institution, this diversion is a manageable fraction of total resources. In a declining institution, the fraction grows because the institution's internal complexity increases faster than its external effectiveness. More meetings. More reports. More compliance requirements. More layers of approval. Each addition consumes time and attention that are not available for the institution's actual work. The people who are best at institutional navigation—the ones who understand the politics, manage the relationships, produce the reports—are promoted, while the people who are best at the institution's actual mission but less skilled at navigating its internal environment are not. Over time, the institution's leadership consists of people who are exceptionally good at running the institution and less interested in or capable of performing the function the institution was created to perform. The institution becomes an organization whose primary product is its own continuation.

The late Ottoman Empire provides a case study in administrative decay so comprehensive that it became a synonym for the phenomenon. By the nineteenth century, the Ottoman administrative apparatus had accumulated centuries of procedural complexity, overlapping jurisdictions, contradictory regulations, and institutional inertia that made governance in the modern sense nearly impossible. Reform efforts were launched repeatedly—the Tanzimat reforms of the mid-nineteenth century were genuine, ambitious, and partially effective—but each reform was implemented through the same decayed administrative apparatus it was trying to reform, which meant the reform was processed, interpreted, and executed by people and procedures that had a structural interest in preventing exactly the kind of change the reform intended. The reform entered the administrative system as a directive for transformation and exited it as a modification of existing practice so modest that the directive was honored in form and defeated in substance. The system did not resist reform deliberately. It metabolized reform automatically, converting demands for structural change into adjustments of procedure that preserved the existing structure. The Ottoman reformers were not incompetent. They were attempting to renovate a building using the building's own construction crew, who understood the old building perfectly and the new blueprint not at all.

COLLAPSE PRECEDES RECOGNITION

The most consistent feature of systemic decline is that the people inside the system are the last to recognize it. This is not because they are stupid, though that is the explanation that subsequent generations tend to prefer. It is because the information environment inside a declining system is structurally hostile to accurate assessment. The incentives favor optimism. The career path rewards loyalty. The institutional culture penalizes dissent. The data that would reveal decline is either not collected, not analyzed, not communicated, or not believed. And the cognitive biases that afflict all human decision-making—normalcy bias, confirmation bias, sunk cost reasoning, status quo preference—operate with particular force in institutional settings where the stakes of acknowledging failure are personal as well as professional. The official who acknowledges that the system is failing is acknowledging that the system they have served, the career they have built, and the identity they have constructed around that career are all implicated in the failure. The psychological cost of this acknowledgment is enormous, and the human capacity to avoid enormous psychological costs is, as a matter of empirical observation, very nearly unlimited.

The result is that decline becomes visible from the outside long before it is acknowledged on the inside. External observers—competitors, critics, historians, ordinary citizens who interact with the institution and experience its dysfunction firsthand—detect the deterioration while insiders are still describing the situation as challenging but manageable. The gap between external perception and internal narrative is itself a diagnostic indicator. When the institution's self-assessment and the public's assessment diverge dramatically, the divergence is almost always resolved in favor of the public's assessment, because the public is experiencing the institution's actual performance while the institution is experiencing its own narrative about its performance. The narrative can be maintained indefinitely. The performance cannot be faked indefinitely. Eventually, the gap between the two becomes impossible to explain away, and the recognition that the narrative was fiction arrives with a force proportional to the duration of the fiction. The longer the decline was denied, the more dramatic the recognition when denial becomes impossible.

The Soviet Union is the canonical modern example of collapse preceding recognition. Throughout the 1980s, the Soviet system was exhibiting every indicator of advanced decline: economic stagnation masked by unreliable statistics, military overcommitment in Afghanistan, administrative decay across every major institution, a credibility deficit so profound that Soviet citizens had developed an entire culture of ironic disbelief toward official communications, and an information environment so corrupted by institutional incentives that the leadership was making decisions based on data that bore minimal resemblance to reality. Western intelligence agencies, academic analysts, and ordinary observers noted these symptoms throughout the decade. The Soviet leadership did not, or if individuals within the leadership did, the institutional environment prevented their assessments from producing action. Gorbachev's reforms were an attempt to address the decline, but they were launched within a system that was more decayed than the reformers understood, and the reforms destabilized the structure faster than the structure could adapt. The collapse, when it came in 1991, was described as sudden. It was not sudden. That said, the collapse's specific timing and form were not predetermined by the structural decline. Recent scholarship (Stephen Kotkin, Stephen Cohen) emphasizes the contingency of the actual collapse—the decisions Gorbachev made, the alternatives available and not taken, the role of specific personalities at specific moments. The structural account explains why the Soviet system was vulnerable. It does not, on its own, explain why the vulnerability was resolved by dissolution rather than by reform, by 1991 rather than by 1995, or by Yeltsin rather than by someone else. The structural conditions opened a window. What came through the window was contingent. It was the visible manifestation of a decline that had been underway for at least two decades and that had been consistently underestimated by the people responsible for addressing it. The collapse was sudden only in the sense that the acknowledgment was sudden. The reality had arrived much earlier.

The pattern is not limited to states. Corporations exhibit the same lag between collapse and recognition with remarkable fidelity. Kodak's leadership understood, intellectually, that digital photography would displace film. The company invented the digital camera. But the institutional structure—the revenue streams, the manufacturing infrastructure, the organizational hierarchy, the workforce skills, the corporate identity—was built around film, and the recognition that film was dying could not translate into action because the action required dismantling the structure on which the institution depended. The decline was visible to external observers for years before Kodak's leadership acted on it, and by the time action was taken, the window for effective response had closed. The company filed for bankruptcy in 2012, roughly four decades after the first digital camera was built in its own laboratories. The gap between the availability of the information and the institutional capacity to act on it was the gap in which the decline occurred. The information was present. The recognition was not. And the recognition arrived too late because the institution's structure made timely recognition functionally impossible.

BlackBerry's trajectory followed an almost identical pattern at compressed speed. Research In Motion dominated the smartphone market in the mid-2000s with a product—secure email on mobile devices—that defined a category. The company's leadership understood that the iPhone represented a different approach to mobile computing. They had the information. What they could not do was abandon the institutional identity built around physical keyboards, enterprise security, and carrier relationships that had made BlackBerry dominant. The company's response to the iPhone was the BlackBerry Storm—a touchscreen device that preserved enough of the old paradigm to satisfy the existing institutional structure while attempting to compete in the new one. It satisfied neither. By 2013, BlackBerry's market share had collapsed from 50 percent to 3 percent. The decline took roughly six years from peak to irrelevance. The leadership had recognized the threat. The institution could not respond to it, because responding required becoming something other than BlackBerry, and institutions cannot commit suicide even when the alternative is death by irrelevance.

The lag between reality and recognition creates a specific and recurring tragedy: by the time decline is acknowledged, the options for addressing it have narrowed to the point where effective response is no longer possible. The time to reform is when the institution still has the resources, the credibility, and the institutional capacity to implement reform. This is also the time when the institution is least inclined to reform, because the symptoms of decline are mild enough to be explained away and the cost of reform is certain while the cost of inaction is speculative. The time when the institution is most inclined to reform—when the decline has become undeniable—is also the time when reform is least likely to succeed, because the resources have been depleted, the credibility has been spent, and the institutional capacity has decayed to the point where the institution cannot implement the reforms it has finally recognized as necessary. The window for effective reform opens early and closes before most institutions recognize it was open. The window is visible only in retrospect, which is useful for historians and useless for the people who needed to act while the window was available.

This is the structural tragedy of decline: the information needed to prevent it is available before the decline becomes irreversible, but the institutional capacity to process that information is degraded by the same forces that produce the decline. The system that most needs accurate self-assessment is the system least capable of producing it. The leadership that most needs to hear bad news is the leadership that has most thoroughly insulated itself from it. The institution that most needs to reform is the institution whose structure most effectively prevents reform. The contradictions are not accidental. They are structural—built into the logic of institutional self-preservation, which prioritizes the maintenance of the current arrangement over the adaptation that would ensure the arrangement's survival. The institution protects itself from the information that would save it, and the protection is what kills it. This is not irony. It is mechanics.

Some readers will object that this chapter is too deterministic—that decline is presented as inevitable, when in fact many systems of power have reformed themselves successfully and avoided the trajectory described here. The reform record is real, and the chapter does not deny it. Some systems do adapt. Some institutions do renew themselves. What the chapter argues is more limited: that the structural pressures producing decline are continuous, that the renewal effort must therefore be continuous, and that systems which assume their durability is automatic discover, usually too late, that it was not. Reform is possible. Reform is not the default. The default is the trajectory described in this chapter, which is why the systems that escape it are notable.

Decline is not the opposite of power. It is its autobiography, written in the language of accumulating dysfunction and diminishing returns. Every system of power examined in this book contains within it the seeds of its own decline—the overreach that follows success, the credibility erosion that follows hypocrisy, the administrative decay that follows institutional aging, and the recognition lag that prevents timely response. The seeds are not defects. They are features of the same structural dynamics that made the system powerful in the first place. The ambition that drives expansion is the ambition that produces overreach. The institutional self-preservation that ensures continuity is the institutional self-preservation that resists reform. The information control that maintains credibility is the information control that prevents accurate self-assessment. The strengths and the vulnerabilities are the same qualities, viewed from different points in the system's lifecycle.

17

HIDDEN POWER

"Resolve to serve no more, and you are at once freed."

Étienne de La Boétie
Discourse of Voluntary Servitude

THE MOST EFFECTIVE POWER is the power you do not notice. Chapter 2 established the framework: three faces of power, the third operating not by deciding outcomes or controlling agendas but by shaping the preferences through which people understand what is possible, desirable, and natural. The framework names the territory. This chapter maps it. The assumptions that determine which questions are asked and which are not, which options are considered and which are excluded before consideration begins, which arrangements are perceived as natural and which are perceived as political—these are the working surface of hidden power, and their invisibility is what makes them powerful. Power that can be identified can be challenged. Power that cannot be identified cannot.

The person navigating this landscape does not feel controlled. They feel free—free to choose among the options available to them, unaware that the most consequential exercise of power was the determination of which options would be available.

STRUCTURAL INFLUENCE

Structural influence is what happens when the design of a system produces outcomes that consistently favor certain groups over others without anyone in the system intending to produce those outcomes. The intention is irrelevant. The design is what matters. A city designed around automobile transportation does not intend to disadvantage people who cannot afford cars. It disadvantages them anyway, because the design of the transportation system determines who can access employment, education, healthcare, and social life, and the design favors drivers. The zoning code that separates residential areas by lot size does not intend to segregate by income. It segregates by income anyway, because lot size determines housing cost, and housing cost determines who can live where. The hiring process that relies on referral networks does not intend to exclude candidates from outside the existing network. It excludes them anyway, because the network reproduces itself by connecting people who are already connected, which means people who are not connected remain unconnected regardless of their qualifications.

The power of structural influence lies in its impersonality. There is no one to blame, no one to petition, no one to overthrow. The outcomes are produced by systems operating as designed, and the people operating the systems are following procedures that appear neutral, applying criteria that appear objective, and making decisions that appear fair when evaluated individually. The unfairness is visible only in the aggregate—in the statistical patterns that emerge when thousands of individually fair decisions produce collectively unfair outcomes. The loan officer who applies the same credit criteria to every applicant is being fair in the transactional sense. If the credit criteria systematically disadvantage applicants from neighborhoods that were historically redlined, the fairness of the individual transaction coexists with the unfairness of the systemic outcome, and the coexistence is what makes the problem so difficult to address. Fixing the system requires acknowledging that the system is broken, and acknowledging that the system is broken is difficult when every component of the system, examined individually, appears to be working correctly.

The labor market is structured in ways that compound initial advantages with a reliability that would be impressive if it were intentional. A person born into a family with professional connections has access to internships, mentorship, and career guidance that a person born into a family without those connections does not. The connected person enters the job market with a network that the unconnected person must build from scratch, and the time and energy spent building a network is time and energy not spent developing skills, producing work, or advancing in a career. The gap between the connected and the unconnected widens with each year, not because the connected person is more talented but because the structure of the market amplifies initial advantage. The connected person gets the interview because someone in the network recommended them. The unconnected person's application is processed through the standard channel, which means it is evaluated by an algorithm or a recruiter who spends an average of seven seconds on each resume. The process is formally equal. The outcomes are structurally unequal. The inequality is produced not by discrimination but by design, and the design is invisible to the people who benefit from it because the benefits feel like earned rewards rather than structural advantages.

Structural influence extends beyond economic systems into every domain of social life. The educational system that funds schools through local property taxes produces quality differences that track wealth differences, ensuring that children born into wealthy neighborhoods receive better education than children born into poor ones—not because anyone decided that wealthy children deserve better education but because the funding mechanism connects educational resources to local wealth. The healthcare system that ties insurance to employment produces coverage gaps for people in part-time, gig, or informal work—not because anyone decided that part-time workers deserve worse healthcare but because the system was designed around a mid-twentieth-century employment model that assumed full-time, permanent employment as the norm. The political system that allows unlimited campaign spending produces a government more responsive to the preferences of donors than to the preferences of voters—not because the system was designed to be undemocratic but because the interaction between free speech doctrine and campaign finance produces an influence market in which money amplifies voice. In each case, the structure produces the outcome, the outcome serves particular interests, and the interests are served without anyone having to advocate for them explicitly. The structure does the advocacy silently, continuously, and with a persistence that no lobbyist could match.

Agenda Control

The most important form of hidden power is not the power to win arguments but the power to determine which arguments occur. This is agenda control—the capacity to define what is discussed, what is decided, and what is excluded from discussion and decision before anyone notices the exclusion. A legislature that debates tax rates is exercising visible power. The forces that determined that the legislature would debate tax rates rather than the existence of taxation, the distribution of wealth, or the structure of property rights are exercising hidden power. The visible debate occurs within a framework that was established invisibly, and the framework constrains the debate more effectively than any participant within the debate could.

Political scientists Peter Bachrach and Morton Baratz identified this dynamic in the early 1960s as the "second face of power"—the face that operates not through decisions but through non-decisions, the systematic exclusion of issues from the political agenda. A community in which environmental pollution is never discussed is not a community that has decided pollution is acceptable. It is a community in which the forces that benefit from pollution have succeeded in keeping the issue off the agenda, which is a more effective form of control than winning a vote on pollution because winning a vote requires acknowledging that the issue exists and competing in a forum where the outcome is uncertain. Keeping the issue off the agenda eliminates the uncertainty entirely. The vote never occurs. The debate never happens. The status quo is preserved not by defending it but by preventing the conditions under which it would need to be defended.

Steven Lukes extended the framework a decade later, in Power: A Radical View (1974), by identifying a third face: power that operates not by keeping issues off the agenda but by shaping the preferences of the people affected so that issues never arise as grievances at all. The first face wins votes. The second face prevents votes. The third face produces a population that does not want the vote, would not know what to do with it, and considers the existing arrangement so natural that voting against it would feel like voting against the weather. This third face is what the rest of this chapter examines, and it is the most consequential of the three because it is the most invisible to the people exercising it and the people subject to it alike.

Agenda control operates through gatekeeping institutions—the organizations and individuals that determine what receives attention and what does not. Media organizations decide which stories are covered. Editorial boards decide which perspectives are represented. Legislative committees decide which bills reach the floor. Corporate boards decide which proposals are presented to shareholders. Academic journals decide which research is published. In each case, the gatekeeper's power is not the power to determine outcomes within the debate but the power to determine whether the debate occurs. A newspaper editor who decides that a particular issue is not newsworthy has exercised more power over that issue than any commentator who argues about it on the opinion page, because the editor's decision affects whether the public is aware of the issue at all. The commentator influences opinion. The editor influences awareness. Awareness precedes opinion, which means the editor's power precedes and constrains the commentator's.

The digital information environment has altered the mechanics of agenda control without eliminating it. Traditional gatekeepers—editors, producers, publishers—have lost their monopoly on determining what receives public attention. Social media platforms, search engines, and algorithmic content curation systems have created new pathways through which issues can reach public awareness without passing through traditional gatekeeping institutions. This has been celebrated as a democratization of agenda-setting, and in some respects it is. Issues that traditional media ignored—police violence, environmental injustice, corporate misconduct—have reached mass awareness through social media channels that bypassed editorial gatekeepers. But the new system has its own gatekeepers, and their power is in some respects greater than their predecessors' because it is less visible. The algorithm that determines which content appears in a user's feed is an agenda-setting mechanism of extraordinary power, affecting the awareness of billions of people, and it operates according to criteria—engagement optimization, advertising revenue, platform growth—that have nothing to do with the public interest and everything to do with the commercial interests of the platform. The traditional editor's agenda-setting power was visible, attributable, and subject to public criticism. The corporate version of this dynamic deserves brief attention here because Hidden Power is where its mechanics are most fully realized. The corporation that lobbies for a regulation is exercising visible power. The corporation that funds the think tank that produces the white paper that the regulator cites is exercising agenda-setting power. The corporation that funds the business schools that train the regulators—and the journalists who cover the regulators, and the consultants who advise the agencies the regulators staff—is exercising the third dimension. None of these activities looks like governance. Each of them is governance, and the cumulative effect is a regulatory environment in which the regulated entity has shaped, often imperceptibly, the conceptual frame within which its own oversight operates. The algorithm's agenda-setting power is invisible, unattributable, and subject to no accountability mechanism that a user can access. The gatekeeping has not been eliminated. It has been automated and hidden behind an interface that presents the curated result as a neutral reflection of the user's interests.

NORMALIZATION

The deepest form of hidden power is normalization—the process by which a particular arrangement comes to be perceived not as one option among many but as the way things are. An arrangement that is perceived as natural does not need to be defended because it does not appear to be a choice. It appears to be reality, and reality does not require justification. The Italian theorist Antonio Gramsci called this hegemony—a form of power that operates not through coercion but through the naturalization of particular arrangements as common sense. Hegemonic power is invisible power, exercised not by forcing compliance but by shaping the conceptual framework through which people understand their situation. The feudal peasant who accepted serfdom as the natural order of things was not consenting to serfdom in any meaningful sense. The peasant was living in a world where serfdom was the background condition of existence, as unremarkable as gravity. The modern worker who accepts that employers determine working conditions, that healthcare is tied to employment, and that housing costs consume a third of income is not consenting to these arrangements either. The worker is navigating a world in which these arrangements are the background conditions of economic life, and the effort of imagining alternatives exceeds the effort of continuing to participate.

Normalization operates through repetition, familiarity, and the absence of visible alternatives. An arrangement that has existed for a generation is an arrangement. An arrangement that has existed for three generations is tradition. An arrangement that has existed for ten generations is the natural order. The content of the arrangement has not changed. The perception of it has, and the perception determines whether the arrangement is subject to political challenge or accepted as a feature of the world that political challenge cannot reach. Slavery was normalized for millennia—perceived not as a political institution that could be abolished but as a natural condition that some people were born into. The normalization did not make slavery morally acceptable. It made slavery politically invisible—an arrangement so deeply embedded in the social fabric that questioning it required a conceptual revolution before it could produce a political one. The abolitionists' first task was not to organize a movement. It was to denormalize slavery—to make visible what had been invisible, to reframe a natural condition as a political choice, to transform background into foreground. The denormalization was arguably a greater achievement than the abolition itself, because abolition followed from denormalization as a logical consequence, while denormalization required challenging a perception so fundamental that most people had never questioned it.

The normalization of contemporary arrangements is no less comprehensive and no less invisible to the people living within them. The arrangement in which a small fraction of the population owns a large fraction of the wealth is perceived not as a political outcome that could be different but as an economic reality that reflects natural variation in talent, effort, and luck. The arrangement in which corporations are legally entitled to the same rights as persons is perceived not as a specific legal innovation that was contested when introduced but as a foundational feature of the economic system. The arrangement in which nations control borders and restrict movement is perceived not as a relatively recent development in human history—passports became standard only in the twentieth century—but as an obvious and permanent feature of international order. Each of these arrangements is contingent. Each could be different. Each serves specific interests. And each is perceived as natural by a population that has never known anything else, which is the definition of successful normalization.

Denormalization—the process of making a normalized arrangement visible as a choice rather than a condition—is the prerequisite for every significant structural reform in history. Before a system can be changed, it must be recognized as a system rather than as reality itself. This recognition is the most difficult and most consequential step in any reform process, because it requires people to see the water they swim in, and fish are famously bad at seeing water. The process typically begins at the margins—with people whose experience of the arrangement is sufficiently negative that the arrangement's naturalness is not convincing. The enslaved person did not need to be told that slavery was a political institution rather than a natural condition. The factory worker in nineteenth-century Manchester did not need to be told that the distribution of wealth was a political outcome rather than an economic inevitability. The person excluded from the arrangement's benefits has a perspective on the arrangement that the person included in its benefits does not, and that perspective is the raw material from which denormalization is constructed. The challenge is communicating that perspective to a population that has internalized the arrangement so thoroughly that the perspective sounds not like insight but like complaint. The normalized arrangement has a built-in defense against denormalization: the people who benefit from it experience it as normal, and any challenge to normality feels abnormal, disruptive, and vaguely threatening. The defense is not organized. It does not need to be. It operates automatically, through the psychological resistance that every person feels when asked to recognize that the world they have taken for granted is not given but constructed.

DEEP STRUCTURES OF ADVANTAGE

Some forms of hidden power persist across centuries, surviving revolutions, reforms, and comprehensive changes in the formal structure of governance. These are the deep structures—patterns of advantage so embedded in the social fabric that they reproduce themselves through mechanisms that operate independently of any specific institution, law, or policy. Land ownership patterns established in the colonial era persist in postcolonial societies long after independence. Wealth concentrations established during industrialization persist through economic transformations that have rendered the original industries obsolete. Educational advantages established when universities served exclusively elite populations persist through admissions processes that formally welcome all applicants while structurally favoring those whose preparation reflects advantages accumulated over generations. The formal barriers have been removed. The structural advantages remain, transmitted not through law but through culture, networks, capital, and the accumulated effects of compounding returns on initial advantage.

The mechanism of deep structural advantage is compounding. An advantage at time zero—better nutrition, better education, better connections, more capital—produces better outcomes at time one. Better outcomes at time one produce greater advantages at time two. Greater advantages at time two produce still better outcomes at time three. The compounding operates across generations through inheritance—not only of money, though money is the most visible vehicle, but of knowledge, networks, cultural capital, health outcomes, and the psychological confidence that comes from growing up in an environment where success is the expected outcome rather than the hoped-for exception. The child raised in a household with books, conversation about ideas, and the assumption that college is not a question but a destination arrives at the starting line of adult life with advantages that no amount of individual effort by a child raised without these things can replicate. The starting line is not the same starting line. It has never been the same starting line. And the fiction that it is—the meritocratic narrative that attributes outcomes to individual effort and talent—is itself a form of hidden power, because it makes the structural advantage invisible by attributing its effects to the personal qualities of the people who benefit from it.

The meritocratic narrative deserves particular attention because it is the primary mechanism through which deep structural advantage is hidden in contemporary societies. The narrative says: the system rewards talent and effort. The reality is: the system rewards talent and effort as they are expressed through structures that amplify some people's talent and effort and diminish others'. The talented child in a well-funded school with experienced teachers, small class sizes, and enrichment opportunities will develop their talent more fully than the equally talented child in an underfunded school with inexperienced teachers, large class sizes, and no enrichment opportunities. The first child's subsequent success will be attributed to talent. The second child's relative failure will be attributed to insufficient talent or effort. The structural difference will be invisible in the narrative, not because it is hidden deliberately but because the meritocratic narrative does not have a place for it. The narrative recognizes individuals. The structure operates on populations. The mismatch between the narrative's unit of analysis and the structure's unit of operation is what makes the structure invisible.

Deep structures are resistant to reform for reasons that go beyond the political power of those who benefit from them, though that power is considerable. They are resistant because they operate through so many simultaneous channels that addressing any single channel leaves the others intact. A reform that equalizes school funding addresses the educational channel but leaves the network channel, the cultural capital channel, the health channel, and the financial inheritance channel untouched. A reform that increases inheritance taxes addresses the financial channel but leaves every other channel intact. The deep structure is not a single mechanism. It is a system of interlocking mechanisms, each of which reinforces the others, and the resilience of the system derives from the redundancy of its components. Disable one mechanism, and the others compensate. The structure reproduces the advantage through whichever channels remain available, like water finding its way around an obstruction. The obstruction is real. The water's destination is unchanged. Comprehensive reform would require addressing all channels simultaneously, which would require a political mobilization of a scale and coherence that the structure itself makes unlikely, because the people who would need to support the reform are the people whose position within the structure makes the reform appear unnecessary. They are succeeding. The system must be working. The evidence of the system's failure is located in the experience of people whose voices the structure has not amplified sufficiently to be heard.

A familiar objection is that calling something "hidden power" risks conspiracism—that once power is defined as invisible, any outcome can be attributed to it without evidence, and the analysis becomes unfalsifiable. The risk is real, and it is why this chapter has tried to identify hidden power through specific mechanisms—agenda control, normalization, deep structural advantage—rather than through general claims about shadowy forces. Hidden power is not conspiracy. It is most often the unintended cumulative effect of many uncoordinated decisions made by people pursuing visible interests within structures whose deeper logic they do not see clearly themselves. The fish are not in on it. They are also not free of the water.

Hidden power is the most important form of power for the simple reason that it is the form that most people encounter most often without recognizing it as power at all. The visible forms—the state, the law, the military, the corporation—are experienced as power and can therefore be engaged, contested, and reformed. The hidden forms—the structures that determine which options are available, the agendas that determine which issues are discussed, the norms that determine which arrangements feel natural, the deep patterns that reproduce advantage across generations—are experienced not as power but as the way things are. Engaging them requires first recognizing them, and recognizing them requires a conceptual effort that the structures themselves make difficult because they have shaped the concepts through which recognition would occur. The fish must see the water. The challenge is that the water is also shaping the fish's eyes.

18

POWER AS CYCLE

*"All things from eternity are of like forms and come
round in a circle."*

Marcus Aurelius
Meditations, Book II (c. 170 CE)

H ISTORY DOES NOT REPEAT itself, but power does. The specific actors change. The specific institutions change. The specific technologies, ideologies, and justifications change. The structural pattern does not. Power concentrates. The concentration produces advantages that accelerate further concentration. The acceleration generates resistance. The resistance produces reform, revolution, or collapse. The resulting redistribution creates a new arrangement in which power begins to concentrate again, through different mechanisms, in different hands, toward the same structural outcome. The cycle is not a metaphor. It is the most consistent pattern in the political record, visible across every scale from the village to the empire, across every era from the Bronze Age to the present, and across every domain from military force to economic wealth to cultural authority. The fourteenth-century scholar Ibn Khaldun identified this pattern in his theory of dynastic cycles, observing that ruling groups rise through solidarity and cohesion, accumulate power and wealth, grow complacent in luxury, lose their cohesion, and are displaced by new groups whose solidarity is intact—a cycle he saw repeating across the Islamic world's political history. Cyclical theories of historical change have a long pedigree — Khaldun in the fourteenth century, Vico in the eighteenth, Spengler and Toynbee in the twentieth — and a notorious problem: they tend to over-pattern. Recent comparative-historical scholarship (Walter Scheidel, Jack Goldstone, Bryan Ward-Perkins) emphasizes contingency over cycle, arguing that what looks like a recurring pattern is often the artifact of selecting cases for their fit. This book's use of the cycle is meant to flag a real recurring tendency in how power formations rise and fall, not to claim that the cycle is law-like or that any given case must follow it. The cycle is a useful pattern. It is not a destiny. The pattern he identified in medieval dynasties operates in modern democracies, corporations, and institutions: concentration, decay, displacement, reconcentration. If there is a single structural truth about power that this book has been building toward, it is this: power is not a possession. It is a process, and the process is cyclical.

ACCUMULATION PATTERNS

Power accumulates the way capital does—slowly at first, then with increasing speed, through mechanisms that convert existing advantage into greater advantage with a reliability that resembles compound interest. The person with power attracts allies who want access to that power. The allies provide resources that increase the power. The increased power attracts more allies. The cycle is self-reinforcing and, in the absence of external constraint, self-accelerating. A lord who controls a fertile valley attracts farmers who need land. The farmers produce surplus. The surplus funds soldiers. The soldiers control more territory. The territory attracts more farmers. The lord who began with a valley ends with a kingdom, not because of any particular genius but because the dynamics of accumulation converted an initial advantage into a cascading series of advantages, each building on the one before.

The accumulation pattern operates through several distinct mechanisms that recur across every form of power examined in this book. The first is resource conversion—the ability to translate one form of power into another. Military power converts into territorial control, which converts into economic extraction, which converts into patronage, which converts into political loyalty, which converts into the institutional authority to deploy military power. The conversion chain is circular, which means a system that possesses any single form of power in sufficient quantity can, given time and competence, acquire every other form. This is why power concentrations in history tend toward comprehensiveness. The wealthy become politically powerful. The politically powerful become militarily dominant. The militarily dominant become culturally authoritative. Each conversion reinforces the others, producing a concentration that spans domains and becomes progressively more difficult to challenge because challenging it in any single domain leaves the other domains intact.

The second mechanism is barrier construction. As power accumulates, the holders of power invest in mechanisms that prevent others from accumulating similar power. The medieval guild restricted access to skilled trades. The modern professional licensing system restricts access to lucrative occupations. The incumbent corporation lobbies for regulations that raise the cost of market entry. The established political party designs electoral rules that disadvantage new parties. The university with a large endowment uses the returns to attract better faculty, which attracts better students, which attracts more donations, which increases the endowment—while universities without endowments compete for the remaining resources in an environment where the rules were established by the institutions that already had endowments. Barrier construction is not always deliberate. Sometimes it is the automatic consequence of scale—the large organization's mere existence creates barriers that smaller competitors cannot overcome. But deliberate or automatic, the effect is the same: accumulated power protects itself by raising the cost of competition, which ensures that the accumulation continues.

The third mechanism is narrative legitimation—the construction of stories that make the existing concentration of power appear natural, deserved, or inevitable. The feudal lord's power was legitimated by divine ordination. The industrial magnate's power was legitimated by the gospel of wealth. The modern billionaire's power is legitimated by the meritocratic narrative that attributes wealth to talent and effort rather than to the structural dynamics of accumulation that this chapter describes. Each narrative serves the same function: it converts a structural outcome into a moral story, which makes the concentration appear to be the result of virtue rather than of dynamics, and which makes challenging the concentration appear to be an attack on virtue rather than an adjustment of dynamics. The narrative does not cause the accumulation. It protects the accumulation by making it appear legitimate, which reduces the resistance it would otherwise generate. A population that believes the rich are rich because they deserve to be is less likely to demand redistribution than a population that believes the rich are rich because the system is designed to make them so. The narrative is the accumulation's immune system, and it is remarkably effective.

The accumulation pattern produces a characteristic shape that is visible across historical periods and institutional domains: a long period of gradual concentration followed by a short period of crisis, followed by a redistribution that initiates a new cycle. The Gilded Age concentrated wealth over decades and was followed by the Progressive Era and the New Deal, which redistributed it. The contemporary cycle is running, with familiar visibility, through the corporate form—the running example introduced in Chapter 2. The accumulation that produced the railroads, the steel trusts, the oil empires, and the auto giants is now producing the platform monopolies, and the resistance that broke the earlier concentrations is being assembled, with the same lag and the same difficulty, around the current ones. The vehicle has changed. The pattern has not. The postwar consensus distributed economic gains relatively broadly for a generation and was followed by a period of reconcentration beginning in the late twentieth century that has produced inequality levels comparable to those of the Gilded Age. The pattern is not identical in its details—the mechanisms differ, the timescales differ, the specific actors differ—but the shape is the same: accumulation, crisis, redistribution, accumulation. The shape suggests that concentration is the default trajectory and redistribution is the exceptional event, which has implications for anyone hoping to produce lasting equality: the effort must be continuous, because the forces producing concentration never stop operating.

RESISTANCE PHASES

Resistance to concentrated power follows a developmental sequence that is as predictable as the accumulation it opposes, though considerably less orderly. The sequence has identifiable phases, each with characteristic features, and the phase a resistance movement occupies at any given moment determines what it can achieve, what it cannot, and what structural conditions must change before it can advance to the next phase. Understanding the sequence does not guarantee success. It does explain why most resistance efforts stall where they stall and why the efforts that succeed tend to share certain characteristics that distinguish them from the efforts that do not.

The first phase is awareness—the recognition that the existing arrangement is a product of power rather than a condition of nature. This is the denormalization described in the previous chapter, and it is the necessary prerequisite for everything that follows. Before people can resist a power structure, they must perceive it as a power structure rather than as the way things are. The awareness phase is slow, uncertain, and typically initiated by people whose experience of the arrangement is sufficiently negative that its naturalness is unconvincing. The enslaved person who recognized slavery as a political institution. The worker who recognized poverty wages as a distributional choice. The colonized subject who recognized foreign domination as an arrangement that could be changed. In each case, the awareness preceded the resistance by years or decades, because awareness had to spread from the people who experienced the arrangement's costs to the broader population that experienced it as background. The spreading was not automatic. It required articulation—intellectuals, writers, speakers, organizers who could translate individual experience into collective understanding. Without articulation, awareness remained individual and politically inert. With articulation, it became the foundation for collective action.

The second phase is organization—the conversion of shared awareness into coordinated capacity. Awareness without organization is complaint. Organization without awareness is bureaucracy. The combination is a movement, and the movement's effectiveness depends on its ability to coordinate action across a population large enough to challenge the existing structure. Organization requires leadership, resources, communication infrastructure, and a strategic framework that translates diffuse grievance into specific demands and specific demands into achievable objectives. The phase is unglamorous. It consists largely of meetings, fundraising, network-building, and the slow construction of institutional capacity that can sustain coordinated action over time. Most resistance efforts that fail do so in this phase, not because their cause lacks merit but because the organizational challenge is enormous and the resources available to meet it are modest compared to the resources available to the structure being challenged. The existing structure has institutions, money, media access, and the inertia of the status quo. The resistance has conviction and numbers, which are powerful but require organization to deploy effectively.

The third phase is confrontation—the direct challenge to the existing structure through collective action. This is the phase that makes history: the march, the strike, the boycott, the revolution, the election that overturns the incumbent order. The confrontation is the most visible phase and the most misunderstood, because observers who focus on the confrontation miss the awareness and organization that made it possible. The march did not appear spontaneously. It was organized over months by people who had been building networks for years in communities where awareness had been developing for decades. The confrontation is the iceberg's tip, and the iceberg is the organizational and intellectual infrastructure beneath it. This is why attempts to replicate successful movements by replicating their confrontational tactics without replicating their organizational foundations consistently fail. The tactic without the foundation is theater. The foundation without the tactic is potential. The combination is power.

The fourth phase is institutionalization—the conversion of confrontational gains into durable structural change. This is the phase described in the chapter on popular power, and its importance cannot be overstated. The confrontation creates a window. The institutionalization determines what is built during the window. Movements that convert their gains into law, policy, institutional reform, and organizational permanence lock in achievements that survive the dissipation of the energy that produced them. Movements that do not—that spend the window on symbolic victories, internal debates, or escalating demands without securing institutional commitments—find that the window closes and the status quo reconstitutes itself around the temporary disruption. The existing structure is patient. It can wait out a confrontation that does not produce institutional change. It cannot undo a legal reform that has been implemented, staffed, and embedded in the administrative apparatus. The institutionalization phase is where resistance becomes durable, and it is the phase that most resistance movements are least prepared for, because the skills required—legislative drafting, administrative design, coalition management, bureaucratic navigation—are fundamentally different from the skills that powered the confrontation.

The fifth phase, which is less a phase than a permanent condition, is maintenance—the ongoing effort to preserve institutional gains against the forces of reconcentration that begin operating the moment the redistribution is achieved. The New Deal's regulatory framework was eroded over decades by the industries it regulated. The Voting Rights Act's protections were weakened by judicial decisions that narrowed its scope. Labor law's guarantees were undermined by legislative changes that shifted bargaining power from workers to employers. In each case, the institutional gains achieved during the confrontation and institutionalization phases were degraded by the same accumulation dynamics that had produced the original concentration. The maintenance phase requires permanent organizational capacity—ongoing advocacy, monitoring, and political engagement that sustains the reform after the emotional energy of the movement has dissipated. This is the least dramatic and most important phase, because it determines whether the cycle's redistribution phase produces lasting change or merely a temporary interruption in the accumulation pattern. Most redistributions are temporary. The ones that endure are the ones that built the organizational infrastructure to maintain them.

TRANSFER MECHANISMS

Power does not disappear when a system declines. It transfers—from one set of holders to another, from one institutional form to another, from one justificatory framework to another. The transfer is rarely clean. It is typically messy, contested, and incomplete, with elements of the old system persisting within the new in ways that shape the new system's character long after the old system has been officially declared dead. Understanding the mechanisms of transfer explains why new arrangements so often resemble old ones in ways that disappoint the people who fought for change and gratify the people who study structural continuity for a living.

The first transfer mechanism is institutional capture—the process by which the personnel and practices of the old system colonize the institutions of the new. A revolution that replaces a government but retains the civil service has replaced the faces at the top while leaving the operational structure intact. The civil servants who administered the old regime's policies will administer the new regime's policies using the same procedures, the same institutional culture, and the same habits of mind that were formed under the old regime. The new policies will be interpreted through the old framework, implemented through the old channels, and modified by the institutional inertia that the old regime created and the new regime inherited. The French Revolution replaced the monarchy with a republic and retained the administrative apparatus that had governed France under the monarchy. Napoleon formalized this retention, building his centralized state on the administrative foundations that the Bourbons had laid. The administrators changed their letterhead. Their methods did not change, because the methods were institutional rather than personal, embedded in procedures and organizational structures that survived the revolution as thoroughly as the buildings that housed them.

The second mechanism is wealth persistence. Political revolutions redistribute political authority. They rarely redistribute wealth with comparable thoroughness, because wealth is distributed across assets, relationships, and knowledge that are more difficult to confiscate than political offices. The aristocratic families of Europe lost their formal political privileges over the course of the nineteenth and twentieth centuries. Many retained their economic position—their land, their investments, their social networks, their cultural capital—and used that position to maintain influence within the new political arrangements that had formally displaced them. The British House of Lords was reformed, diminished, and stripped of most of its legislative power. The families that had populated it continued to exercise influence through economic power, social networks, and the educational institutions that trained the governing class. The political form changed. The social structure that had produced the political form persisted, adapted to the new environment, and continued to generate advantages for the same populations it had always served. The transfer was formally complete and structurally partial.

The third mechanism is conceptual inheritance—the persistence of the old system's categories, assumptions, and frameworks within the new system's thinking. A colonial power that withdraws politically leaves behind not only institutions and infrastructure but a conceptual framework—categories of identity, models of governance, economic assumptions, legal principles—that continues to shape how the postcolonial society understands itself and organizes its affairs. The newly independent nation operates within borders drawn by the colonial power, uses a legal system inherited from the colonial power, conducts commerce in a language established by the colonial power, and evaluates its economic performance against metrics developed in the colonial power's universities. The political transfer is complete. The conceptual transfer is ongoing, and it operates beneath the level of conscious recognition, which makes it more durable than any institution and more influential than any policy. The colony was governed by foreign administrators for decades. The colony's self-understanding was shaped by foreign concepts for generations, and the concepts persist long after the administrators have gone home.

The fourth mechanism is the most counterintuitive: legitimacy inheritance. The new system borrows legitimacy from the old, either by claiming continuity with it or by defining itself in opposition to it—which is itself a form of dependence, because the new system's identity is constructed in relation to the old rather than independently. The Chinese Communist Party derived its initial legitimacy from its opposition to the Nationalist government and the imperial system before it. The opposition defined the Party's identity, its narrative, and its justification for authority. Decades later, the Party began incorporating elements of traditional Chinese governance—Confucian values, historical continuity, civilizational identity—into its legitimacy narrative, borrowing from the very traditions it had initially defined itself against. The transfer of legitimacy was not a reversal. It was an evolution in which the new system gradually absorbed the old system's sources of authority because those sources retained their cultural resonance. The revolution rejected the old order's institutions. It could not reject the old order's cultural foundations without rejecting the culture itself, and no government that depends on popular support can reject the culture of the population it governs. The old order's legitimacy was recycled into the new order's vocabulary, and the recycling was so thorough that the boundary between the two orders became, over time, a matter of scholarly debate rather than lived experience.

The political sociologist Theda Skocpol, in States and Social Revolutions, demonstrated that successful revolutions—the French, Russian, and Chinese cases she examined—share a structural pattern that has nothing to do with the ideologies the revolutions advanced. They occur when an existing state has been weakened by external pressure, the dominant class has fragmented or lost confidence, and a peasant population has the autonomy to organize collective action outside the state's control. When all three conditions hold, revolution becomes possible. When any one is absent, revolutionary energy produces unrest but not transformation. The implication for the cycle described in this chapter is that resistance succeeds in producing structural change only under narrow conditions, and that those conditions are mostly produced by forces other than the resistance movement itself. The revolution does not cause the conditions; the conditions produce the opening into which a revolutionary movement can step. This is why the same ideological commitment, in different structural conditions, produces wildly different outcomes—and why the people inside a revolution cannot tell, until afterward, whether they are riding a structural opening or staging a doomed protest. The cycle is real. The conditions under which the cycle produces change rather than merely repetition are real and narrow.

ADAPTATION OVER REPLACEMENT

The most important observation about the power cycle is also the most disillusioning: genuine replacement is rare. What appears to be replacement—revolution, regime change, institutional overhaul—is more often adaptation, the existing structure of power modifying its form while preserving its substance. The faces change. The rhetoric changes. The institutional names change. The underlying distribution of advantage changes less than any of these, because the forces that produced the distribution are structural rather than personal, and structural forces survive personnel changes with the same indifference that a river survives changes in the boats on its surface. The river's current was not produced by the boats. Removing the boats does not alter the current.

The pattern is visible at every scale. The French Revolution abolished the aristocracy and produced, within a generation, a new elite whose composition was modestly different from the old and whose structural position—at the top of a centralized, hierarchical system that extracted surplus from a large population for the benefit of a small one—was identical. The Russian Revolution abolished the bourgeoisie and produced, within a generation, a nomenklatura whose privileges—access to scarce goods, superior housing, preferential education, foreign travel—mirrored the privileges of the class it had replaced with eerie precision. The decolonization movements of the mid-twentieth century replaced colonial administrators with national leaders and frequently preserved the economic structures—export-oriented agriculture, extractive industries, dependency on former colonial markets—that the colonial system had established. In each case, the political transformation was genuine. The structural transformation was partial at best, because the structural forces that had produced the old arrangement continued to operate under the new one, producing outcomes that converged toward the same distributional patterns through different institutional mechanisms.

This convergence is not evidence that change is impossible. It is evidence that change is harder than changing the people in charge. Structural change requires changing the rules, the incentives, the institutional designs, and the resource distributions that produce outcomes—not just once, during the revolutionary moment, but continuously, against the forces of reconcentration that begin operating the instant the redistribution is achieved. The societies that have produced the most durable structural change—the Scandinavian social democracies are the most commonly cited example—did so not through revolution but through sustained institutional reform maintained over decades by organized political constituencies that understood the reform as a permanent project rather than an accomplished fact. Sweden's Rehn-Meidner model, for instance, combined centralized wage bargaining, active labor market policies, and progressive taxation—implemented in the 1950s and maintained through the sustained power of organized labor and social democratic parties that treated these reforms not as achievements to celebrate but as arrangements to defend. The institutional mechanisms included strong union density (exceeding 70 percent of the workforce), corporatist bargaining structures that gave labor formal power in economic decision-making, and welfare state provisions funded by tax rates that remained high even as other developed nations reduced theirs. The result was not permanent—Sweden's model has eroded since the 1990s—but it demonstrates that decades of structural difference are possible when institutional reforms are continuously defended rather than simply enacted. These decades matter—not merely as data points in a structural analysis but as generations of people who lived without the grinding poverty their grandparents endured, who sent their children to university on scholarships rather than to factories at fourteen, who retired with pensions rather than dying at their workstations. The structural improvements were also reductions in suffering, and the suffering reduced was real. The reform was never complete. It was continuous, adaptive, and defended by organizations whose existence was predicated on maintaining it. The result was not equality—no society has achieved equality—but a distribution significantly different from what the unregulated dynamics of accumulation would have produced, sustained over a period long enough to demonstrate that structural change is possible, difficult, and never finished.

The tendency toward adaptation rather than replacement has implications for how we understand the power cycle itself. The cycle is not a circle that returns to its starting point. It is a spiral—each iteration resembling the previous one in structure while differing in specifics. The feudal lord and the industrial magnate and the technology billionaire occupy structurally analogous positions—at the top of systems that concentrate resources and convert those resources into political, cultural, and social influence—but the systems themselves are different in ways that matter. The technology billionaire's workers are not serfs. The industrial magnate's employees were not chattel. The conditions at each stage of the spiral are better, by most measures, than the conditions at the previous stage, not because the power dynamics have changed but because the resistance at each stage produced institutional reforms that improved the terms on which power was exercised even if it did not fundamentally alter the distribution. The spiral moves. It does not move as far as the revolutionaries hoped. It moves farther than the cynics expected. It moves because the cycle includes resistance as a structural feature, and resistance, even when it falls short of its aspirations, produces incremental improvements that accumulate across iterations.

The recognition that power operates cyclically is uncomfortable because it denies the possibility of a permanent solution. There is no institutional design, no constitutional arrangement, no revolutionary achievement that eliminates the dynamics of accumulation permanently. Every solution is temporary—effective for a period, eroded by the forces it was designed to constrain, and eventually replaced by a new solution that addresses the current iteration's specific pathologies while containing within it the seeds of the next iteration's. This is not a failure of human ingenuity. It is a feature of human organization, as fundamental as the tendency of entropy to increase in closed systems. The response to entropy is not despair. It is maintenance—the continuous input of energy required to sustain order against the forces that degrade it. The response to the power cycle is the same: not the pursuit of a permanent solution but the commitment to continuous, adaptive, institutional maintenance that keeps the cycle's worst excesses in check without pretending that the excesses can be eliminated once and for all. The vigilance is the solution. The moment it stops, the cycle resumes.

The cyclical reading invites a serious objection: that emphasizing recurrence underplays genuine progress, and that the conditions of life under a twenty-first-century democracy are sufficiently better than those of a medieval kingdom that the language of "cycle" obscures more than it reveals. The objection is correct about progress and wrong about the cycle. Progress is real. The cycle is also real. Each iteration occurs at a higher level than the one before, because the resistance phase produces reforms that improve the terms on which power is exercised even when it does not redistribute power itself. The technology billionaire's workers are not serfs. The improvement is durable, and it was produced by exactly the cycle this chapter describes—not in spite of it.

Power is a cycle, not a story. Stories have endings. Cycles do not. The accumulation that feels permanent is temporary. The redistribution that feels transformative is partial. The new arrangement that feels unprecedented contains more of the old than its architects recognize. These observations are not grounds for resignation. They are grounds for realism—the kind of realism that understands the scale of the challenge, the limits of any single intervention, and the necessity of sustained effort over timescales that exceed individual careers, individual movements, and individual lifetimes. The people who built the institutions that constrain power most effectively were not the people who enjoyed the benefits of those institutions. They built for successors they would never meet, against forces they could not permanently defeat, with the understanding that the work would never be finished. The work is still not finished. It will not be. The value of the work is not diminished by its incompleteness. It is defined by it.

The final chapter synthesizes—identifying the structural constants beneath historical variation, the principles that recur across every form of power examined here, and their implications for understanding how power works, how it's exercised, how it's resisted, and why resistance is neither futile nor final.

CLOSING REFLECTIONS

*"Of making many books there is no end; and much study
is a weariness of the flesh."*

Ecclesiastes 12:12 (KJV)

THIS BOOK BEGAN WITH a definition and ends without a conclusion, because power does not conclude. It persists. It transforms. It migrates from one vessel to another with a fluidity that makes every attempt to contain it a temporary success and every attempt to eliminate it a permanent failure. Eighteen chapters have examined power in its various forms—sacred and secular, military and economic, institutional and popular, visible and hidden, accumulating and declining—and the examination has produced not a theory but an observation, which is more honest and possibly more useful. The observation is this: power is a structural feature of human organization, as fundamental as language and as inescapable as gravity. It can be distributed more broadly or more narrowly, exercised more brutally or more humanely, legitimated more honestly or more deceptively. It cannot be abolished. Every attempt to abolish it has produced a new distribution that its architects did not intend and its beneficiaries did not anticipate.

What follows is not a summary. The chapters speak for themselves, and the reader who has arrived at this point does not need the book recited back to them in compressed form. What follows is a synthesis and then a demonstration—first, the structural constants that recur across every form of power examined in this book, and second, those constants applied to a power system forming in real time. Three observations have emerged with sufficient consistency to warrant elevation from observation to something approaching principle. Power rarely disappears; it transforms. Structures absorb shocks that appear to destroy them. And legitimacy cycles faster than the institutions it sustains. These are not laws in the scientific sense. They are patterns in the structural sense—regularities so consistent across different contexts that ignoring them requires more effort than acknowledging them.

The first principle: power does not disappear when the system that exercises it collapses. It relocates. The mechanism has been visible throughout this book—the Roman administrative apparatus migrating into the Catholic Church, the French centralized state surviving the monarchy's abolition, the colonial economic structures persisting through decolonization. The pattern is structural, not conspiratorial. Power exists because coordination requires it, and when one arrangement for coordinating collapses, the need for coordination does not collapse with it. The vacuum is filled by whoever inherits the resources, expertise, and institutional knowledge of the old system. Destruction produces debris. Debris gets reassembled. Reshaping is slower and more durable than destruction, which is why the societies that have altered power's distribution most successfully did so through sustained institutional redesign rather than revolutionary demolition.

The second principle: structures are more resilient than they appear. Shocks that seem to destroy them more often deform them temporarily before they return to something resembling their previous configuration. This is not because structures are designed for resilience—though some are—but because they are embedded in networks of relationships, dependencies, and interests that pull the deformed structure back toward its prior shape. Revolutions produce genuine change. They also produce continuities. The French Revolution abolished feudal privilege and retained the centralized state. American democracy established self-governance and retained economic hierarchy. Decolonization produced sovereign nations and preserved extractive relationships. The shock bends the structure. The structure absorbs the shock and settles into a new configuration that incorporates elements of both the old arrangement and the new principles—which is neither what the old regime wanted nor what the revolutionaries planned.

The third principle: legitimacy cycles at a different speed than institutions. Institutions accumulate over decades and persist for centuries. Legitimacy can be established in a generation and destroyed in a news cycle. The mismatch is the source of most political instability, because institutions routinely outlive the beliefs that justified them. The Catholic

Church's institutional structures had been built over a millennium. Its legitimacy was undermined by the printing press in decades. The Soviet Union's institutional apparatus was formidable. Its legitimacy had eroded to nonexistence before the structures collapsed. Contemporary democratic institutions remain structurally intact while public trust declines at rates the institutions have not matched with reform. The institution functions. The belief that the function is adequate erodes. The gap between institutional speed and legitimacy speed produces the structurally sound but legitimacy-depleted system—functional, procedurally correct, and operating on borrowed authority that compounds with interest.

These principles are not speculative. They are observable, documented across millennia, and they operate whether anyone acknowledges them or not. The question is not whether they are true. The question is what they explain. The answer is: more than most people find comfortable. Which brings us to the demonstration.

PLATFORM POWER: THE CYCLE IN REAL TIME

The concentration of power in digital platforms over the past fifteen years is not an anomaly. It is the accumulation pattern described in this book, operating at a speed that history rarely permits us to observe in real time. What took the Roman Church centuries and the British Empire decades, the platform companies accomplished in a generation. The speed is new. The mechanism is ancient. And because the mechanism is still operating—because we are living inside the cycle rather than studying it in retrospect—the platform case provides something the historical examples cannot: a demonstration of how the framework works when applied to a system whose outcome is not yet determined.

ACCUMULATION

The accumulation began the way it always does with an advantage that attracted resources that increased the advantage. Facebook had users. Users attracted more users—the network effect, which is the digital equivalent of the lord's fertile valley attracting farmers. The farmers produced surplus. The users produced data. The surplus funded soldiers. The data funded infrastructure—servers, engineers, acquisitions. The soldiers controlled more territory. The infrastructure controlled more of the social graph, the map of human relationships that determines who sees what, who connects with whom, and whose voice reaches an audience. The initial advantage—being first to scale in social networking—converted into a cascading series of advantages, each building on the one before, through the same resource conversion mechanism that has operated in every domain of power this book has examined.

The conversion chain is visible if you know what to look for. User data converts into market dominance—advertising revenue, in the platform model, but the currency is attention, and attention is power in an information economy the same way land was power in an agrarian one. Market dominance converts into political influence. The platform that mediates how billions of people communicate, access information, and form opinions is not a neutral infrastructure. It is a political actor, whether it intended to be one or not, and the recognition of this fact occurred remarkably quickly once the 2016 election made the influence visible. Political influence converts into cultural authority—the platform becomes the arbiter of acceptable speech, the moderator of public discourse, the institution that decides what constitutes misinformation and who gets to participate in the conversation. Cultural authority converts back into user retention and data accumulation, completing the circle. The conversion chain is exactly what this book described in the abstract. The platform economy made it concrete.

Barrier construction followed accumulation the way it always does. Facebook acquired Instagram when Instagram had thirteen employees and no revenue, paying one billion dollars for a company that had no obvious value except as a potential competitor. The acquisition was not about Instagram's current capabilities. It was about preventing Instagram from becoming what Facebook already was—a barrier constructed not against a present threat but against a future one. Google acquired YouTube. Amazon acquired competitors in e-commerce, cloud infrastructure, and logistics. The pattern is so consistent that antitrust regulators eventually noticed, though they noticed decades after the barriers had been constructed and the market structure had calcified around them. The acquisitions were not consolidation. They were barrier construction through the elimination of potential competition, which is considerably more effective than competing with rivals after they have scaled.

The narrative legitimation was, in retrospect, almost too obvious to require documentation. Facebook was connecting people. Google was organizing the world's information. Amazon was obsessed with the customer. The narratives were not false. They were incomplete, emphasizing the consumer benefit while eliding the power concentration, the same way the feudal lord's narrative emphasized protection while eliding extraction. The meritocratic founder myth operated at full strength: the college dropout in the dorm room, the garage startup, the brilliant engineer solving problems through code rather than through the traditional power structures that gatekeepers controlled. The myth was compelling because it contained truth. It was also legitimation, converting a structural outcome—market dominance through network effects and capital access—into a moral story about talent, vision, and disruption. The narrative protected the accumulation by making it appear to be the result of virtue rather than dynamics, which reduced the resistance the accumulation would otherwise have generated. When the resistance eventually came, the narrative was the first line of defense. We built this. We earned this. The users chose us. The choice was real within constraints the users did not set, which is the definition of manufactured consent, and the manufacturing was so effective that most of the governed did not recognize they were being governed until the governance became visible.

TRANSFORMATION

The transformation from neutral platform to political actor occurred in public, which is unusual. Most power transformations happen slowly enough that no one can identify the moment when the merchant became a lord or the lord became a king. The platform transformation was compressed into a span of years short enough that we can date it with reasonable precision. The Cambridge Analytica scandal in 2018 was not the cause of the transformation. It was the moment when the transformation became undeniable—when the fiction that platforms were neutral infrastructure distributing content according to user preference collided with the reality that platforms were curating information environments that shaped elections, and the collision was public, well-documented, and impossible to dismiss.

The transformation had been underway for years before it became visible. Facebook was making algorithmic decisions about what content to surface, what to suppress, and how to weight engagement signals that favored outrage over accuracy. Google was making decisions about search results, autocomplete suggestions, and knowledge panel content that shaped what information billions of people encountered when they asked questions. YouTube was making recommendations that determined what people watched after they finished watching what they had chosen to watch, and the recommendation algorithm had learned that extreme content kept people watching longer, so extreme content was what the algorithm recommended, which was not a political choice in the sense that the engineers were advancing an ideology, but it was a political outcome in the sense that it amplified certain voices, certain perspectives, and certain narratives over others. The platforms were governing—exercising authority over the information environment in ways that shaped public discourse, political behavior, and social norms—long before they admitted they were governing or anyone insisted they were responsible for the outcomes the governance produced.

The admission, when it came, was partial and defensive. Platforms were not publishers, they insisted, because publishers exercised editorial judgment and platforms merely provided infrastructure. The distinction was legally useful and structurally absurd. An algorithm that determines what content appears in a feed, how prominently it appears, and to whom it appears is exercising editorial judgment. The judgment is automated. The effects are editorial. And the insistence that automation absolved the platform of responsibility was the twenty-first-century equivalent of the feudal lord insisting that because the peasants had voluntarily chosen to farm his land, the relationship was one of mutual benefit rather than extraction. The relationship was both, which is how power always works when it has been competently structured.

By 2020, the transformation was complete. Platforms were deciding what constituted election misinformation and removing it. Platforms were banning heads of state from their services based on content moderation policies the platforms had written. Platforms were negotiating with governments about how to handle speech during public health emergencies, international conflicts, and domestic unrest. The platforms had become what the book's earlier chapters described: institutions exercising coordinated authority over large populations, operating according to rules they set, accountable to no one but themselves, and claiming legitimacy based on user consent that was manufactured through terms of service no user read and alternatives no user could practically access. The power had not been seized. It had accumulated through dynamics the platforms had not fully controlled and had eventually recognized they possessed. The transformation was complete. The question was whether the legitimacy would follow.

RESILIENCE

The platform system has absorbed shocks that appeared, at the moment of impact, to threaten its existence. Cambridge Analytica was supposed to be a reckoning. Congressional hearings were convened. Regulatory investigations were launched. Facebook's stock price dropped. Public trust collapsed. And then nothing structural changed. Facebook introduced privacy controls that gave users the appearance of choice while preserving Facebook's data collection apparatus. The company renamed itself Meta, which was not a strategic repositioning but a branding exercise designed to distance the corporate entity from the reputational damage the product had sustained. The shock was real. The structure absorbed it.

The pattern repeated with each subsequent crisis. Antitrust investigations in the United States and Europe produced years of legal proceedings, hundreds of millions of dollars in fines, and exactly zero divestitures. The investigations documented the market dominance. They did not alter it. Apple's iOS privacy changes in 2021 were described as existential threats to the advertising-based business model. Facebook's revenue dipped for a quarter and then resumed growing. The shock was absorbed through adaptation—targeting methods changed, tracking mechanisms evolved, and the fundamental structure of attention-based advertising persisted in modified form. TikTok bans were threatened, debated, and deferred. Each threat produced stock volatility and strategic adjustments. None produced structural change.

The resilience is not mysterious. It is the same resilience this book has documented in every other power structure examined across eighteen chapters. The platforms are embedded in the daily operations of billions of lives. They are infrastructure now—the way people communicate, organize, access information, and navigate the social world. You cannot replace infrastructure while it is in use, and the people using it cannot stop using it long enough for a replacement to be built, so they continue using it while complaining about it, which is the definition of acquiescence, and acquiescence is what this book has identified as the operating system of governance most of the time. The platforms did not plan to become infrastructure. They became infrastructure by being useful, and once they were infrastructure, they became very difficult to dismantle, because dismantling infrastructure disrupts the lives of everyone who depends on it. The users who claim they would leave if there were an alternative are correct that they would leave if there were an alternative. They are incorrect that an alternative can be built while they are still using the existing system, because the existing system's value increases with the number of users, which means every user who stays makes it harder for the alternative to compete, which means the users are trapped by a collective action problem they cannot solve individually. The platforms did not trap them deliberately. The network effect trapped them structurally, and the platforms benefited from a dynamic they did not create but thoroughly understood how to exploit.

The institutional response to platform power has followed the pattern this book described in the chapter on institutional absorption of dissent. Regulate the platforms. The platforms hire the regulators. Constrain their data collection. The platforms modify their data collection in ways that comply with the letter of the regulation while preserving its substance. Require algorithmic transparency. The platforms release reports that describe their algorithms in language too technical for the public and too vague for competitors. The pattern is not unique to platforms. It is the pattern of institutional resilience operating in a digital context, and it works because the platforms have resources the regulators do not, expertise the regulators cannot match, and the capacity to operate at a speed that regulatory institutions—designed for a slower century—cannot follow. The regulation is genuine. The compliance is genuine. And the structure that the regulation was designed to constrain continues operating in ways that the drafters of the regulation did not anticipate and the enforcers of the regulation cannot prevent, because the institution being regulated understands its own operations better than the institution doing the regulating, and understanding is advantage.

LEGITIMACY

The legitimacy crisis is where the platform case most clearly demonstrates the principle this book identified as the source of political instability: legitimacy cycles faster than institutions. The platforms' institutional structures are intact. Their legitimacy is not. Public trust in tech companies has declined precipitously since 2016. The decline is measurable, consistent across demographics, and driven by a gap between what the platforms promised and what they delivered. They promised connection. They delivered filter bubbles. They promised democratized information. They delivered algorithmic curation that amplified outrage because outrage drove engagement and engagement drove revenue. They promised community. They delivered surveillance capitalism, which is not a polemic but a description of a business model in which the product is the user's attention and behavior, and the customer is the advertiser who pays to influence both.

The loss of legitimacy has not produced the loss of users, which is the mismatch this chapter has been describing. People continue using platforms they do not trust because the platforms are infrastructure, and you do not stop using infrastructure because you disapprove of the people who built it. You use the roads even if you dislike the government. You use the platforms even if you dislike the platforms. The usage is not endorsement. It is acquiescence, and acquiescence sustains institutional power long after legitimacy has eroded, because acquiescence is cheaper than the cost of exit and easier than the cost of organizing collective action to demand reform. The platforms understand this. Their entire business model depends on it. The friction of leaving—losing your social graph, your content history, your established presence—is high enough that most users stay despite their dissatisfaction, and the platforms have designed the friction deliberately, which is not conspiracy but strategy. Make it easy to join. Make it costly to leave. The asymmetry is structural, and the structure produces lock-in, and lock-in is power.

The legitimacy deficit is compounding. Each scandal lowers the baseline of trust from which the next scandal is evaluated. Each regulatory failure reinforces the perception that the platforms are too powerful to be constrained. Each content moderation controversy—and there are many, because content moderation at scale is impossible to execute in ways that satisfy everyone—reinforces the belief that the platforms are making political choices disguised as neutral policies. The platforms are making political choices. The disguise is wearing thin. And the public, having recognized that the platforms govern, is beginning to ask the question that every governing institution eventually faces: by what right? The platforms' answer—user consent, market choice, innovation-driven meritocracy—is the same answer that every governing institution provides when its legitimacy is challenged. The answer is not false. It is incomplete, eliding the structural dynamics that produced the concentration and emphasizing the voluntary elements of a relationship that is voluntary within constraints that were not chosen. The answer satisfies people who benefit from the arrangement. It does not satisfy people who recognize that the benefits are asymmetric and the constraints are invisible until you try to violate them.

The trajectory is uncertain because we are living inside it, but the structural position is clear. The platforms are legitimacy-depleted but structurally intact, operating on borrowed authority that diminishes with each cycle. The borrowing can continue for years—possibly decades, because institutions are durable and users are captive. But the interest compounds, and the bill eventually comes due, because systems that govern through manufactured consent rather than genuine accountability produce outcomes that the governed eventually recognize as serving interests other than their own. The recognition does not produce collapse. It produces instability—a condition where the institution's structural resilience and its legitimacy deficit coexist in tension that can be sustained but not indefinitely. How the tension resolves depends on variables this book cannot predict, because they are contingent on choices that have not yet been made. What can be identified is the condition: the platform system is intact, the belief in its justification is eroding, and the gap between the two is widening.

RESISTANCE

The resistance to platform power is following the developmental sequence this book described as predictable. Awareness came first—the recognition, post-2016, that platforms were not neutral infrastructure but power systems that shaped outcomes. The recognition spread from activists and academics to journalists and policymakers and eventually to the public, though the public's recognition is uneven and the platforms' narrative legitimation continues to contest it. Awareness was necessary but insufficient, which is the pattern.

Organization followed awareness, though less effectively than the accumulation pattern would predict. Antitrust coalitions formed. Worker organizing began—warehouse workers striking over conditions, content moderators speaking publicly about psychological trauma, engineers objecting internally to projects they considered unethical. The organization was real. It was also fragmented, under-resourced, and operating against institutions with legal teams that numbered in the hundreds, lobbying budgets that numbered in the tens of millions, and the capacity to absorb, deflect, or outlast most challenges through a combination of strategic concessions and procedural delay. The existing structure has institutions, money, and inertia. The resistance has conviction and numbers, which are powerful but require organization to deploy, and the organization phase is where most resistance efforts stall. Platform resistance has not stalled. It has also not produced the coordinated capacity required to challenge the structure effectively.

Confrontation has occurred in the form of regulatory action, Congressional hearings, and high-profile lawsuits. The confrontation is visible, well-publicized, and less effective than it appears, because the confrontation is operating through institutions designed for a previous era. Antitrust law was designed to address industrial monopolies that competed on price. Platforms compete on features, often offering services for free while extracting value through data and attention. The law is being adapted, slowly, to address this mismatch, but the adaptation is occurring at institutional speed while the platforms operate at market speed, which means the platforms adapt to new constraints faster than the constraints can be updated to address the adaptation. The confrontation is genuine. The outcome is indeterminate.

Institutionalization—the conversion of confrontational gains into durable structural change—has barely begun. Some reforms have been enacted. The EU's Digital Markets Act imposes interoperability requirements and restricts certain practices. State-level privacy laws in the United States provide modest protections. The reforms are real. They are also narrow, difficult to enforce, and operating in an environment where the platforms have more expertise in compliance engineering than regulators have in oversight. Institutionalization requires embedding reforms in administrative apparatus that can sustain them after the political energy that produced them dissipates. The apparatus is being built. It is not yet built, and the platforms are operating as though it will not be, which is a reasonable bet given the historical pattern of institutional lag documented throughout this book.

Maintenance has not arrived, because there is not yet a stable institutional achievement to maintain. The question is whether the resistance will reach that phase before the window closes—before the political energy dissipates, the regulatory attention shifts, and the platforms successfully navigate through the current scrutiny into a new equilibrium in which they are regulated, constrained, and fundamentally unchanged in their structural position. The precedent suggests they will succeed, because the precedent is that structures absorb shocks, and the platform shock absorption has been thorough so far. But precedent is not destiny, and the outcome depends on choices that have not yet been made by people who are reading analyses like this one and deciding whether to believe that structural resilience is permanent or merely durable.

PATTERN RECOGNITION

The platform case demonstrates what this book has been arguing across eighteen chapters and several millennia: the mechanisms are consistent. The speed changes. The technology changes. The specific actors change. The accumulation pattern, the resilience of structures, the cycle speed of legitimacy, the phases of resistance—these do not change, because they are not features of specific systems but properties of coordination itself. Power concentrates because coordination creates advantages that compound. Structures persist because they are embedded in dependencies that pull them back toward equilibrium. Legitimacy cycles quickly because belief is faster than institutions. Resistance follows predictable phases because the phases reflect the structural requirements of converting individual awareness into collective action and collective action into institutional change.

The platform system is not an exception. It is an iteration. The feudal lord, the industrial magnate, and the platform founder occupy structurally analogous positions—at the top of systems that concentrate resources and convert those resources into influence that spans domains. The systems differ in ways that matter. The workers are not serfs. The users are not peasants. The conditions are better, which is progress. The dynamics are the same, which is structure. And the recognition that the dynamics are the same is what allows us to predict, with reasonable confidence, that the platform system will follow the same trajectory as its predecessors: accumulation until the concentration generates resistance, resistance until it produces partial redistribution, redistribution until the forces of reconcentration begin operating again. The cycle continues because the forces that drive it are permanent features of human organization rather than defects that can be engineered away.

The practical implication is that the question is not whether platform power will be constrained. The question is how thoroughly, how durably, and at what cost. Thorough constraint requires structural reform—breaking up the companies, requiring interoperability, democratizing governance, or replacing the advertising model with something less extractive. Durable constraint requires permanent organizational capacity to maintain the reform against erosion. The cost is the disruption to the billions of people who depend on the platforms and the economic reorganization required to build alternatives. The likelihood that the constraint will be thorough, durable, and achieved at acceptable cost is lower than optimists hope and higher than cynics expect, which is the pattern for every significant structural reform this book has examined. The platforms will not be destroyed. They will be regulated, modified, and eventually displaced by something new that will accumulate power through mechanisms we are currently describing as decentralization or democratization or user ownership, and which will, in time, produce concentrations that resemble the concentrations we are currently trying to constrain. The cycle is not a failure. It is a feature. And understanding it is the prerequisite for engaging with it effectively rather than repeatedly.

The platform landscape has not stood still since this case was first developed. TikTok operates a substantially different model from the Western platforms — its governance is state-adjacent rather than corporate-autonomous, and the structural relationship between platform and state takes a form the Western cases have not produced. X, under different ownership since 2022, demonstrates a third pattern: idiosyncratic individual control over a platform that previously exhibited the institutional-corporate dynamics described above. And the rise of generative-AI platforms — OpenAI, Anthropic, Google's AI products, Meta's open-weight releases — is reshaping the platform layer in real time, in ways that the social-network model does not capture. None of these developments invalidates the structural framework. Each of them is the framework operating on different inputs. The accumulation, the legitimacy production, the resistance, the regulatory response — they recur, with different actors and different specific dynamics, in every variant. The platform case is not Facebook. The platform case is the structural pattern that Facebook exemplified for a decade and that subsequent platforms are exemplifying in updated form. The cycle continues, faster than the regulatory imagination can keep up.

Closing

A candid note about what kind of book this has been. The structural view is not a neutral stance. It is a particular politics, and a serious reader is owed the acknowledgment. To a conservative temperament, the structural account confirms that grand reform projects are difficult and that the existing arrangement is the product of durable forces; this can be read as quietism, and the reading is not entirely wrong. To a progressive temperament, the structural account can read as despair-inducing — if the cycle continues regardless of effort, what is the work for? To a radical temperament, the structural account looks like ideology in the bad sense, naturalizing the very conditions that radical politics is trying to denaturalize. Each of these readings has something to it. This book has chosen the structural stance over the alternatives because it is the stance that takes the actual record of human power formations most seriously — the long history of revolutions that produced new ruling classes, of reforms that were absorbed by the institutions they tried to reform, of liberations that became the next regime's bureaucracies. The structural view is not optimism, not pessimism, and not neutrality. It is the view that takes durability seriously without confusing durability for legitimacy. Whether the view is correct is the kind of question that a book cannot resolve. Whether the view is useful — to readers who want to engage with the world they actually inhabit rather than the world they would prefer it to be — is the wager this book has made. The reader will judge.

Power is not a subject that yields to conclusions. It yields to observations, and the observations, accumulated across eighteen chapters, several millennia of evidence, and one contemporary demonstration, converge on a picture that is neither optimistic nor pessimistic but structural. Power concentrates because the dynamics of human organization reward concentration. Concentration generates resistance because the costs fall on the many while the benefits accrue to the few. Resistance produces redistribution, partial and temporary, because the structures that produced the concentration absorb the shock and reconstitute themselves in modified form. The cycle continues because the forces that drive it—the need for coordination, the advantages of scale, the self-reinforcing dynamics of accumulation—are permanent features of human organization rather than defects that can be engineered away.

The structural view is uncomfortable because it denies the possibility of a final victory. There is no constitution that permanently prevents the concentration of power. There is no revolution that permanently redistributes it. There is no institutional design that permanently solves the problem of who governs and on what terms. Every solution is temporary, every arrangement is contingent, and every generation inherits a distribution of power that was shaped by forces it did not create and that it will modify, incrementally, for the benefit of generations it will never meet. The work is not futile. It is essential, precisely because the forces that produce concentration never rest. The constraint must be continuous because the force it constrains is continuous. The maintenance must be permanent because the degradation it counters is permanent. The effort must be renewed because the conditions it addresses are renewed.

The platform case makes this concrete. The accumulation is visible in real time. The resilience is documented in regulatory failures. The legitimacy crisis is measurable in polling data. The resistance is organized but incomplete. And the outcome is undetermined, which means the people reading this analysis have agency in shaping it, which is the only useful thing a book about power can offer: not prediction, but framework. Not certainty, but clarity. Not solutions, but understanding of the machinery.

This is not a story with a moral. It is an analysis with an implication, and the implication is practical rather than inspirational: understand the machinery. Not the personalities, not the ideologies, not the dramatic moments that make good narratives and bad predictions. The machinery—the structural dynamics that produce concentration, the mechanisms that sustain it, the forces that challenge it, the patterns through which it transforms. The machinery operates regardless of who is in charge, regardless of what they believe, regardless of what they promise. Understanding it does not guarantee better outcomes. It guarantees better questions, which is the prerequisite for better outcomes and is, in any case, all that a book can honestly provide.

The machinery is running. It has always been running. It will continue to run after this book is closed and the reader returns to the world it describes. The platform case will resolve one way or another. Another system will accumulate power. Another resistance will form. Another cycle will complete. The question is not whether to engage with the machinery. The question is whether to engage with it informed or uninformed, with structural literacy or with the narratives that power tells about itself, with recognition that the work is never finished or with the expectation that any single victory will be permanent.

This book has been an argument for structural literacy, for informed engagement, and for the recognition that the work is continuous. The choice, as always, belongs to the reader. That choice—the decision to understand or to remain within the narrative, to engage with the machinery or to be moved by it—is itself an exercise of power, small in scale but meaningful in aggregate. The aggregate is where structural change happens. The aggregate is where this book ends and where the reader's engagement with its subject begins. The machinery is running. The question is what you do with that knowledge. The answer, whatever it is, will matter less than you hope and more than you think, which is an accurate description of most things that matter, and is probably as close to wisdom as a book about power can get.

Acknowledgements

This book began long before the first chapter was written. It began in observation — in noticing, early, that the people who hold power and the people who shape it are not always the same, and that the machinery underneath rarely matches the appearances on top. That noticing became a habit. The habit became a question. The question became the chapters that follow.

To my children — each of you, in different ways, has taught me more about how power actually works than any history book ever did. Patience, persuasion, leverage, dissent, the long negotiation that masquerades as bedtime — I have watched all of it unfold in real time. You grew up while I was learning to pay attention. Much of what I claim to understand about influence, authority, and consent, I learned first by watching you become yourselves.

To everyone I have worked alongside over the years — across offices, industries, decisions, and the long arguments that often produced more truth than the meetings that followed them — thank you. I have seen power exercised generously and ungenerously, openly and quietly, well and badly. The players change. The forms change. The patterns underneath keep their appointments. Much of what is collected here was first understood in rooms most of you will recognize.

This is also the opening volume of a thematic series, and a companion to the Nomical History monthly book series The calendar volumes follow time. This series follows mechanism. Different lenses, same world, same suspicion that the polished version of events is almost never the accurate one.

And to the reader — power notices you whether or not you notice it. Reading this is one of the cheaper ways to even the score.

— Joel Thomas

Sources & Further Reading

If you'd like to explore the events beyond my commentary, here are the main sources and references used:

General Theory of Power

Niccolò Machiavelli, *The Prince*

Thomas Hobbes, *Leviathan*

John Locke, *Two Treatises of Government*

Jean-Jacques Rousseau, *The Social Contract*

Bertrand Russell, *Power: A New Social Analysis*

Hannah Arendt, *On Violence*

Steven Lukes, *Power: A Radical View*

Michel Foucault, *Discipline and Punish*

Michael Mann, *The Sources of Social Power, Volumes 1 and 2*

Joseph Nye, *Soft Power: The Means to Success in World Politics*

Visible and Invisible Power

Peter Bachrach and Morton S. Baratz, *"Two Faces of Power" (American Political Science Review, 1962)*

Steven Lukes, *Power: A Radical View*

John Gaventa, *Power and Powerlessness*

Philip J. Stern, *The Company-State: Corporate Sovereignty and the Early Modern Foundations of the British Empire in India*

Pre-State Societies

Christopher Boehm, *Hierarchy in the Forest*

Marshall Sahlins, *Stone Age Economics*

Elman Service, *Origins of the State and Civilization*

Morton H. Fried, *The Evolution of Political Society*

Jared Diamond, *Guns, Germs, and Steel*

SACRED POWER

Max Weber, *The Sociology of Religion*

Mircea Eliade, *The Sacred and the Profane*

Jan Assmann, *The Mind of Egypt*

Karen Armstrong, *A History of God*

Robert Bellah, *Religion in Human Evolution*

MILITARY POWER & STATE FORMATION

Carl von Clausewitz, *On War*

John Keegan, *A History of Warfare*

Azar Gat, *War in Human Civilization*

Charles Tilly, *Coercion, Capital, and European States*

Martin van Creveld, *The Rise and Decline of the State*

POLITICAL POWER

Aristotle, *Politics*

Max Weber, *Economy and Society*

Robert A. Dahl, *Who Governs?*

C. Wright Mills, *The Power Elite*

Daron Acemoglu and James A. Robinson, *Why Nations Fail*

ECONOMIC POWER

Karl Marx, *Capital, Volume I*

Joseph Schumpeter, *Capitalism, Socialism and Democracy*

Karl Polanyi, *The Great Transformation*

Thomas Piketty, *Capital in the Twenty-First Century*

IMPERIAL POWER

Ibn Khaldun, *The Muqaddimah*

Paul Kennedy, *The Rise and Fall of the Great Powers*

Eric Hobsbawm, *The Age of Empire*

INSTITUTIONAL POWER

Douglass North, *Institutions, Institutional Change, and Economic Performance*

Francis Fukuyama, *The Origins of Political Order*

James C. Scott, *Seeing Like a State*

KNOWLEDGE AS POWER

Michel Foucault, *Power/Knowledge*

Walter J. Ong, *Orality and Literacy*

Elizabeth Eisenstein, *The Printing Press as an Agent of Change*

Benedict Anderson, *Imagined Communities*

CULTURAL POWER

Antonio Gramsci, *Selections from the Prison Notebooks*

Pierre Bourdieu, *Language and Symbolic Power*

Edward Said, *Orientalism*

Raymond Williams, *Culture and Society*

TECHNOLOGICAL POWER

Lewis Mumford, *Technics and Civilization*

Langdon Winner, *The Whale and the Reactor*

Shoshana Zuboff, *The Age of Surveillance Capitalism*

POPULAR POWER

Mancur Olson, *The Logic of Collective Action*

Theda Skocpol, *States and Social Revolutions*

Charles Tilly, *Social Movements, 1768-2012*

Frances Fox Piven and Richard Cloward, *Poor People's Movements*

Erica Chenoweth and Maria Stephan, *Why Civil Resistance Works*

POWER AND FEAR

Hannah Arendt, *The Origins of Totalitarianism*

Corey Robin, *Fear: The History of a Political Idea*

POWER AND CONSENT

Walter Lippmann, *Public Opinion*

Edward S. Herman and Noam Chomsky, *Manufacturing Consent*

James C. Scott, *Domination and the Arts of Resistance*

POWER IN DECLINE

Joseph Tainter, *The Collapse of Complex Societies*

Jared Diamond, *Collapse*

Peter Turchin, *War and Peace and War*

HIDDEN POWER

Peter Bachrach and Morton S. Baratz, *Power and Poverty*

John Gaventa, *Power and Powerlessness*

G. William Domhoff, *Who Rules America?*

POWER AS CYCLE

Robert Michels, *Political Parties*

Peter Turchin and Sergey Nefedov, *Secular Cycles*

Walter Scheidel, *The Great Leveler*

INDEX

slavery, 119, 183, 184, 193

social contract, 154, 155

soft power, 115

Solon, 71

Southeast Asia, 81, 147

Soviet Union, 8, 84, 85, 146, 147, 172, 204

Spain, 77, 78, 84

Spanish Crown, 81

Spanish Empire, 54, 84

Spruyt, Hendrik, 48

Standard Oil, 89

standing armies, 49, 50

Stasi (East German), 123

state formation, 34, 48, 49

Sui dynasty, 59

Sumer, 58, 60, 98

surveillance, 8, 55, 104, 123–125, 128, 143, 147, 210

Sweden, 199, 200

T

Tang dynasty, 59

Tanzimat reforms, 170

technological power, 121, 127

television, 99, 114, 115, 143, 167

Terror, Reign of (French Revolution), 134

Terror, War on, 147

Thebes (Egypt), 39

Tilly, Charles, 48

Trajan, 84

treason, 52, 142

tribute systems, 48, 79, 80, 86

Tunisia, 131

Twelve Tables, 60

U

United States, 48, 54, 70, 84, 85, 89, 91, 109, 112–116, 123, 135, 144, 146–148, 204, 209, 213

Ur-Nammu, 60

V

Victorian Britain, 109

visible power, 2, 18, 107, 180, 181

Voting Rights Act, 135, 136, 195

W

Walmart, 20

warlords, 48

Weber, Max, 59

Western Roman Empire, 42

William the Conqueror. *See* Norman Conquest

About the Author

Joel Thomas writes about power the way an engineer writes about bridges: not whether they are beautiful, but whether they will hold. His work examines the structural forces that shape human organization—the accumulation patterns, resistance cycles, and institutional dynamics that recur across centuries and contexts with a consistency that defies the narratives power tells about itself.

He is the creator of the Nomical History series, a calendar-based collection that tracks how revolutions, collapses, and institutional transformations unfold when systems meet their limits. His approach combines rigorous historical analysis with the kind of clarity that comes from refusing to mistake ceremony for explanation or intention for outcome.

Power: How Influence, Authority, and Control Shaped Civilizations is his first book-length treatment of a single subject, synthesizing decades of pattern recognition across empires, corporations, movements, and states into a framework for understanding how power concentrates, transforms, and reconstitutes itself regardless of who claims to hold it. The work that began with daily histories of particular moments has become an examination of the forces that operate beneath all of them.

Thomas writes from the conviction that structural literacy matters more than moral judgment, that understanding how power works is the prerequisite for engaging with it effectively, and that the most useful thing a book can provide is not inspiration but analytical tools sharp enough to cut through the stories systems tell about themselves.

He works between archives, case studies, and the recognition that every structural pattern described in this book is still operating somewhere, right now, whether anyone is paying attention to it or not.

Learn more and connect at:
NomicalBooks.com or contact@nomicalbooks.com

Nomical History

Scan the QR code above for more books in the Nomical History Series.

NOTES

The notes that follow document the principal sources for specific claims, figures, and historical episodes referenced in the text. They are organized by chapter and keyed to the passage they support. Where a claim is widely accepted in the scholarly literature, the note identifies the most authoritative or accessible treatment; where the claim is contested, the note flags the disagreement. The general theoretical framework behind each chapter draws on the works listed in the Sources & Further Reading section; the notes here are reserved for specific evidentiary anchors.

CHAPTER 1: POWER DEFINED

"Power is control over outcomes." The functional definition adopted here draws most directly on Robert Dahl, *"The Concept of Power,"* *Behavioral Science* 2 (1957): 201–215, modified by the relational and structural considerations developed in Steven Lukes, *Power: A Radical View* (1974; expanded ed. 2005).

"Influence is the capacity to shape decisions without direct control... Dominance is the ability to override resistance." These distinctions follow Bertrand Russell, *Power: A New Social Analysis* (1938), and are refined in Hannah Arendt, *On Violence* (1970), which argues that power and violence are conceptually distinct rather than points on a continuum.

"The most successful exercise of control is the one that never has to be exercised at all." The point that non-events are themselves exercises of power is developed in Peter Bachrach and Morton Baratz, *"Two Faces of Power,"* *American Political Science Review* 56 (1962): 947–952, and forms the basis for Lukes's "third face" formulation revisited in Chapter 17.

CHAPTER 2: VISIBLE AND INVISIBLE POWER

"The political theorist Steven Lukes formalized this layered structure as the three faces of power... The framework has organized political-science thinking about power for fifty years." Steven Lukes, *Power: A Radical View* (1974; expanded ed. 2005). On the first and second "faces" that Lukes builds on, see also Peter Bachrach and Morton Baratz, *"Two Faces of Power,"* *American Political Science Review* 56 (1962): 947–952 (cited in Chapter 1 notes); the application of the framework to specifically hidden or structural forms of power is developed at length in Chapter 17 notes.

"The East India Company most spectacularly, but also the Dutch East India Company, the Hudson's Bay Company, the Royal African Company—exercised governmental power across continents." On the corporate-sovereign hybrids of the early modern period, see Philip J. Stern, *The Company-State: Corporate Sovereignty and the Early Modern Foundations of the British Empire in*

India (2011). The detailed history of the East India Company in particular is treated in Chapter 8 notes.

CHAPTER 3: POWER BEFORE STATES

"The earliest human social groups were small bands of perhaps twenty to fifty individuals, rarely exceeding a hundred and fifty." The cognitive ceiling of roughly 150 stable relationships is associated with Robin Dunbar, *Grooming, Gossip and the Evolution of Language* (1996), and "Neocortex Size as a Constraint on Group Size in Primates," *Journal of Human Evolution* 22 (1992): 469–493.

"Anthropologist Elman Service's classification of human political organization—from bands to tribes to chiefdoms to states." Elman R. Service, *Primitive Social Organization: An Evolutionary Perspective* (1962), and *Origins of the State and Civilization: The Process of Cultural Evolution* (1975). Morton H. Fried's *The Evolution of Political Society* (1967) offers the parallel egalitarian-ranked-stratified-state typology.

"The potlatch ceremonies of the Pacific Northwest, the feast-giving traditions of Melanesian big men, the meat-sharing norms of African foraging bands." On potlatch as competitive gift-giving, see Marcel Mauss, *The Gift* (1925), and Marshall Sahlins, *Stone Age Economics* (1972). On the Melanesian "big-man" complex, see Marshall Sahlins, "*Poor Man, Rich Man, Big-Man, Chief: Political Types in Melanesia and Polynesia,*" *Comparative Studies in Society and History* 5 (1963): 285–303.

"The anthropologist Christopher Boehm documented extensive evidence of what he called reverse dominance hierarchies." Christopher Boehm, *Hierarchy in the Forest: The Evolution of Egalitarian Behavior* (1999), particularly chapters 3-4 on leveling mechanisms.

"The transition was contested at every stage... The state was not adopted. It was, in most cases, imposed." On resistance to state formation, see James C. Scott, *The Art of Not Being Governed: An Anarchist History of Upland Southeast Asia* (2009), and *Against the Grain: A Deep History of the Earliest States* (2017).

CHAPTER 4: SACRED POWER

"The concept of the divine king... appeared independently in nearly every early civilization. Egypt had it. Mesopotamia had it. China had it. Mesoamerica had it. The Polynesian islands had it." The cross-cultural pattern is treated in A. M. Hocart, *Kingship* (1927), and reassessed in Nicole Brisch, ed., *Religion and Power: Divine Kingship in the Ancient World and Beyond* (2008). For Polynesian sacred chieftainship, see Patrick V. Kirch, *How Chiefs Became Kings* (2010).

"Egyptologist Jan Assmann's analysts of divine kingship... the pharaoh was the living embodiment of Horus and the intermediary between the human world and the divine order, or

*Ma'at."*Jan Assmann, *The Mind of Egypt: History and Meaning in the Time of the Pharaohs* (2002), and Ma 'at: Gerechtigheit und Unsterblichkeit im alten Agypten (1990).

"Mesopotamian theology allowed for divine displeasure in ways Egyptian theology generally did not." On Mesopotamian conceptions of divinely sanctioned and divinely revocable kingship, see Henri Frankfort, *Kingship and the Gods* (1948), still the standard comparative treatment.

"China's Mandate of Heaven offered a variation that introduced something genuinely novel." The doctrine (tianming) is set out in the Book of Documents (Shujing) and analyzed in David S. Nivison, The Ways of Confucianism (1996), and Yuri Pines, Envisioning Eternal Empire (2009).

"The history of ancient Egypt includes multiple periods where priestly power rivaled or exceeded royal authority, particularly during the late New Kingdom when the priests of Amun at Thebes accumulated enough wealth and influence to effectively govern Upper Egypt independently." On the rise of the High Priests of Amun and the Twenty-First Dynasty division, see Karl Jansen-Winkeln, "Das Ende des Neuen Reiches," Zeitschrift fiir Agyptische Sprache und Altertumskunde 119 (1992): 22–37, and Aidan Dodson, Afterglow of Empire (2012).

"In Mesoamerica, the ritual calendar was so central to social organization that political decisions, military campaigns, and economic activities were timed to align with ceremontal cycles." On the 260-day tonalpohualli and 365-day xiuhpobualli and their political functions, see Anthony F. Aveni, Skywatchers of Ancient Mexico (2001).

*"The Hindu caste system, formalized through religious texts and reinforced through ritual practice, persisted for millennia."*On varna, jati, and karmic legitimation, see Louis Dumont, Homo Hierarchicus (1970), and Nicholas B. Dirks, Castes of Mind (2001), which emphasizes the role of British colonial administration in fixing what had been more fluid categories.

"The medieval Church operated the closest thing to a welfare state that existed in Europe for centuries. On the Church's social provision, see R. W. Southern, Western Society and the Church in the Middle Ages (1970), and Brian Tierney, Medieval Poor Law (1959).

CHAPTER 5: MILITARY POWER

"The sociologist Charles Tilly compressed this insight into a sentence... war made the state, and the state made war." Charles Tilly, "Reflections on the History of European State-Making," in The Formation of National States in Western Europe (1975), 42, and developed at length in *Coercion, Capital, and European States*, AD 990–1992 (1990). Tilly's "war made the state" thesis is sometimes paired with his observation that early states resembled "protection rackets" — see "War Making and State Making as Organized Crime" in Peter Evans et al., eds., Bringing the State Back In (1985).

"The earliest states that left clear archaeological and documentary evtdence—in Mesopotamia, Egypt, China, and the Indus Valley—all show the marks of this military origin." See Bruce Trigger, Understanding Early Civilizations (2003), for the comparative evidence on fortifications and martial iconography.

"The Praetorian Guard in Rome made and unmade emperors with the casual efficiency of a hiring committee that also handled terminations." On the Praetorians' political role, see Sandra Bingham, The Praetorian Guard: A History of Rome's Elite Special Forces (2013); the auction of the empire to Didius Julianus in 193 CE is the canonical illustration.

"Roman legions were stationed far from their regions of recruitment. Ottoman janissartes were deliberately separated from their families and communities of origin. Chinese dynasties rotated regional military commanders." On the devsirme and the separation logic of janissary recruitment, see Gilles Veinstein, "On the (ifilik Debate," and the relevant chapters in Halil inalcik, The Ottoman Empire: The Classical Age 1300–1600 (1973). On Roman legionary deployment, see Edward Luttwak, The Grand Strategy of the Roman Empire (1976).

"Roman soldiers received land grants upon retirement." On the praemia militiae and the political consequences of Augustan military settlement, see Lawrence Keppie, Colonisation and Veteran Settlement in Italy 47–14 B.C. (1983).

"The Assyrian Empire... practiced deportation on a massive scale." On Assyrian deportation policy and ideological warfare, see Bustenay Oded, Mass Deportations and Deportees in the Neo-Assyrian Empire (1979), and Simo Parpola, Letters from Assyrian Scholars to the Kings Esarhaddon and Assurbanipal (1970–83).

"The Norman conquest of England was accomplished by cavalry in 1066 and maintained by a legal and administrative system that eventually made Norman authority feel indigenous." On the post-conquest administrative consolidation, see George Garnett, Conquered England: *Kingship*, Succession, and Tenure 1066–1166 (2007).

"The Crusader states in the Levant held territory for roughly two centurtes without ever establishing genuine legitimacy among the majority population." The kingdom of Jerusalem (1099–1291) is treated in Joshua Prawer, The Latin Kingdom of Jerusalem (1972), and Christopher Tyerman, God's War:.A New History of the Crusades (2006).

CHAPTER 6: POLITICAL POWER

"Sociologist Max Weber analyzed this transition as the shift from charismatic to legal-rational authority." Max Weber, Economy and Society, ed. Guenther Roth and Claus Wittich (1922 [1978]), Vol. 1, ch. 3, and The Theory of Social and Economic Organization (1947). Weber's three ideal types — traditional, charismatic, and legal-rational — frame the analysis throughout this book.

"When a scribe in Ur recorded grain deliveries to a temple storehouse in 2500 BCE." Mid-third-millennium temple accounting tablets from Ur and Lagash are catalogued in I. J. Gelb, P. Steinkeller, and R. M. Whiting, Earliest Land Tenure Systems in the Near East: Ancient Kudurrus (1991). For the broader administrative role of scribes, see Eleanor Robson, Mathematics in Ancient Irag (2008).

"China produced the most sophisticated early bureaucracy... The imperial examination system, formalized during the Sut and Tang dynasties." On the keju system, its formalization between 605

and 960 CE, and its administrative consequences, see Benjamin A. Elman, A Cultural History of Civil Examinations in Late Imperial China (2000), and Ichisada Miyazaki, China's Examination Hell (1976).

"The Ottoman Empire achieved something similar through a mechanism that was considerably more unsettling. The devsirme system." On the child-levy system, its scale, and its administrative function, see V. L. Ménage, "Some Notes on the Deoshirme," Bulletin of the School of Oriental and African Studies 29 (1966): 64–78, and Halil Inalcik, An Economic and Social History of the Ottoman Empire (1994).

"The earliest known legal codes—Ur-Nammu in Sumer, Hammurabi in Babylon, the Twelve Tables in Rome." The Code of Ur-Nammu (c. 2100 BCE) is the earliest extant legal code; see Martha T. Roth, Law Collections from Mesopotamia and Asia Minor (1995). On Hammurabi (c. 1754 BCE), see Marc Van De Mieroop, King Hammurabi of Babylon (2005). On the Twelve Tables (451–450 BCE), see Michael Crawford, ed., Roman Statutes (1996).

"The Napoleonic Code" (referenced obliquely in the discussion of legal systematization). The Code civil des Frangats of 1804 is the standard modern example of comprehensive codification; see Jean-Louis Halpérin, L impossible Code civil (1992).

CHAPTER 7: ECONOMIC POWER

"The temple granaries of ancient Mesopotamia were not merely storage facilities. They were power centers." On the redistributive function of Sumerian temple complexes, see A. Leo Oppenheim, Ancient Mesopotamia: Portrait of a Dead Civilization (rev. ed. 1977), and Marc Van De Mieroop, The Ancient Mesopotamian City (1997).

"In classical Athens... Liturgies—mandatory public contributions for festivals, warships, and infrastructure—fell disproportionately on the rich." On the liturgia system (trierarchies, choregia), see Matthew R. Christ, The Bad Citizen in Classical Athens (2006), and Peter Wilson, The Athenian Institution of the Khoregia (2000).

"The Roman Republic was explicitly structured around wealth. Citizens were organized into classes based on property holdings, and voting power was weighted accordingly." On the comitia centuriata and its property-graded structure, see Andrew Lintott, The Constitution of the Roman Republic (1999).

"Karl Marx built an entire theoretical framework around this observation." Karl Marx, Capital, Volume I (1867), particularly Part III on the working day and Part VII on accumulation. The dependency analysis here is closer to the structural argument than to its prescriptive conclusions.

"Ancient Rome's latifundia—vast agricultural estates worked by slaves and tenant farmers." On the latifundia and their displacement of small landholding, see Keith Hopkins, Conquerors and Slaves (1978), and Peter Garnsey, Famine and Food Supply in the Graeco-Roman World (1988).

"Economist Thomas Piketty documented this pattern extensively." Thomas Piketty, *Capital in the Twenty-First Century* (2014), particularly Part Three on the structure of inequality and the relation r > g.

"The Babylonian misharum edicts, the biblical Jubilee, Solon's setsachtheia in Athens." On Mesopotamian misarum and andurarum debt cancellations, see Michael Hudson, ...and forgive them their debts (2018), and J. J. Finkelstein, "Some New misharum Material," Assyriological Studies 16 (1965): 233–246. On the Jubilee, see Leviticus 25; on Solon's seésachtheia (594 BCE), see Aristotle, Constitution of the Athentans, 5-12.

"The Medici did not rule Florence through military conquest or divine mandate. They ruled through banking." On the Medici Bank's political mechanics, see Raymond de Roover, The Rise and Decline of the Medici Bank, 1397–1494 (1963).

"The Fugger banking family of Augsburg financed the election of Charles V as Holy Roman Emperor." The 1519 imperial election cost roughly 850,000 florins, the bulk advanced by Jakob Fugger; see Mark Haberlein, The Fuggers of Augsburg (2012).

"The Glorious Revolution of 1688... was also and perhaps primarily a

" triumph of creditors over a king who could not be trusted to repay his debts. The fiscal-political reading is developed in Douglass C. North and Barry R. Weingast, "Constitutions and Commitment: The Evolution of Institutions Governing Public Choice in Seventeenth-Century England," *Journal of Economic History* 49 (1989): 803–832.

CHAPTER 8: IMPERIAL POWER

"The British Empire repeated the pattern with steam engines and better record-keeping. At its peak, Britain governed roughly a quarter of the world's land surface and a quarter of its population." Standard figures from John Darwin, The Empire Project: The Rise and Fall of the British World-System, 1830–1970 (2009).

"The Persian Empire under Darius I organized its territory into satraptes, each assigned a specific tribute obligation denominated in silver talents." The tribute lists are recorded in Herodotus, Histories, III.8997. On the satrapy system, see Pierre Briant, From Cyrus to Alexander: A History of the Persian Empire (2002).

"The British East India Company did not establish itself in Bengal to improve Bengali living standards. It established itself to redirect Bengali revenue to company shareholders." On the post-Plassey extraction (1757 onward) and the Bengal famine of 1770, see William Dalrymple, The Anarchy (2019), and Tirthankar Roy, The East India Company: The World's Most Powerful Corporation (2012).

"Historian Paul Kennedy analyzed this phenomenon as 'imperial ove rstretch.'" Paul Kennedy, The Rise and Fall of the Great Powers: Economic Change and Military Conflict from 1500 to 2000 (1987), particularly the concluding chapter.

"At its territorial peak under Trajan in 117 CE, Rome controlled the entire Mediterranean basin, most of Western Europe, significant portions of the Near East, and a strip of North Africa." Standard treatment in Edward Gibbon, The Decline and Fall of the Roman Empire (1776–88); for modern scholarship on Trajanic frontiers, see David Mattingly, Imperialism, Power, and Identity: Experiencing the Roman Empire (2011).

"Spain's acquisition of American silver in the sixteenth century produced a windfall that appeared to solve the resource problem permanently." On the Potosi silver economy and its inflationary consequences, see Earl J. Hamilton, American Treasure and the Price Revolution in Spain, 1501–1650(1934), and Kris Lane, Potost: The Silver City That Changed the World (2019).

"The Soviet commitment to maintaining a global ideological empire…

consumed resources that the Soviet economy could not sustainably generate." On Soviet imperial overstretch, see Stephen Kotkin, Armageddon Averted: The Soviet *Collapse*, 1970–2000 (2001).

CHAPTER 9: INSTITUTIONAL POWER

"Economic historian Douglass North analyzed how institutions persist through the creation of formal rules and informal constraints." Douglass C. North, Institutions, Institutional Change and Economic Performance (1990).

"Christianity 1s the most consequential example of this transition in human history… Within three centurtes, it became the official religion of the empire that had executed its founder." The Edict of Thessalonica (380 CE) under Theodosius I established Nicene Christianity as the state religion; see Peter Brown, The Rise of Western Christendom (1996), and Robert Louis Wilken, The First Thousand Years: A Global History of Christianity (2012).

"Standard Oil outlived Rockefeller's direct management because its organizational structure— the trust, the holding company, the divisional hierarchy—could function without Rockefeller in the room." On the structural innovations of Standard Oil, see Ron Chernow, Titan: The Life of John D. Rockefeller, Sr. (1998).

"Alexander the Great built the largest empire the ancient world had seen and left behind no institutional framework for governing it." On the Diadochi succession and Alexander's institutional gap, see A. B. Bosworth, The Legacy of Alexander (2002).

"English courts have operated continuously since the twelfth century… The ship that sails today shares no planks with the ship that launched in 1154." Henry II's reforms (1154–1189) are conventionally dated as the foundation of English common law; see John Hudson, The Oxford History of the Laws of England, Volume II: 871–1216 (2012).

"The Hudson's Bay Company was chartered in 1670 and is still operating." On the company's chartered structure and longevity, see Stephen R. Bown, The Company: The Rise and Fall of the Hudson's Bay Empire (2020).

"The British monarchy is a masterclass in legitimacy recycling. The original claim—divine right of kings—was formally abandoned after the Glorious Revolution of 1688." On the constitutional reconfiguration after 1688, see J. C. D. Clark, English Society 1660–1832 (rev. ed. 2000), and David Cannadine, "The Context, Performance and Meaning of Ritual: The British Monarchy and the 'Invention of Tradition,' c.

1820–1977," in Eric Hobsbawm and Terence Ranger, eds., The Invention of Tradition (1983).

CHAPTER 10: KNOWLEDGE AS POWER

"Sumerian cuneiform involved hundreds of symbols. Egyptian hieroglyphics involved hundreds more. Chinese characters required memorizing thousands." On the deliberate complexity and access-restriction of early writing systems, see Jack Goody, The Logic of Writing and the Organization of Soctety (1986).

"Medieval European Christianity concentrated literacy overwhelmingly within the clergy, who read and interpreted the Bible in Latin." On clerical literacy as an instrument of authority, see M. T. Clanchy, From Memory to Written Record: England 1066–1307 (3rd ed. 2013).

"When Gutenberg's press made it possible to produce books in large quantities at reduced cost." The standard treatment is Elizabeth L. Eisenstein, *The Printing Press as an Agent of Change* (1979). On the speed of Lutheran pamphlet distribution after the Ninety-Five Theses (1517), see Andrew Pettegree, Brand Luther (2015).

"Political scientist James C. Scott documented how states have systematically used information collection—censuses, surveys, cadastral maps, standardized measurements—to make populations legible' and therefore governable." James C. Scott, *Seeing Like a State*: How Certain Schemes to Improve the Human Condition Have Failed (1998), particularly chapters 1-2.

"The census—an instrument so ancient that it appears in both the Bible and Chinese records from the third millennium BCE." On Mesopotamian and Egyptian population accounting, see the Yu Gong tradition discussed in Mark Edward Lewis, The Construction of Space in Early China (2006); for biblical references, see Numbers 1 and 2 Samuel 24.

"The Domesday Book, compiled for William the Conqueror in 1086, was the most comprehensive survey of English wealth and landholding ever attempted." See Sally Harvey, Domesday: Book of Judgement (2014).

"The American Medical Association has spent a century carefully managing the supply of physicians." On the AMA, the Flexner Report (1910), and physician supply, see Paul Starr, The Social Transformation of American Medicine (1982).

CHAPTER 11: CULTURAL POWER

"Antonio Gramsci analyzed this phenomenon as cultural hegemony." Antonio Gramsci, *Selections from the Prison Notebooks*, ed. Quintin Hoare and Geoffrey Nowell Smith (1971), particularly the sections on the "war of position" and the role of intellectuals.

"The Confucian examination system in imperial China demonstrates how a single norm—filial piety—sustained political hierarchy for more than a millennium." On xiao (filial piety) as political ideology, see Keith Knapp, Sedfless Offspring: Filial Children and Social Order in Medieval China (2005). For the longue durée of the examination system, see Benjamin Elman (cited in Chapter 6 notes).

"Victorian Britain deployed the code of respectability as a dass-discipline mechanism." On respectability as social control, see F. M. L. Thompson, The Rise of Respectable Society: A Social History of Victorian Britain, 1830–1900 (1988).

"Postwar American homeownership norms illustrate how cultural assumptions shape political allegiance." On the GI Bill, FHA mortgages, and the political construction of American homeownership, see Kenneth T. Jackson, Crabgrass Frontier: The Suburbanization of the United States (1985), and Richard Rothstein, The Color of Law (2017).

"Sociologist Pierre Bourdieu analyzed how cultural knowledge functions as capital." Pierre Bourdieu, Distinction: A Social Critique of the Judgement of Taste (1979), and "The Forms of Capital" in John G. Richardson, ed., Handbook of Theory and Research for the Sociology of Education (1986): 241–258,

"France's revolutionary and post-revolutionary governments pursued the elimination of regional languages, Breton, Occitan, Basque, Alsatian." On the Abbé Grégoire's report (1794) and subsequent linguistic centralization, see Eugen Weber, Peasants into Frenchmen: The Modernization of Rural France, 1870–1914 (1976).

"William Randolph Hearst did not need to hold office to shape American politics." On Hearst's papers and the construction of mass-market journalism, see David Nasaw, The Chief: The Life of William Randolph Hearst (2000).

"The term 'soft power,' coined by the political scientist Joseph Nye. Joseph S. Nye, Jr., Bound to Lead: The Changing Nature of American Power (1990), and *Soft Power: The Means to Success in World Politics* (2004).

CHAPTER 12: TECHNOLOGICAL POWER

"The stirrup gave mounted cavalry an advantage that reshaped Eurasian warfare." Lynn White Jr., Medieval Technology and Social Change (1962), advanced the strong claim linking the stirrup to feudalism. The thesis has been contested; see Bernard S. Bachrach, "Charles

Martel, Mounted Shock Combat, the Stirrup, and Feudalism," *Studies in Medieval and Renaissance History* 7 (1970): 47–75. The text's claim is the modest one — that the stirrup mattered, not that it caused feudalism.

"The cotton gin made slavery more profitable at the precise historical moment when moral arguments against it were gaining traction." On Eli Whitney's 1793 invention and its economic consequences for the cotton South, see Gavin Wright, Slavery and American Economic Development (2006), and Sven Beckert, Empire of Cotton: A Global History (2014).

"The Hyksos in Egypt, the Huns in Europe, the Mongols across Eurasia—each represented a case in which a technological advantage inverted the existing power hierarchy." On the Hyksos and the chariot's introduction to Egypt (Second Intermediate Period, c. 1650–1550 BCE), see Manfred Bietak, Avaris, the Capital of the Hyksos (1996). On Mongol cavalry and composite-bow logistics, see Timothy May, The Mongol Art of War (2007).

"The Maxim gun didn't cause imperialism—it made imperialism efficient." The Maxim, patented 1884, is treated in Daniel R. Headtick, The Tools of Empire: Technology and European Imperialism in the Nineteenth Century (1981); the Battle of Omdurman (1898), at which roughly 10,000 Mahdist troops died against minimal British casualties, is the iconic illustration.

"The East German Stasi, perhaps the most thorough surveillance apparatus of the pre-digital era, employed an estimated ninety thousand full-time agents and recruited roughly one informant for every sixty-three citizens." Figures from Anna Funder, Stasiland (2003), and Mary Fulbrook, The People's State (2005). The informant ratio is approximate; estimates of Inoffizielle Mitarbeiter numbers range from 173,000 to over 200,000 at the apparatus's peak.

"China's social credit system represents the most ambitious attempt to operationalize comprehensive surveillance as a governance tool." On the system's variegated implementation, see Rogier Creemers, "China's Social Credit System: An Evolving Practice of Control," SSRN (2018), and Jeremy Daum's reporting at China Law Translate, which corrects the more lurid Western accounts.

"The revelations of the early 2010s documented intelligence programs that collected communications data on a scale that previous generations of intelligence officials would have considered technically impossible." The Snowden disclosures, beginning June 2013, are documented in Glenn Greenwald, No Place to Hide (2014), and Barton Gellman, Dark Mirror (2020).

"Five companies—Alphabet, Amazon, Apple, Meta, and M1crosoft—control the platforms, the data, the algorithms, and the infrastructure on which an increasing share of economic and social life depends." Market share figures (e.g., Google's >90 percent search share in most markets, Amazon's roughly 40 percent U.S. e-commerce share, Meta's three billion-plus monthly active users across platforms) reflect 2023–2024 reporting from the U.S. House Subcommittee on Antitrust, Statcounter, and company filings; figures shift, but orders of magnitude are stable.

CHAPTER 13: POPULAR POWER

"The economist Mancur Olson formalized this logic in The Logic of Collective Action." Mancur Olson, *The Logic of Collective Action*: Public Goods and the Theory of Groups (1965).

"The self-immolation of Mohamed Bouaztzi in Tunisia did not create the conditions for the Arab Spring." Bouazizi set himself on fire on 17 December 2010 in Sidi Bouzid; he died on 4 January 2011. On the subsequent diffusion across the region, see Marc Lynch, The Arab Uprising (2012).

"The French Revolution, the most analyzed popular uprising in Western history, lasted in its radical phase roughly five years—from the storming of the Bastille in 1789 to the fall of Robespierre in 1794." Standard chronology in William Doyle, The Oxford History of the French Revolution (1989). Robespierre was guillotined on 28 July 1794 (10 Thermidor Year II).

"The Russian Revolution of 1917 followed a structurally similar trajectory at higher speed and greater scale." The Romanov dynasty had ruled since 1613. On the February and October revolutions, see Sheila Fitzpatrick, The Russian Revolution (rev. ed. 2017), and Orlando Figes, A People's Tragedy (1996).

"The Iranian Revolution of 1979 was a broad coalition of secular liberals, leftists, students, workers, merchants, and clerics united by opposition to the Shab." On the coalition dynamics and clerical capture, see Ervand Abrahamian, Iran Between Two Revolutions (1982), and_A History of Modern Iran (2008).

"The Egyptian revolution of 2011... removed Mubarak in eighteen days." Mubarak resigned on 11 February 2011, eighteen days after the 25 January demonstrations. On the SCAF's subsequent role and the Sisi takeover (2013), see Jason Brownlee, Tarek Masoud, and Andrew Reynolds, The Arab Spring: Pathways of Repression and Reform (2015).

"The civil rights movement in the United States provides the clearest positive example of a movement that understood this dynamic." On the strategic deliberateness of the 1963 Birmingham campaign and its connection to the Civil Rights Act of 1964 and Voting Rights Act of 1965, see Taylor Branch, Parting the Waters (1988) and Pillar of Fire (1998), and Aldon D. Morris, The Origins of the Civil Rights Movement (1984).

CHAPTER 14: POWER AND FEAR

"Crucifixion was not merely a method of execution. It was a technology of communication." On crucifixion's communicative function in the Roman penal system, see Martin Hengel, Crucifixion in the Ancient World and the Folly of the Message of the Cross (1977).

"Michel Foucault argued that the shift from public punishment to prtvate incarceration in the eighteenth and nineteenth centuries represented a fundamental change in the nature of power." Michel Foucault, *Discipline and Punish*: The Birth of the Prison (1975; English trans. 1977), particularly Part I on the spectacle of the scaffold and Part III on panopticism.

"Research consistently demonstrates that certainty of punishment deters more effectively than severity." The classical empirical finding is summarized in Daniel Nagin, "Deterrence in the Twenty-First Century," Crime and Justice 42 (2013): 199–263. The point dates to Cesare Beccaria, On Crimes and Punishments (1764).

"The British response to the Easter Rising of 1916 provides a textbook example." The Rising began 24 April 1916; sixteen leaders were executed between 3 and 12 May. On the radicalizing effect of the executions, see Charles Townshend, Easter 1916: The Irish Rebellion (2005), and Fearghal McGarry, The Rising: Ireland: Easter 1916 (2010).

"The American war on drugs, launched in the early 1970s and escalated over the following decades, produced an expansion of law enforcement power, incarceration capacity, and survetllance authority." President Nixon's 1971 declaration is the conventional starting point. On the structural consequences, see Michelle Alexander, The New Jim Crow (2010), and Michael Javen Fortner, Black Silent Majority (2015).

"The Department of Homeland Security... is now a permanent fixture of the federal government with a budget exceeding fifty billion dollars and a workforce exceeding two hundred thousand employees." DHS was established by the Homeland Security Act of 2002. FY2024 enacted budget authority is approximately $61 billion; total workforce is roughly 260,000. Figures from DHS Budget-in-Brief documents.

CHAPTER 15: POWER AND CONSENT

"Hobbes, Locke, and Rousseau each proposed versions of an original agreement." Thomas Hobbes, *Leviathan* (1651); John Locke, *Two Treatises of Government* (1689); Jean-Jacques Rousseau, *The Social Contract* (1762). The most rigorous modern critique of the historical-contract reading is in David Hume, "Of the Original Contract" (1748), which the chapter's argument echoes.

"The phrase 'manufacturing consent' entered the political vocabulary through Walter Lippmann, who used it approvingly, and Noam Chomsky, who used it as an indictment." Walter Lippmann, *Public Opinion* (1922), 158, used "the manufacture of consent" approvingly as a feature of modern democracy. Edward S. Herman and Noam Chomsky, *Manufacturing Consent*: The Political Economy of the Mass Media (1988), inverted the framing.

"Communication scholars call framing....A frame is a conceptual structure that organizes information and determines its meaning." On framing theory, see Robert M. Entman, "Framing: Toward Clarification of a Fractured Paradigm," Journal of Communication 43 (1993): 51–58. On agenda-setting, see Maxwell McCombs and Donald L. Shaw, "The Agenda-Setting Function of Mass Media," *Public Opinion Quarterly* 36 (1972): 176–187.

CHAPTER 16: POWER IN DECLINE

"The Roman Empire in the third century was not less competent than the empire in the first century. It was more committed." On the third-century crisis (235–284 CE), see David S. Potter, The Roman Empire at Bay, AD 180–395 (2004), and Peter Heather, The Fall of the Roman Empire (2005).

"The late Ottoman Empire provides a case study in administrative decay so comprehensive that it became a synonym for the phenomenon." On the Tanzimat (1839–1876) and the structural limits of Ottoman reform, see Roderic H. Davison, Reform in the Ottoman Empire, 1856–1876 (1963), and M. Şükrü Hanioğlu, A Brief History of the Late Ottoman Empire (2008).

"The Soviet Union is the canonical modern example of collapse preceding recognition." The 1991 dissolution is treated in Serhii Plokhy, The Last Empire: The Final Days of the Soviet Union (2014), and Stephen Kotkin (cited in Chapter 8 notes). On the gap between Western and Soviet self-assessment, see the CIA's own retrospective: Gerald K. Haines and Robert E. Leggett, eds., Watching the Bear: Essays on CIA's Analysis of the Soviet Union (2003).

"Kodak's leadership understood, intellectually, that digital photography would displace film. The company invented the digital camera... The company filed for bankruptcy in 2012, roughly four decades after the first digital camera was built in its own laboratories." Steven Sasson built Kodak's first digital camera prototype in 1975; the company filed for Chapter 11 on 19 January 2012. On the strategic-failure analysis, see Rebecca Henderson, "The Innovator's Dilemma as a Problem of Organizational Competence," Journal of Product Innovation Management 23 (2006), 5-11.

"BlackBerry's trajectory followed an almost identical pattern at compressed speed... By 2013, BlackBerry's market share had collapsed from 50 percent to 3 percent." Smartphone market share data from IDC and Gartner; for the strategic narrative, see Jacquie McNish and Sean Silcoff, Losing the Signal: The Untold Story Behind the Extraordinary Rise and Spectacular Fall of BlackBerry (2015).

CHAPTER 17: HIDDEN POWER

"The political theorist Steven Lukes called this the 'third face of power.'" Steven Lukes, *Power: A Radical View* (1974; expanded 2005). The "three faces" framework treats decision-making, agenda-setting, and preference-shaping as analytically distinct dimensions.

"Political scientists Peter Bachrach and Morton Baratz identified this dynamic in the early 1960s as the 'second face of power.'" Peter Bachrach and Morton S. Baratz, *"Two Faces of Power,"* American Political Science Review 56 (1962): 947–952, and Power and Poverty (1970).

"The Italian theorist Antonio Gramsci called this hegemony." The concept of egemonia runs through the Prison Notebooks; the most useful single entry point remains *Selections from the Prison Notebooks* (1971), pp. 12–13 and 181–182.

"The arrangement in which nations control borders and restrict movement is perceived not as a relatively recent development in human history—passports became standard only in the twentieth

century." On the post-World War I generalization of the passport regime, see John Torpey, The Invention of the Passport: Surveillance, Citizenship and the State (2000).

"Land ownership patterns established in the colonial era persist in postcolonial societies long after independence." On the persistence of colonial land tenure, see Mahmood Mamdani, Citizen and Subject (1996), and on Latin American latifundia continuities, John Tutino, From Insurrection to Revolution in Mexico (1986).

CHAPTER 18: POWER AS CYCLE

"The fourteenth-century scholar Ibn Khaldun identified this pattern in his theory of dynastic cycles." Ibn Khaldûn, *The Muqaddimah*: An Introduction to History, trans. Franz Rosenthal (1958), particularly Books II-III] on asabiyya (group solidarity) and the dynastic life-cycle.

"The Gilded Age concentrated wealth over decades and was followed by the Progressive Era and the New Deal." On the long inequality cycle, see Walter Scheidel, *The Great Leveler* (2017), and the data series in Piketty, *Capital in the Twenty-First Century* (cited above), which document the U-shaped twentieth-century pattern in U.S. and European top-income shares.

"The Russian Revolution abolished the bourgeoisie and produced, within a generation, a nomenklatura whose privileges... mirrored the privileges of the class it had replaced." Milovan Djilas, The New Class: An Analysis of the Communist System (1957), is the foundational analysis.

"The Scandinavian social democracies are the most commonly cited example... Sweden's Rehn-Meidner model." The Rehn—Meidner framework, designed by LO economists Gösta Rehn and Rudolf Meidner in the late 1940s and operative from the 1950s, is treated in Lennart Erixon, "The Rehn-Meidner Model in Sweden: Its Rise, Challenges and Survival," Journal of Economic Issues 44 (2010): 677–715. Swedish union density peaked above 80 percent in the 1980s before declining to roughly 65 percent by the 2010s.

"The French Revolution replaced the monarchy with a republic and retained the administrative apparatus that had governed France under the monarchy. Napoleon formalized this retention." On the institutional continuity from Bourbon centralization through the Revolution to the Napoleonic state, see Alexis de Tocqueville, The Old Regime and the Revolution (1856), the original statement of the thesis, and Isser Woloch, The New Regime: Transformations of the French Civic Order, 1789–1820s (1994).

"The Chinese Communist Party derived its initial legitimacy from its opposition to the Nationalist government and the imperial system before it. Decades later, the Party began incorporating elements of traditional Chinese governance." On the post-1989 turn toward Confucian and civilizational legitimation, see Daniel A. Bell, The China Model (2015), and Sébastien Billioud and Joël Thoraval, The Sage and the People: The Confucian Revival in China (2015).

CLOSING REFLECTIONS

"The Roman administrative apparatus migrating into the Catholic Church." On the institutional inheritance from Roman provincial structure to ecclesiastical organization, see Peter Brown, The Rise of Western Christendom (cited in Chapter 9 notes), and Chris Wickham, The Inheritance of Rome (2009).

"The concentration of power in digital platforms over the past fifteen years is not an anomaly. It is the accumulation pattern described in this book, operating at a speed that history rarely permits us to observe in real time." On platform accumulation as a specifically network-effect phenomenon, see Shoshana Zuboff, *The Age of Surveillance Capitalism* (2019); for the antitrust analysis, see Lina M. Khan, "Amazon's Antitrust Paradox," *Yale Law Journal* 126 (2017): 710–805, and the U.S. House Subcommittee on Antitrust, Investigation of Competition in Digital Markets (October 2020).

"Contemporary democratic institutions remain structurally intact while public trust declines at rates the institutions have not matched with reform." Long-run trust data are tracked in the Pew Research Center's "Public Trust in Government" series (1958-present), the American National Election Studies, and the OECD's Trust in Government indicators.